The Philosophical Athlete

The Philosophical Athlete

Heather L. Reid

CAROLINA ACADEMIC PRESS

Durham, North Carolina

ISBN 0-89089-405-1
LCCN 2002103371

CAROLINA ACADEMIC PRESS
700 Kent Street
Durham, North Carolina 27701
Telephone (919) 489-7486
Fax (919)493-5668
www.cap-press.com

Printed in the United States of America.

To My Students

Contents

Preface

What Is a Philosophical Athlete?

The concept of a philosophical athlete goes back to ancient Greece and a young wrestler named Plato who would go on to be counted among the greatest thinkers of all time. Plato liked to describe philosophical dialogue in terms of wrestling moves and strategies.[1] To him, and many others in ancient Greece, the philosophical struggle for truth was absolutely akin to the athletic struggle for victory. Sport and philosophy were for Plato, as they are for this book, the twin pillars of education.

So it's not merely coincidence that western philosophy and competitive athletics have a common origin. Ancient Greek society provides a real-world model for how the synthesis of sport and philosophy can fuel the pursuit of personal excellence (*areté*) and the dynamic, thriving happiness the Greeks called *eudaimonia*. Education was for them, as it is for us, aimed at achieving a good and happy life. The problem is that in modern society we've retained our athletic programs but lost sight of the connection between education, excellence, and happiness.

Of course, few modern athletes are more than vaguely aware of their connection to Plato and the ideals of ancient Greece. As a collegiate cyclist churning out lonely miles in the hill country around Charlottesville, Virginia, I thought little about such matters—beyond their obvious connection to the Olympic games. For me, cycling was more than an escape from the books and lecture halls of the university, it provided a formidable challenge—a set of tangible standards by which I could test my personal mettle.

I dreamt, like so many others, of an Olympic medal.

---

1. See, for example, *Euthydemus* 277d.

But as I pedaled along, imagining myself atop the Olympic podium, head bowed to receive a cold disc of gold, my visions were less about the medal than about the "I" capable of winning it. The real task was to create the Olympian self, to cultivate the virtues — the discipline, the courage, the self-knowledge — I believed all Olympians had.

Somehow I sensed that happiness would come not from the wealth or adoration victories can bring, but from *being the kind of person* who is capable of winning in the first place. On those long painful climbs or the cold wet mornings when I knew others stayed in bed, I hoped ultimately to become the kind of person who deserved a medal — this much more than the medal itself.

Now, as a middle-aged college professor who never did stand upon that Olympic podium, I can nevertheless say that sport brought me a long way toward being the kind of self I hoped would win a medal. Looking back at my early athletic career through the lens of my academic training, I now see the connections to Platonic ideals, Aristotelian virtue-ethics, and Stoic self-creation. I can say I was a philosophical athlete before I understood Plato, or the Greek conceptions of excellence, education, and happiness.

I can also say that, at the time, I felt alone as a philosophical athlete. People understand the goal of an Olympic medal, college scholarship, or professional career, but no one seemed to fathom the sheer beauty of conquering a challenge and experiencing, if only for a moment, the dynamic perfection we so doggedly seek.

Even athletes avoid talking about such moments among themselves. It's easier not to deviate publicly from what one is expected to say. So I kept my personal thoughts about sport and the intoxicating struggle for excellence to myself. Professors couldn't understand my devotion to sport and coaches derided my emphasis on academics. I felt like I was the only person in the world who saw the connection.

It wasn't until I began teaching a course in the subject that I realized I was far from alone in my philosophical approach to sport. Reflected in my students' eyes (many of whom are active athletes harboring the same lofty goals I once did) I see the desire for personal excellence shine through the frustration of being asked to articulate their reasons for participating.

Initial responses to the question 'Why sport?' cluster around extrinsic rewards such as wealth or admiration from others. Students cite their scholarships, hopes for professional careers, or desire to please parents, coaches, and peers as their reasons for playing sport. As the class wears on, however, they talk more freely about such intrinsic rewards as self-knowledge, individual accomplishment through hard work, and personal confidence.

Obviously not every student who takes my class ends up a philosophical athlete, but nearly all gain a healthy perspective on the practice to which they devote so much of their time and energy.

I am writing this book in the hope that many more can benefit from taking a philosophical approach to sport. After taking my class, students often end their post high school hiatus from sport. Others persist past collegiate team-sports to begin individual athletic activities such as running, swimming, or cycling.

Misguided motivations such as wealth, fame, or pleasing Mom and Dad sputter in the high school and college years as our childhood dreams fade and the reality of adulthood sets in. But a philosophical athlete focuses on the intrinsic rewards of sport such as self-knowledge, ethical virtue, and learning to work with others as a team. These rewards pay off endlessly in terms of useful living skills and personal happiness.

This book will try to cultivate the philosophical perspective that empowers sport to enhance life. The philosophical athlete knows that the greatest opponent is the self, the greatest challenge personal excellence, and the greatest reward true happiness. By taking a philosophical approach to sport, athletes of all ages, shapes, and sizes can reclaim the educational value of athletics as it was championed in ancient Greece by such great thinkers as Plato, the wrestler.

Acknowledgments

I can only mention a few of the many who have helped me with this book. Thanks, first of all, to my advisor Gareth B. Matthews, who encouraged me to develop my first course on philosophy and sport, and kudos to the students in those courses who worked with me to develop, and challenged me to communicate, these concepts. Thanks also to Morningside College in Sioux City, Iowa, for providing the support necessary to complete the manuscript, and to my students and colleagues there who offered their criticism and expertise. In addition to Matthews, I am grateful to R. Scott Kretchmar, Lillian J. López, Bruce Forbes, and Jan Hodge, for their helpful comments on the manuscript. I am also indebted to Lynn Kogelmann for her caring assistance through the entire project. Finally, special thanks go to my husband, Larry Theobald, for his generosity, patience, and support.

The Philosophical Athlete

Introduction

What We Can Learn from Sport

In the final chapter of their groundbreaking study on college sports and educational values, *The Game of Life*, James L. Shulman and William G. Bowen offer a series of propositions for curing what ails the modern college-sports machine. First and foremost among those propositions is the following:

> The growing gap between college athletics and educational values is a major, unavoidable, issue for the academy; it must be understood and addressed. The objective should be to reinvigorate the contribution of intercollegiate athletics to the achievement of educational goals.[1]

For many a modern athlete, education and athletics are experienced as competing imperatives. Many student athletes face huge demands on their time and energy from powerful coaches and professionally marketed "programs." To them, collegiate sport can feel less like a playful co-curricular activity, than an arduous job—a job paid in academic opportunities that the student may be too exhausted to really benefit from. Meanwhile, those athletes no longer in school who pursue athletic goals for the sake of personal development are pressured by a derisive social attitude that perceives recreational sport as a frivolous waste of time and energy.

In this book I argue that a philosophical approach to sport can help to bridge the gap between educational values and athletic excellence. Philosophical athletes know how sport can benefit them *as* human beings, beyond social and financial rewards—even beyond physical

---

1. Shulman and Bowen (2001, 294).

health. For thinking people in high-school, college, and beyond, a philosophical perspective can greatly enhance our ability to learn from and improve through the athletic experience.

The Philosophical Approach

The first thing to note here is that there is nothing elusive or mystical about the term "philosophical." Literally, a philosopher is anyone who loves and pursues wisdom—a person with a drive for truth: about the self, about others, about the world.

Put simply, philosophers ask questions—continually trying to discover the truth about a thing. They alter their perspective on an issue by stepping back and looking at the "big picture" or zooming in to contemplate the details (see the section "Thinking Activity").

Some say that philosophers go asking questions where things are better left unexamined. Socrates says that the unexamined life is not worth living.[2] Whom do you believe?

To be sure, a philosophical approach to sport may lead us to questions we're uncomfortable answering. Other questions simply cannot be answered, and still others have obvious or uninteresting answers. The value of all these questions is that they keep our minds open and ready for the truth. The philosophical approach to sport maximizes what we can learn from it and gives us the best chance for leading better lives because of it.

It is an admittedly huge leap from the practice of philosophical questioning to the promise of leading a better life. What exactly can we learn by taking a philosophical attitude toward sport, and how will that help us to lead better lives? The full answer to that question encompasses this whole book, but here's a general road map to give you an idea of the journey.

The book focuses on four basic areas of learning:
Self-discovery
Responsibility
Respect
Citizenship

This sequence is important because authentic self-knowledge is an essential foundation for effectively dealing with the personal and social

---

2. See Plato, *Apology* 38a.

challenges faced by philosophical athletes. Specific issues such as violence, racism, and performance-enhancing drugs will be discussed in their relevant contexts. But philosophical athletes focus on the big picture, approaching each issue within the context of a complete vision of themselves, their moral commitments, and their roles in society.

Thinking Activity: A Philosophical Perspective on Sport

Taking a philosophical approach to sport is largely a matter of practice. Philosophers have a particular way of observing and thinking about things. Throughout the book you'll find "thinking activities" to guide you though philosophical analysis of key issues.

To demonstrate, let's imagine a photograph of Jesse Owens winning the 100 meter race at the 1936 Olympics in Berlin—an event not only significant within sport, but with great social and political dimensions as well.

Question: Philosophical analysis always begins with a question. Let's ask, "What is the significance of this image?"

Observe: Next, take a moment to observe. Mentally zoom in on the picture, stripping it down to its most basic parts: a human being, running, crosses a chalk line on the ground.

Analyze: Think about the stripped-down image and decide what it means. If you were from another galaxy and you saw a snapshot of a humanoid running across a chalk line, what might you conclude? Little or nothing. The acts of crossing a finish line, shooting a ball into a net, or breaking the plane of a goal line are insignificant when stripped of their context. These sporting feats that we so ardently dream of and strive for mean nothing in and of themselves.

Question Again: So where does the meaning come from?

Observe: Zoom out a notch and consider Owens' victory within the context of the sport itself.

Analyze: Someone carefully constructed a set of written rules and artificially delineated a course 100 meters long with specific methods governing the start, timing, and finish of the task. The object of all this artifice is to determine which man can run the fastest over this distance under these specific conditions. Within this purely sporting context, our image of Owens crossing the line gains significance because he is the first among all men in the race to do so and according to the rules, he is thereby designated the "winner" of the race.

Question Again: But why on earth is "winning" so important? What is it about covering 100 meters on a specially designed track faster than the handful of other men that makes someone so deserving of praise?

Again, to answer these questions we need to zoom out once more and think about why the human qualities associated with sporting victory are so valued in society. As we continue to zoom out and fill in the bigger picture, questions of ethics and fair play, then of society and politics will present themselves for thought.

The basic idea is that the better and more authentically you know yourself, the better decisions you will be able to make in your life. The better decisions you make in your life, the happier you are likely to be.

Clearly, not all factors contributing to happiness are within an individual's control. However, barriers to personal happiness are often based on lack of self-understanding—as in never reflecting upon what really makes you happy, or mistakenly believing that happiness comes from such things as wealth and fame. The dozens of maladjusted and depressed millionaire sports icons are testament to this phenomenon.

Self-Discovery

Sport provides special opportunities for individuals to come to know themselves. Every sporting practice is filled with what I call "moments of challenge"—times when an athlete finds him- or herself alone, faced with a particular task and the very real possibilities of success or failure.

Imagine the basketball player attempting a game-winning (or losing) free-throw, the batter with a full count and two outs in the bottom of the ninth, or the racer who sees a key competitor start to pull away up the road. I've heard athletes describe these as times when you "meet your maker," but in fact it is your *self* that you face at this moment.

At first, you might not even recognize the self you meet at the moment of challenge because you are removed from the social context that tries to define you from without. Within the moment of challenge, you experience yourself as an embodied whole; you are forced to bridge the mind-body gap instead of identifying with one or the other as we humans are so wont to do.

Most strikingly you realize that you are terrifyingly free—free to fail as the limited, imperfect, mortal that you are. And free to succeed, even to transcend your apparent limits and to resemble, if only for a moment, infallible gods. Athletes like to call this momentary, transcendent state of perfection "the zone" and almost all of them claim to have experienced it at one time or another.

As beautiful as it is to watch an athlete face these defining moments in sport, there is no substitute for experiencing them in person—for finally confronting yourself from the inside-out. In contrast to the outside-in conceptions of ourselves so many of us co-opt from our social evaluators, the self we get to meet within the practice of sport is inevitably more authentic—more true to ourselves.

The reason is simple: a real self emerges from real tests with real criteria for success and failure. I may imagine myself as a perfect free-throw shooter, I may even have the kind of statistics that make my success at this moment highly probable. Ultimately, however, my image, my statistics, my race, my gender, my hours of practice, my perfectly-timed ritual can't shoot the ball for me. *I* have to shoot it, alone—and in this moment I learn important things about myself that cannot be hidden, imagined, or faked.

Responsibility

With the awareness of freedom, however, there comes a newfound sense of responsibility. Moments of challenge reveal both crushing limitations and unfathomable possibilities—leaving athletes responsible to make what we can of them.

In sport, athletes face death—metaphorically in the case of losing, and literally in the genres of extreme and risk-sports. Tellingly, we relish this opportunity to take responsibility for our lives. Sport helps to reveal the extent to which we ourselves control our actions and attitudes.

The sense of responsibility we develop in these moments of challenge provide a foundation for our ethical and social selves, as well as playful self-expression and independent self-direction. How? As philosophical athletes develop a sense of personal responsibility, we also learn to reflect upon and articulate meaningful values and goals.

As I described in my personal example, the philosophical athlete is engaged in the act of creating and cultivating the self he or she wants to be. These hard-won conceptions of who we are and want to be take on preeminent value in our lives. They are primary goods that provide meaning; therefore they won't be compromised for secondary or extrinsic goods such as notoriety or cash rewards.

Respect

Largely, this ethical strength is a matter of self-respect. For example, Ben Johnson wants to be Olympic champion. He discovers that by adding steroids to his regimen he can achieve that goal. Because he is focused on victory rather than excellence, he is willing to sacrifice his own integrity—to settle for the external *image* of an Olympic champion and for the mere spoils of victory. But, he must sacrifice the possibility of actually being the kind of person who deserves those spoils.

One explanation for this is that whatever conception he had of himself, he was willing to falsify it for an image of something he was not. When he was caught and the steroid abuse was revealed, the gap between what he really was and what he wanted people to believe he was became apparent not only to him but to the world. He failed to respect himself, his competitors, even the ideals of sport itself.

An athlete with a strong conception of self will not sacrifice that for a misleading public image or temporary financial payoff. Even if the truth is never revealed to the public, he will always know that he is something less than what he wants to be, and the charade will never be as satisfying as true self-respect.

Sport teaches ethics not so much by prescribing particular answers to moral dilemmas, but by helping philosophical athletes to find our own best answers. Once we realize our stake in the outcome—not just of the game, but of the personal struggle for excellence—we might ultimately find the strength to resist external pressures and to follow through with what we know to be right.

The logical follow-up to self-respect is respect for others, which is based on the philosophical athlete's understanding of how he or she relates to other individuals on both a personal and social level. The athlete has important relationships with teammates, coaches, and competitors.

Again, a philosophical approach can reveal the intricacies of these relationships and provide a guideline for making them healthy. Consider, for example, the relationship between tennis competitors Chris Evert and Martina Navratilova. What do these women do for one another? Most obviously, when one hits the ball, the other returns it. This fact is important to reflect upon because it shows us that without an opponent, the test of hitting a ball over a low net would not be much of a challenge.

In tennis, as in many other sports, the competitor provides the challenge. A good competitor provides a good challenge, one that pushes us to our limits while keeping the possibilities of success and failure as even as possible. Martina actually provides Chris with the *opportunity* to test herself, to learn about herself, to become the kind of self she strives so hard to be.

Yes, Martina is in some sense an *obstacle* to Chris' goal of winning the championship, but she also is essential to Chris' primary goal of personal excellence. If she played easy or threw the match or tried to deny Chris the chance to play by injuring her with a shot to the eye, Martina would be harming the contest. But by playing hard and challenging Chris as much as possible, she is in fact *helping* her to achieve her primary goal. A little perspective yields a lot more respect for others in the life of the philosophical athlete.

Citizenship

Ultimately, there is the question of the individual's role in the larger community. A developing sense of our desired selves can only be complete when it includes an understanding of our function in society. Conveniently, the sporting experience places individual athletes in a myriad of micro-communities, from teams working together to achieve particular goals to groups representing neighborhoods, schools, colleges, cities, states, and even nations in the mini-United Nations that is international athletics.

Elusive concepts such as justice, fairness, and human equality can be explored through the medium of sport, while tangible social issues such as race, gender, economic and cultural differences are also encountered. The sporting context limits the scope of these social and political concepts, enabling the philosophical athlete to test and develop different opinions and approaches to them.

This experience helps to form a foundation for involvement in larger social and political communities. The use of athletes as political pawns, as in the 1980 U.S. boycott of the Moscow Olympic games, is testament to their political power. Ideally, philosophical athletes can use reflection about events within sport to form a basis from which we can reclaim our political power and use it thoughtfully.

Real Life

There's no question that this book's vision of what can be learned from sport is ambitious and far-reaching. The reality of modern athletes as they are typically depicted and understood seems to contradict the claim that sport has such great educational potential.

After all, doesn't athletic success usually come to people with extraordinary physical gifts who simply coast on their talents all the way to fame? And aren't athletes notorious for their immature and sometimes depraved responses to the wealth and adulation showered upon them? Doesn't it seem like professional and collegiate athletes are more likely to be substance abusers, spouse abusers, and generally devoid of ethical sense?

I concede that these images exist and that they are at least based on real incidents. But there are two key reasons why this does not destroy my thesis about what can be learned from sport. First, this image is derived chiefly from a small group of professional and collegiate athletes in major team sports. Even if this group has been accurately characterized by the media, it still makes up only a small fraction of all the athletes in the world.

What we're dealing with is a very visible minority who are visible because they are involved in sports associated with extrinsic rewards (wealth and fame), which are only of secondary importance to a *philosophical* athlete. Although these high-profile sports can and do attract philosophical athletes, they are more likely to attract those primarily enamored with the spoils of victory rather than the internal rewards.

Second, the larger sports world is actually full of examples of athletes who demonstrate personal virtue and thoughtful approaches to life: speedskaters Johan Olav Koss and Bonnie Blair, cyclist Lance Armstrong, skier Manuela Di Centa, track athletes Gail Devers and Jackie-Joyner Kersee are just a few of those we know about—and we only know them because they won important international events that received extensive media coverage, including in-depth profiles and interviews.

To these famous competitors, add the millions of thoughtful and fulfilled athletes whose sports never see the spotlight or who never win the major competitions and the number of philosophical athletes who can testify to the educational potential of sport swells enormously. A glimpse of their world may be seen through the pens of such authors as George Sheehan, Stephen Kiesling, and Alan Sillitoe.[3]

By far the best way to experience the life of a philosophical athlete, however, is quite simply to live it. This book is intended to help all athletes, great and small, to achieve just that.

---

3. An annotated bibliography of philosophical sports writing appears at the end of each chapter.

Four Characteristics
of a Philosophical Athlete

1. Values the sports experience as an opportunity to learn about himself as a person.

2. Takes responsibility for her actions, her attitudes, and the pursuit of meaningful goals.

3. Shows respect for himself, those around him, and the ideals of his sport.

4. Understands the values of her sports community and seeks to preserve them.

Part One

Discovering Your Self

Section Preview

Introduction:
"Know Thyself"

> *While a game allows one to see what man can do, a contest,*
> *instead, offers an occasion for self-discovery*
>
> —Paul Weiss

At the ancient Greek city of Delphi, just below the stadium where heroes were made in the Pythian games, stood the sacred temple of Apollo, god of music and light.[1] The temple housed the oracle that declared no man wiser than Socrates.[2] Perhaps more important were the words of wisdom inscribed on its walls:

"Know Thyself."

This profound exhortation can, and has been, understood many ways. There's no doubt it was meant to be open to interpretation; after all, questions about meaning are doorways to understanding. On the other hand, the statement says much just taken at face value: self-knowledge is the foundation of human wisdom.

The inscription's message rings true today, not only for philosophers but for philosophical athletes as well. An examined life in sport begins with examination of oneself. But seeing ourselves as we really are is something inherently difficult to achieve—even more so in this modern world of constant distractions and external stimulation. We're al-

---

1. The Pythian games, honoring Apollo, were second in prestige only to the Olympics. See Mechikoff and Estes (1998, 45).
2. See Plato, *Apology*, 21a.

13

ways listening to stereos, watching television, talking to friends. We need some place where we can listen to our bodies, watch our dreams, talk to ourselves. We need a place to tune out from the external world and tune in to who we are as individuals. The philosophical athlete can find such a place through a mindful approach to sport.

In sport we encounter ourselves as alone, embodied, and free. The aloneness, often, is just figurative—a feeling of isolation born of the responsibility we feel to perform as individual athletes. The ball comes to me and now I must shoot it. This is an "I" in some sense isolated from outside concerns, from social labels, and even from past experience.

An athlete encounters the "I" in a novel way, not only in relative isolation from external contexts, but also from a new perspective—from the *inside out*.[3] In everyday life, we tend to see ourselves as others see us—reflected through such mirrors as race, gender, and social status. These mirrors can distort our understanding of ourselves, giving us only a view from the outside in. Getting to know this stripped-down "I" encountered in sport is the first step toward becoming a philosophical athlete.

Athletes also encounter their embodiment in the sporting experience. We tend to identify our minds with ourselves, viewing our bodies as mere objects. This mind-over-matter philosophy has justified not only an insensitive tendency to view athletes' bodies as laboratory specimens, it has also cast doubt upon their intelligence as a group. Brains and brawn are thought to be mutually exclusive, so the genius of a running back is shrugged off as mere skill, while his coach, seated in a skybox, gets credit for a "brilliant" play. Philosophical athletes can take back their bodies as subjects and reinterpret "intelligence" from the stance of embodied unity. Sport helps us to accept our selves as wholes—mind and body together.

Perhaps the greatest feeling we experience in sport is freedom. The sense of freedom an athlete discovers derives from the uncertainty of each sporting moment. Indeed sport seems to be created as a diversion from the demands and predictability of everyday life. It brings us face to face with our freedom. In sport we manipulate time, space, and gravity to create a virtual escape from the inevitabilities of nature. We also retreat from social definitions and determinations; from the psychological limitations that we place upon ourselves.

---

3. I owe this locution to Michael Novak (1988, 162).

Athletes cannot ignore their freedom of choice. Philosophical athletes learn that choice actually creates freedom. In this way we prepare ourselves to choose who we will become.

Section Preview List

- What is the nature of your true self? (Chapter 1)
- Is being an athlete a matter of mind? Body? Or both? (Chapter 2)
- What is the significance of our experience of freedom in sport? (Chapter 3)

Chapter 1

Discovering Yourself as Unique

Chapter Preview

Introduction:
The Art of Being Who You Are

> *Delfon has been working out all summer at Oberlin... "This race is very important to me," he says. "It's a pride race."*
>
> *His fists and knees are pumping high and hard, and finally he pulls ahead of Joe. Delfon has learned how to hold on. He stayed in school when he felt like quitting. He chose life when he felt like dying.*
>
> *When he felt lost, he held on and eventually met his father and Jackie Elliott and Erica Wright, missing pieces in his life. And when he met them, he met himself, because they told him who he was and what he should do. Go to school, they said. Run. Hold on.*
>
> —Duane Noriyuki, "Let the Games Begin"

In his article "Let the Games Begin," Duane Noriyuki tells the true story of a 100 meter race between three runners on a worn asphalt track in the wasteland of inner-city Detroit. There are no electronic timers, no starting blocks, no finishing tape. It's an annual neighborhood race that means nothing—and at the same time it means everything.

The meaning of this race comes from the contestants' opportunity to discover themselves. In the race, they will confront who they are and what they have become.

The three young men all grew up in this neighborhood together, but have since forged divergent paths in life. Joe is a high-school dropout and former crack-dealer, struggling to turn his life around. Snook is a

17

dishwasher at a local hotel; he partied late the night before the race. Delfon attends college and runs track at Oberlin, an achievement due in part to the inspiration provided by this race.

A fourth competitor was gunned down the night before.

You might think that Delfon's status as a student-athlete should be enough to prove who he is to his "homies." But there's a truth to be found in the race—in *this* race against old friends in his old neighborhood—that can't be discovered elsewhere.

Titles, diplomas, and shiny new cars may say something about you to others who take notice. But to get in touch with yourself—to find out who you really are beneath all those external labels—you must search from the inside out.

The starting gun fires, the race begins. Delfon falls behind and confronts the reality that he might lose. His scholarship to Oberlin, the expectations of his father and coach, the grudging respect of the dope-dealers, the admiration of the neighborhood children—all these things threaten to fade from existence unless he can find the strength to run faster at this moment.

Somewhere on that track, Delfon risks his reputation and even his self-concept to ask himself the question, "Who are you?" The response to this question cannot be a fairy-tale; it must be answered with his legs—now, on this track, today.

Delfon wins the race, and reaffirms his identity.

The losing contestants asked the same question of themselves. And the answers they discovered, though not exactly what they'd hoped, are no less accurate. In the race, everyone has learned something about himself.

You don't have to be an athlete to ask the question, "Who am I?" But being an athlete can help you to discover an answer.

Our lives, our roles, our identities are so heavily directed by external customs and social expectations that our paths through life can feel as confining as a train-ride conducted by somebody else. For runner-philosopher George Sheehan, the ticket off that train was sport. Once he "stepped off that train and began to run," he says, "I began to find out who I was."[1]

Sport provides so many opportunities to encounter the "naked self." Imagine the experience of shooting a free-throw. Fingering the familiar roughness of the basketball, you look down at the blue stripe

---

1. Sheehan (1975, 3).

painted on the tan wood floor and carefully toe the line. Methodically, you bounce the ball exactly three times, look up at the basket and set your body for the shot. Then, there is a moment of peace at the center of this tension as you come face to face with your self. This is just one example of what I call the "moment of challenge."

At the moment of challenge in sport, philosophical athletes confront the question of *personal identity* and begin to develop an authentic self-knowledge that will become the foundation for their social and ethical existence. Here, we encounter the question of *reidentification*—finding a constant and unchangeable element to the self that represents "who you really are." We also face the question of *individuation*—distinguishing ourselves from others like us. And finally, there's the question of our *inner and outer selves*—in which we evaluate the origin and authenticity of who we have become.

Indeed, the moment of challenge is itself a kind of question, a *lived question* that initiates the philosophical process of self-discovery in sport.

Chapter Preview List

- Can sport help us get to know our true selves?
- How does an athlete distinguish himself from others?
- Does sport provide an opportunity to see ourselves from the inside out?

1.1 Moments of Challenge: A Lived Question

Uncertainty Is Opportunity

Every sport has its moments of challenge, intersections of time and spirit when athletes encounter a specific task, know exactly what they must do to succeed, and face the reality of actually performing. These moments can happen at third down and long in American football, on the edge of a high-rise diving platform, or just before a difficult reach in rock climbing. Some moments of challenge are fleeting and hardly noticed, while others seem to last an eternity. They come in all shapes and sizes, and every athlete experiences them.

The essence is that the athlete is challenged in a very specific and personal way—a challenge characterized above all by uncertainty. Philosophers recognize that our desire to know is motivated by uncertainty: an awareness that we don't know. Uncertainty destroys all illusion of knowledge and opens the athlete's soul to the reality of unknown truth.

The uncertainty experienced at the moment of challenge is as much uncertainty about *who I really am* as it is about whether I will succeed. As long as I think I know who I am, I have little desire to find a new answer. Since sport in general and the moment of challenge in particular are characterized by uncertainty about outcomes, they force athletes to confront their imperfections, come to terms with limitations, and explore potential.

This encounter with the self is embedded in a further question about what that self is. Think again about a basketball player on the free-throw line. Imagine that she is making a crucial shot in her high-school state championship. She looks inside at this moment of challenge worried about what she might see. Maybe, for a moment, she wishes she weren't herself. Maybe she wishes to be Michael Jordan. But what does that mean?

Perhaps she wishes to have his brain transplanted in her body? Or maybe she wants her brain transplanted in his body. Maybe she just wants to *feel* the kind of confidence and power he must feel on the free throw line. But to get this would she need to have his memories, his training, his quirky habits? And if she had all that, could she still be herself? Would she feel as though *she* had taken the shot?

This puzzle reveals that uncertainty about the self begins with uncertainty about what the self *is*. What does it mean to be me and not someone else? What is essential to my "I" that remains over time?

Philosophical Background:
Personal Identity

"Who am I?" is a fundamental philosophical question that can be approached on several different levels. Before we can even ask that question, however, we must establish that there is some particular enduring "I" to discover. Philosophers know this as the problem of reidentification — retaining a single identity despite changes that occur over time.

The problem has its roots in puzzles about how objects retain their identity when parts are replaced: can I say I own the bike that Fausto Coppi rode to victory in the Tour de France if over the years, one by one, I have replaced all of its parts? If not, at what point did it cease to be Coppi's bicycle? When I replaced the first tire? When less than half the parts were original? When I removed the last original part?

How *can* humans claim identity over time? It is said that all the cells in our bodies are replaced every seven years. Maybe it's the unique genetic code stored in our DNA that holds the key to our identities. But are you really the same person you were when you were 2 or 7? This problem became serious for a roommate of mine on a school trip to Russia in the early 1980's. The picture on her passport had been taken nearly 10 years earlier when she was only 8 years old. The border guard simply did not believe that she was the same person in the picture. How would you prove to a guard your identity over time?

One solution to our personal identity crisis is the Buddhist doctrine that we have no self at all. Western philosophy has sought to preserve the concept of personal identity, however, by dissociating the self from the body and identifying it with consciousness and memory. In his 1698 *Essay Concerning Human Understanding*, Englishman John Locke concluded,

> For, since consciousness always accompanies thinking, and it is
> that which makes every one to be what he calls self, and thereby
> distinguishes himself from all other thinking things: in this alone
> consists personal identity... [2]

By severing a constant concept of self from our ever-changing bodies, Locke was able to solve the problem of reidentification. He observed that physical changes did not threaten the identity of an object so long as they were expected for the type of substance the thing is. Flowers, for example, are expected to grow, then wilt and lose their

---

2. Locke (1689a, 335).

petals. Humans increase in height (and girth) as time wears on, their hair changes color and skin becomes looser, but these changes don't affect their identity.

Since Locke believes individuals are identified with consciousness, bodily concerns become secondary. He illustrates with a story of a prince and a cobbler who trade bodies one night. When the prince wakes up in the cobbler's workshop and the cobbler wakes up in the palace, we cannot say, despite his physical appearance, that the man in the cobbler's bed is in fact the cobbler. After all, he has no knowledge of shoe-making and none of the rest of the cobbler's memory needed to make sense of his new surroundings.[3] In summary then, for Locke, our personal identity boils down to consciousness and memory.

The Power of the Question

An athletes' search for an enduring and authentic idea of self is motivated by the experience of sport. The moment of challenge forces us to admit a kind of ignorance about ourselves. I may convince myself without a shadow of a doubt that I can run 400 meters in under a minute. I cannot step on that starting line, however, without admitting the possibility that I might fail. To actually run the race is to *ask a question* about myself.

A challenge is, almost by definition, some task for which there is doubt about one's ability to perform. Even the most confident athletes know deep inside that the outcomes they seek are never guaranteed. This is precisely the allure of sporting challenges—the opportunity to test and learn some truth about yourself. If you were absolutely sure you could make that free throw, there'd be no point in trying. If we were absolutely sure what the meaning of life is, there'd be no point in asking. But we don't know so we ask, we attempt, we enter contests.

That tension in your gut at the moment of challenge—no, not the butterflies, that almost burning sensation at your geographical center—you've felt that tension before and it's a good thing. It's desire. Sure, there's fear and nervousness and anxiety, but strongest is the desire to succeed, to complete the task, to swish the shot. Ultimately, this desire is directed toward truth—we desire to answer the question asked at the moment of challenge: "Who am I?"

This desire is also the driving force of philosophy: the desire to know, to learn, to become wise. All athletes experience the desire to

---

3. Try a similar thought experiment under "thinking activities," below.

perform well and attain victory. What sets philosophical athletes apart is their understanding of the overarching desire to achieve wisdom. A philosophical athlete recognizes the desire present at the moment of challenge not only as a desire for athletic success, but ultimately as a desire to learn and know.

The Encounter with Oneself

Whether I make the shot, win the race, or nail my dismount from the balance beam is not meaningful *in itself*. My desire to succeed at sporting tasks like these is really a desire to know myself. Sports tasks are just proxy for some truth about the kind of person I am in relation to the kind of person I believe myself to be. I begin with the desire to be a certain kind of person, then ascertain that this task (i.e. running a marathon) is something achievable for that person. In discovering whether I can meet my particular sporting challenge, I thereby discover something about myself.

All athletes gain information from the challenges faced in sport. They find out whether a 78% free-throw percentage can be achieved, whether the ankle injury is affecting their shooting, whether the team will end its losing streak, whether they can go to the playoffs. Philosophical athletes learn even more. We learn not only the statistical outcomes produced in sport, we learn about ourselves—and not only in terms of athletic ability—we learn something about *who we are.*

In the lived question of the moment of challenge, philosophical athletes recognize two great opportunities: one, the chance to encounter ourselves as we really are, and two, the possibility to express that true self through our performance. Unlike the statistical banalities learned through a conventional approach to sport, what philosophical athletes seek is lived knowledge—things personally experienced rather than merely known.[4]

My performance within sport always reveals some truth about me. It is rarely a matter of debate whether I passed my particular challenge—often the answer is on public display. The lack of ambiguity in a failed free-throw attempt can be harsh, even brutal, but it is refreshingly clear.

Frequently what we discover in sport is that we fall short of our personal expectations. We learn that we still haven't become the person we are striving to become. We sometimes discover that we are much

---

4. Kretchmar (1994, 162–164) explains the value of personally experienced vs. impersonally absorbed knowledge.

farther from that goal than we thought. Along with the initial disappointment of the dropped ball or lost race, however, comes a quiet pleasure. Ultimately there is beauty in discovering the truth, even when it's not what you hoped for. It's a liberation from illusion, a freedom from confusion.

At the moment of challenge we experience our selves, with all our limitations and possibilities. This may be the only way to *know* who we really are. Philosophical athletes consciously look for truth in the moment of challenge, a lived truth about ourselves.

Thinking Activity: Who Am I?
Question: Who are you? There are many ways to ask this question with many meanings attached—the way that you answer can reveal a lot.
Observe: Take a blank sheet of paper and answer the question "Who am I?" by listing 3–5 characteristics. Try to list things you think are essential by using the criterion: "If this thing changed, I wouldn't be the same person."
Analyze: Next, analyze your list—what sort of things did you put down?
   Designators: names, nicknames, serial numbers
   Bodily Characteristics: gender, size, age, the colors of your hair, eyes, or skin
   Mental Characteristics: smart, clever, good sense of humor, sly, devious
   Social Roles: student, shortstop, cashier, daughter, brother, New Yorker, friend
   Internal Characteristics (how you feel inside): happy, confident, strong, fearful
   External Characteristics (how you appear to others): cheerful, smiling, arrogant
Question Again: What do these answers tell you about the way you see yourself? Are you focused more internally or externally? Do you identify more with your body, your mind, your emotions? Do you define yourself with reference to your family, your profession, your sport? Are you more worried about how you appear than how you really feel inside? Finally, see if you observe a difference between the description you wrote on the paper and the way you really see yourself? Analyze what the differences are. Ask yourself why.

1.2 Alone with Oneself

Alone in a Crowd

Of the many things to be encountered within a moment of challenge, one a philosophical athlete is sure to experience is being alone. At the moment of challenge we are isolated, stripped by uncertainty from prediction and pretension and extracted by responsibility from the masses surrounding us. Whatever I may think of myself, whatever the statistics may show about free-throw percentages for college players, for my team, or even for me based on past performance—at the moment of challenge I do not know what will happen. Reputation, probability, and illusion evaporate like sweat off my skin on a cool Fall evening.

As William A. Harper puts it, we are "alone" in sport:

> Man is alone in sport. When he is actively involved, his personal success or failure depends solely upon him. The man in sport cannot shirk being alone; he cannot defer this state in preference for a public substitution. His only choice is to play or not to play. If he chooses the former, he is condemned to solitude.[5]

Harper perceives this solitude as nothing less than a blessing. The fact is that this modern world can suck the individuality right out of a person. Our everyday lives are lived among a herd of nearly indistinguishable others. Like some generic sedan caught in a massive L.A. traffic jam, we live our lives as one of a mass of students, or workers, or "the television audience."

One fundamental human desire is to distinguish ourselves from the herd we live in. We seek to discover ourselves as unique and to do this we must feel alone. In the athletic moment of challenge we are alone—even while dressed identically to our teammates on a crowded field or court. As soon as the ball comes sailing my direction, there's no-one in the world but me and the challenge I face.

Philosophical Background:
Individuation

This experience of aloneness in sport helps the philosophical athlete to deal with the problem of individuation—distinguishing ourselves from others who are like us. When the animated toy space ranger, Buzz Lightyear, wanders into Al's Toy Barn in *Toy Story II*, he comes face to face with a towering display of factory-fresh Buzz Lightyears identical to himself, and he undergoes an existential crisis.

---

5. Harper, (1969, 57).

Of course persons are not made on assembly lines like toys, but the desire to find our uniqueness runs deep. A clear sense of personal identity is increasingly difficult to achieve, especially in a modern world where we are most often identified by social security numbers, credit-card codes, or DNA. There aren't many places in this modern world where we can feel solitary and original among the crowd.

Locke's association of identity and memory doesn't solve the problem by itself. His contemporary, David Hume, agreed that consciousness was the place to search for personal identity, but he disagreed that it could simply be memory and ended up skeptical about whether there was such a thing at all.

In his 1739 *Treatise of Human Nature,* Hume stipulates that a true *self* must "continue invariable the same, through the whole course of our lives; since the self is supposed to exist in that manner"[6]

But Hume was an *empiricist,* that is, he believed knowledge comes from sense-impressions, and quite simply he failed to find any constant and invariable impression of the self. Says Hume:

> There are some philosophers, who imagine we are every moment intimately conscious of what we call our Self...[but] I never can catch myself at any time without a perception, and never can observe any thing but the perception.[7]

To understand this idea better, think of your life like a reel of film, each frame representing some sense-impression you've had. In a lifetime you will have literally millions of these impressions, but there is no idea of yourself independent of these impressions and the sense of self you might find in each individual frame is constantly changing, like the point of view of the camera. Hume concluded that our selves could be no more than "bundles of impressions" with no sameness and no identity.[8]

Breaking Out of the Herd

Hume's skepticism about the possibility of personal identity is confirmed by experience. Almost nothing is unique to us. Our jobs can be done by others, maybe robots. Our homes share common floor plans

6. Hume (1739, 251).
7. Hume (1739, 251–2).
8. Hume (1739, 253).

and are distinguished only by paint and numbers. Our food is cooked in factories or industrial-size vats, neutralized in flavor to be acceptable to most everyone but truly savored by no one. Our clothes are mass-produced — one size fits thousands. Athletic gear is uniform in brand, color, and style. Even our thoughts tend to conform to the opinions and values of the dominant culture as spewed forth though television, newspapers, and ubiquitous social small talk.

So who am I really? Which thoughts are mine? Is there anything in this world that I can claim for myself, even my *self* itself?

Socrates made it clear that being a philosopher meant becoming independent from the homogenized thinking of the masses or *hoi polloi*. Much later, existentialist philosophers reemphasized his point, seeing that the industrial revolution had further robbed humanity of its sense of individuality. Existentialists called this social force *the herd, the other,* or simply *the they* and explained that the individual must detach himself from the group, at least mentally, in order to recover the subjectivity and sense of self necessary for a good life. The philosophical athlete, at the moment of challenge, can find just the kind of seclusion Socrates and the existentialist philosophers demanded.

Only You Can Fail

The catalyst for this isolation is the real possibility of failure and the acute sense of personal responsibility that accompanies it.[9] I know that the basketball game is a team effort, that I had no control over the opponent who fouled me, no say in the decision of the referee to award me these free shots. But even while I know that I'm not responsible for this opportunity to win or lose the game, I cannot avoid the reality that I am personally and individually responsible for whether or not I make the shots.

It's as if a long line of falling dominoes leading up toward our victory in the game has now come to a single domino that I must personally push over in order to continue the sequence. No one else can shoot for me and there is no hiding my success or failure. In this gym filled with screaming humanity, I am utterly alone at this moment of challenge.

Philosophical athletes welcome this isolation and responsibility because it opens the door at last to the experience of being truly ourselves. By isolating us from the herd we live in, the moment of challenge strips away obstacles to self-knowledge.

---

9. This is artfully articulated in Harper (1969).

An Asian woman, for example, can escape the stereotypes about her race and gender by participating in sport where her actual performance quickly supercedes social assumptions about what she ought to be able to achieve. As she slide-tackles the soccer ball from a charging opponent, assumptions about her lack of speed and timidity must be left behind—even by her. She becomes what she does and escapes the labels assigned to her socially.

Finally, if she's a philosophical athlete, she recognizes this opportunity and seeks it out. She uses sport as a kind of private classroom, where she can be alone and learn about her self.

Thinking Activity: The First-Person Self
Question: How authentic is my self?
Observe: Choose a moment that stands out in your memory. Maybe you have clear memories of an event that happened when you were playing your sport. Take some time and develop the image as much as you can. Include all the senses, what you see, smell, feel, hear, taste. Include how you feel emotionally, what you think and say. Recite these to a friend or write them down.
Analyze: Return to your description with fresh eyes, or trade with another person and see what you can learn from the description. Is the description from the first person (internal) point of view, or from a third person (external) point of view? Even if you used the pronoun "I" you may have been picturing yourself from the outside, from a god's-eye point of view, through the lens of an imaginary camera, or from the point of view of others in your scene. Are you looking at yourself from someone else's point of view? Who? What do they see? What are they looking for?
Question Again: What have you learned from your analysis of this event? Does the you seem more "real" than your everyday self? Are you willing to share your "inner-self" with others? Why or why not?

1.3 Confronting Oneself from the Inside-Out

A New Perspective on the Self

The self we encounter at the moment of challenge might be unfamiliar at first. This shouldn't be a surprise. So much of our lives are spent wearing masks. We worry about how we appear to others so we spend much of our time constructing and projecting a persona that we think will be pleasing to them. This is the problem of inner and outer selves.

In fact, many of us have an elaborate array of different personae tailored to different audiences or different situations: one for our mother, another for our coach, another for our teacher or employer, and yet another for hanging with our pals.

You may remember the episode of TV's *Seinfeld* in which the character of George Costanza tries desperately to keep his fiancée away from Jerry because the persona of "Relationship George" he projects around her is nothing like the "Raunchy George" persona he adopts with Jerry. It's important to recognize that you have these different personas, simply because they can get in the way of understanding who you really are—your authentic self.

Sports psychologists have identified the ability to get past our social personas as an important component of *flow*—the mental state associated with peak athletic performance.[10] By liberating ourselves from concern about what others expect of us, we are better able to focus on what we are actually doing, and to *be* who we "really are."

Philosophical Background:
Our Inner and Outer Selves

Confusion about "the real you" is a third dimension of the problem of personal identity. It might occur when you catch a glimpse of yourself in a mirror, see yourself in a photograph, or hear your recorded voice on tape. You ask yourself, if only for a moment, "Is that me?"

There's a fairly wide gulf between how we experience ourselves in the first person—from the inside-out—and how others experience us in the third person—from the outside-in. Of course we're aware of how we appear to others, indeed we often take great pains to project a particular image to the world. But do we ever confuse that self with our real self?

Maybe we do. The question of who or what our innermost "self" might be and how on earth it generates the "selves" we experience and project everyday has been simultaneously clarified and made more complex by the findings of psychological theory, brain research, and discoveries about such phenomena as multiple personality disorder.

How have these findings affected philosophy? Contemporary philosopher Derek Parfit observed that neurosurgeons had been able to split the brain and produce two separate streams of consciousness. He

---

10. Jackson and Csikszentmihalyi (1999, 66 f.).

concluded, like Hume and the Buddha before him, that personal identity is not possible.[11]

On the other hand the distinction, drawn by famed psychologist Karl Jung and others, between the persona we project to others and our deeper, more authentic selves not only makes the question of personal identity more complex, it opens up the possibility of finding and becoming our true selves.

Of course, the psychologist Sigmund Freud's discovery of the unconscious showed that these inner selves may not be so accessible as we might hope. Nevertheless, there seems to be some consensus in modern psychoanalytic theory that the "I" is at least partially a self-generated construct. That is, to a certain degree, I can *create* my own self. [12]

Psychology's discoveries about the elusiveness and flexibility of personal identity open up new possibilities for understanding and even shaping who we are. This makes the philosophical athlete's project of self-discovery and self-direction all the more plausible.

The Courage to Be Yourself

Runner/philosopher George Sheehan says it took him until middle age to get up the courage to be himself:

> At the age of reason, I was placed on a train, the shades drawn, my life's course and destination already determined. At the age of 45, I pulled the emergency cord and ran out into the world. It was a decision that meant no less than a new life, a new course, a new destination. I was born again in my 45th year.[13]

Running was the catalyst for this rebirth because it forced him to act in accordance with who he knew himself to be. Sheehan says that his "previous 'me' was not me" because it was thrust upon him by others. His educational and career paths, his personal choices about marriage and family had all been conditioned by external forces.

He found running to be an activity in which he couldn't avoid himself. Truths about his temperament, his body-type, his capacities, and his limitations forced themselves to the fore. Once he came to terms

---

11. Parfit (1987, 19).

12. For more on the relationship between modern psychoanalytic theory and the philosophical problem of personal identity, see Kolak (1993).

13. Sheehan (1975, 3).

with this genuine self, he began to live in accordance with it. And by living "authentically," he found freedom and happiness.

As athletes, we know that honestly assessing the truth about our physical strengths and weaknesses, then playing in accordance with that knowledge, leads to better performance. The short, quick basketball player who models his play after Shaquille O'Neal will never maximize his potential. The challenge for philosophical athletes is to apply that principle beyond sport and *live* according to our knowledge of ourselves—to be *authentic*.

The problem for most people, according to the French existentialist philosopher John-Paul Sartre, is that we identify too closely with the role or function given to us by society and sacrifice our sense of subjectivity, our unique selves, to that function.[14] It's easy in society to hide from yourself, to become so absorbed in what you are expected to be or what you are trying to be on the outside that you forget who you really are on the inside.

Responsibility and Authenticity

Just as the Fosbury flop represents a unique interpretation rather than a rejection of the rules of the high jump, being yourself requires independence from rather than abandonment of social roles. The trick is to take what you learn about being yourself in sport and retain that sense of unique identity as you perform your social functions.

Like Sartre's waiter in the story below, authentic individuals must not confuse who they are on the inside with the role they are playing for others. At the same time, they should find a way to express their individuality within social roles.

> *Let us consider the waiter in a café.* His movement is quick and forward, a little too precise, a little too rapid. He comes toward the patrons with a step a little too quick. He bends forward a little too eagerly; his voice, his eyes express an interest a little too solicitous for the order of the customer... All his behavior seems to us a game... He is playing; he is amusing himself. But what is he playing? We need not watch long before we can explain it: he is playing at being a waiter in a café.[15]

---

14. Sartre (1956, 58 f.).
15. Sartre (1956, 59), emphasis the author's.

Many athletes find ways to express their individuality within sport. They adopt particular styles such as a distinctive batting stance, or invent particular moves such as a signature slam-dunk. In sport, we're most comfortable—and most successful—when our actions express our unique selves.

We also know that it takes time and experience to develop a signature playing style. Likewise, it takes time and experience to be yourself in society. It also takes courage to accept the personal responsibility implied by a moment of challenge in sport. Philosophical athletes can develop and harness that courage earned at moments of challenge to accept personal responsibility for who they are in life. Ultimately, they may learn to live authentically based on the self-knowledge discovered in sport.

Thinking Activity: Be Like Mike

Question: What would it take not just to "be like Mike" but to actually be Michael Jordan—that is, to have his personal identity?

Observe: You've heard of sports video games where they put electrodes on real athletes' bodies to computerize and duplicate their movements on screen. Imagine an elaborate virtual-reality game that could interface with your brain at exactly the right places in a way that gave you all the sense experiences Michael Jordan has when he takes off through the air for a spectacular dunk. Perhaps the programmers planted a recording device in Jordan's brain, then simply replayed that data into a similar device hooked up to your brain.

Analyze: Does this scene have all the elements necessary for identity transfer? Hume says that our selves are just bundles of perceptions. So if all the perceptions that Jordan has somehow became mine, on what basis could we claim to be different persons? Locke equates personal identity with memory. Would the virtual reality game have to transfer all Mike's memory data as well as his perceptions in order for the identity transfer to be complete? What about the body? Of course my body remains silent, still, and 5'6" tall during this experience—does that matter as long as I receive the signals from Mike's body? Do I also need the rewards to truly be Mike? Do I need the applause of the crowd? The championship trophy? The salary and endorsements? Do I deserve *them?*

Question Again: Ask yourself what this exercise has taught you about your view of personal identity. What does it reveal about what really matters in being a great athlete? Would you really give up being yourself forever, in order to be like Mike?

Chapter Review

Summary

The many and varied moments of challenge in sport provide philosophical athletes with a starting gate for our pursuit of self-knowledge. These challenges function as lived philosophical questions that demand an admission of uncertainty and create a heartfelt desire to learn. Here, a philosophical athlete begins to struggle with questions of personal identity. We find the opportunity to access and reidentify the constant and unchangeable dimension of our inner selves. The sense of aloneness felt at the moment of challenge helps us to individuate ourselves from the masses, and to experience ourselves as isolated individuals.

The personal responsibility for success or failure accepted at the moment of challenge reveals the subjective, first-person perspective on life so often lost in society. In sport we are forced to see ourselves from the inside out, to deal with the problem of inner and outer selves. As an athlete, I am not an actor playing the part of a free-throw shooter, I *am* a free-throw shooter, *this* free-throw shooter, *myself*. Even if I fail in accomplishing my task, the truth of the moment has beauty. I have learned something about myself and satisfied, if only for a moment, my overriding thirst for wisdom.

Further Reading

Philosophy

Hume, David. [1739] 1978. "Of Personal Identity." Section VI of *A Treatise of Human Nature*, edited by L. A. Selby-Bigge, 2nd ed. Oxford: Clarendon Press, 251–255. In this brief selection, Hume articulates the problem of finding some invariable entity we can call the self. Hume's famous conclusion that we are "bundles of impressions" requires a brief introduction to empirical thought, but proves dissatisfying in a provocative way.

Kolak, Daniel. 1993. "Finding Our Selves: Identification, Identity, and Multiple Personality." In Kolak and Martin, ed., 94–113. Kolak gives a useful overview of the impact of advances in modern psychology on the philosophical problem of personal identity.

Locke, John. [1689] 1975. "Of Identity and Diversity." Book II, Chapter 27 of *An Essay concerning Human Understanding*, edited by Peter H. Nidditch. Oxford: Clarendon Press, 328–348. This selection offers a relatively concise solution to the problems of personal identity based on the theory that persons are essentially consciousness and identity is memory.

Sartre, Jean-Paul. 1956. *Being and Nothingness.* Translated by Hazel E. Barnes. New York: The Philosophical Library, Inc. The existentialist concept of authenticity is not unique to Sartre, but his account of it in this classic work is among the most accessible and inspiring.

Philosophy of Sport

Harper, William. 1969. "Man Alone." *Quest* XII: 57–60. Using existentialist text from Heidegger and Sartre, Harper emphasizes the human need to isolate ourselves from others in the process of finding our identities. He identifies the individualizing experience of sport as way to do this in the modern world.

Novak, Michael. 1988. "Self-Discovery." In *The Joy of Sports: End Zones, Bases, Baskets, Balls, and the Consecration of the American Spirit.* Lanham, NY: Hamilton Press, 158–166. Novak offers an inspired explanation of what it means to experience yourself "from the inside out" in sport.

Sheehan, George. 1975. "Myself and Yourself." In *Dr. Sheehan on Running.* New York: Bantam, 3–12. This is an autobiographical essay that explains how running was the medium for Sheehan's mid-life self-discovery and a new expression of personal independence.

Journalism and Literature

Noriyuki, Duane. 1990. "Let the Games Begin." Originally published in *The Detroit Free Press Magazine.* Reprinted in Halberstam, ed., 48–61. This is a non-fiction news feature about a 100m race among three young men from a rough Detroit neighborhood. Their performances in the race neatly reflect their individual personalities.

Chapter 2

Discovering Yourself as Embodied

Chapter Preview

Introduction:
My Body, My Mind, Myself

> *The marvels of the body are short-lived, reminding us of our own mortality. Becoming an athlete is then the building of a new self-confidence, a confidence exclaiming to the world that this body can withstand anything the world has to offer, but which can only briefly cover up the real sources of insecurity.*
>
> —Stephen Kiesling, *The Shell Game*

For athletes, the relationship between mind and body is much more than an academic question. We are identified in society by our bodily dimensions—described in terms of height, weight, circumference of the biceps. It's not surprising, then, that some athletes derive their sense of worth from their bodies—even to the extent that they may ignore or even hide their real selves.

Erstwhile Big-10 football player Elwood Reid explains:

In high school, my scrawny body filled out as I moved from junior varsity to varsity and then to captain of a mediocre football team. College scouts came to time me in the forty-yard dash, watch me lift weights and eye me coming out of the shower as if I were a horse they might someday bid for at auction. I can't say I didn't enjoy the attention, but I began to realize that as a potential college-football recruit, I was expected to behave like one...I had to be smart but not too smart...I couldn't tell them that I didn't care who won the

Super Bowl, that what really mattered to me was books. That when I finished *One flew Over the Cuckoo's Nest* or *Heart of Darkness*, my heart beat faster than it ever had on the football field. I knew I had to keep this part of me hidden and let the scouts and coaches see the bright-eyed athlete they wanted to see.[1]

Reid goes on to describe the experience of being a slave to his body, then having his body enslaved by coaches and a brutal game that nearly squelched the book-loving student inside and left him "with a clear-cut of a body, a burned-out village that I sacked for a sport."[2]

Embedded within the question "Who am I?" is the *metaphysical* question, "What am I?"[3] And, just as the moment of challenge in sport provides a starting point for the philosophical athlete's exploration of personal identity, it also provides fertile ground for coming to understand the nature of that "I."

In philosophy, debate about the nature of human beings focuses on the *mind-body problem*. We appear to have minds and to have bodies, but what are they made of and how are they related? To many, these seem to be questions better suited to science than philosophy. However, if you think that human beings have a mystical dimension such as soul or spirit, empirical science will not get you too far. You must ask the question philosophically: what am I, exactly?[4]

In sport, athletes face mind-body problems of their own: getting their bodies to do what their minds ask. How often we apprehend, envision, even rehearse an athletic move in our minds only to have our bodies fall short. How seldom we experience the seamless cooperation of mind and body some call "the zone."

Athletes' and philosophers' mind-body problems *are* connected, but not in the way you might think. Western philosophy's view of the mind-

---

1. Reid (1998, 119).

2. Reid (1998, 131).

3. *Metaphysics* is the philosophical study of the nature of reality. So the metaphysical study of human beings involves questions about the nature of our material and immaterial existence and their relation.

4. The most common answer I hear to this question is "body, mind, and spirit," an answer heavily influenced by modern western religions. It's worth noting that, for philosophers, the task of distinguishing among mind, soul and spirit is of much less interest than distinguishing between mind and body. One reason for this is that Plato, who postulated a real distinction between body and mind, had a conventional idea of body but a very complex idea of mind that incorporated most of the characteristics we now might attribute to soul or spirit.

body problem has so influenced the beliefs, perspective, and even language of western culture that it may actually *create* the athletes' mind-body problem.

Compare western athletes' complaints about their bodies refusing do what their minds command with the Zen approach to sport found in many eastern cultures. Zen athletes seek to eliminate the distinction between themselves and external objects. "Don't just see the ball," they say, "*be* the ball." Western athletes who complain about disobedient bodies not only make a distinction between subjects and objects, we also make a distinction between our*selves* and our bodies! We view our bodies as objects to be used by our minds. It's important to understand that we do this because mind/body division is engrained into our schooling, language, and philosophical heritage.

Now the task of philosophical athletes is to seek knowledge about ourselves through our experience in sport. Just as the moment of challenge provides an opportunity to encounter oneself from the *inside out,* it also gives us a chance to address the question of mind and body away from the influence of culture and upbringing.

Social assumptions about mind and body act like 3D glasses that influence our view of everything, including ourselves. By understanding the way philosophy influences our perceptions, we may liberate ourselves from such illusions and attempt to observe our experience in sport with fresh eyes.

So the mind-body problem for philosophical athletes is really an intellectual challenge—a challenge to answer the question "What am I?" by observing and evaluating our experience in sport free from distorting influences.

Chapter Preview List

- Is being an athlete more about the body or the mind?
- Is intelligence in athletics different from intelligence elsewhere?
- Do you view your body as friend or foe?

2.1 Athletic Bodies: From Divine Images to Lab Specimens

The Athletic Body-Object

Next time you have a chance, take a close look at some ancient Greek statues. You will see some of the most beautiful athletic bodies imaginable. Finely muscled, perfectly proportioned, these statues are still awe-inspiring as reflections of ideal physical beauty. What you may not realize is that many of these statues depict gods.

Ancient Greeks imagined their gods in human form, great athletes capable of competing in battles alongside their favorite mortals. Athletic contests such as the Olympics were organized specifically to honor the gods, who were presumably pleased by the athletes' efforts to approximate divine perfection. But this emphasis on the physical prowess and beauty of the gods was eventually eroded—first by Plato, who emphasized the divinity of intellect, then by religions that associate the body with sin. The ancient Olympic games were abolished for religious reasons.[5]

Although the beauty of athletic bodies is still widely prized, the idea that bodies and minds are distinct from one another has had a profound and often damaging impact on athletics and human movement in the modern western world.

If you view success in sport as an issue of mind over matter, you may very well be just another athletic legacy of *dualism* (the view that mind and body are two distinct things). Consider such terms as "physical education," such expressions as "keeping your mind in the game," such slogans as "a sound mind in a sound body." As we eventually learned from our struggle with racial segregation, what is separate cannot be equal. Whether the body or the mind is regarded as more important, the whole person eventually suffers.

Philosophical Background: Descartes' Mind-Body Dualism

By far the most famous argument for dualism comes from the 17th century French philosopher René Descartes. Famous for saying, "I think,

---

5. See Swaddling (1980, 78–79).

therefore I am," Descartes arrived at the conclusion that human beings are essentially 'thinking things' by employing a scientific "method of doubt."

In the *Meditations,* Descartes searches after certain truth by eliminating every idea that can be doubted for any reason. Since so many of our thoughts come to us through the senses (sight, smell, taste, touch, and hearing), which are notoriously fallible, they must all be eliminated as candidates for truth. Included among these are all thoughts about the body:

> Therefore I will suppose that all I see is false. I will believe that none of those things that my deceitful memory brings before my eyes ever existed. I thus have no senses: body, shape, extension, movement, and place are all figments of my imagination. What then will count as true? Perhaps only this one thing: that nothing is certain...[6]

As it turns out the only thing Descartes can be sure about is his thinking. Even if *what* he thinks is completely wrong, it is still true that he is thinking. A "great deceiver" could be creating every thought in his head like some cosmic virtual reality game—but he would still exist if only as the passive recipient of all this false input.

> Deceive me as he will, he can never bring it about that I am nothing so long as I shall think that I am something. Thus it must be granted that, after weighing everything carefully and sufficiently, one must come to the considered judgment that the statement, "I am, I exist" is necessarily true every time it is uttered by me or conceived in my mind.[7]

Once Descartes identified thinking as the solitary indubitable truth about his nature, it wasn't a huge leap to the idea that "I" am (like all humans) essentially a thinking thing—a *mind*. Furthermore, since material things like bodies are by nature so uncertain, the minds we identify with can't just be brains, they must be immaterial.

> Here I discover that thought is an attribute that really does belong to me. This alone cannot be detached from me. I am; I exist; this is certain. But for how long? For as long as I think. Because perhaps it could also come to pass that if I should cease from all think-

---

6. Descartes (1993, 17).
7. Descartes (1993, 18).

ing I would then utterly cease to exist. I now admit nothing that is not necessarily true. I am therefore precisely only a thing that thinks; that is, a mind, or soul, or intellect, or reason — words the meaning of which I was ignorant before. Now, I am a true thing, and truly existing; but what kind of thing? I have said it already: a thing that thinks.[8]

Descartes' observation provides an *epistemological* rationale for the widespread belief that our bodies are extended (space-occupying), material substances, while our minds are unextended, non-physical thinking things.[9] The mind is, of course, in charge of the body. This dualistic account may be illustrated by the image of a ghost (immaterial mind) driving a car (material body). The athlete's body would be a kind of machine operated by a mysterious immaterial force.

There are problems with this account, just as there would be problems getting a ghost to drive a car. How can an immaterial mind make a material thing like my body move? Descartes thought the two interfaced somewhere in the brain, but science can neither confirm nor deny his explanation. Furthermore, athletic experience tells us that the mind/body interface is more complex and less reliable than ordinary life would make it seem. Will the nature of the mind-body connection forever be a mystery?

A Love-Hate Relationship with Our Bodies

When René Descartes identified "I" as an unextended thinking-thing, his mind became the subject and his body the object. On this view, the body is something owned, operated, and controlled by the mind — a hierarchy that fits well with religions and philosophies that view the mind as divine and eternal, the body as base and ephemeral.

But in practice we find it difficult to identify with our minds over our bodies. Hunger, thirst, and sexual drives sometimes seem to control us. Our gender, race, and physiques seem inseparable from who we are.

---

8. Descartes (1993, 19).

9. *Epistemology* is the philosophical study of knowledge. Since Descartes finds thought to be known with more *certainty* than matter (which is only known through unreliable senses) his argument that we are our minds is knowledge-based, or *epistemological.*

Our understanding of genetic codes link physical reality to personal destiny. If I am subject and my body object, it sure seems as if my body is pulling "me" around, like an unruly St. Bernard on a leash.

This dualistic confusion that permeates western culture has resulted in what sport-philosopher Lynne Belaief calls athletes' love-hate relationship with their bodies.[10] On the one hand, we love our athletic bodies for their power, grace, and finely proportioned beauty. On the other hand, we resent that same bodily power as demonically violent, or crude and unfeminine in women. Men may worry that their grace is "effeminate." Physical beauty can become an unattainable ideal that engenders anxiety or eating disorders.

Even highly successful and widely admired athletes can have tortured relationships with their bodies. Triathlete Paula Newby-Fraser, for example, doesn't like the look of her legs and buttocks despite the fact that they have propelled her to victory in several Ironman races.[11]

One way to deal with mind/body bifurcation is to reject claims about the superiority of the mind and identify specifically with our bodies. This approach is associated with traditional physical education, whose roll-calls and jumping jacks nearly all of us have endured. According to this paradigm, our bodies are still objects but they are objects to be prized and developed—separately from the mind.

Arguably, however, the widespread failure of traditional PE to encourage human health is due to its acceptance of mind-body separation. It failed to improve the body (which it viewed as an object/machine) because it neglected to engage the mind, which it viewed as separate and irrelevant to its goal.[12] How many still view physical exercise as "mind-numbing" drudgery?

The same mistake is being made by several contemporary attempts at motivating people to exercise. There is the focus on physical beauty and sex-appeal that spawned so many trendy athletic clubs in the 1980s. Ultimately the singles' bar effect became more important than the exercise. Lately there has been a focus on personal health. With obesity, cancer, and heart disease rates rising, exercise is repeatedly prescribed as the only effective prevention. Still, success is limited. Dieting

10. Belaief (1977, 414).
11. See Burton-Nelson (1991, 52).
12. An articulate account of this crisis can be found in Leonard (1975, chapter 1).

is infinitely more popular than exercise, and obesity rates continue to swell among old and young alike.

The fact is that few people will continue to exercise unless they find some *meaning in their movement*.[13] To do that we must engage the mind in movement, rather than distracting it with music, television, or reading. Philosophical athletes should treasure our workouts as quality times with our selves—a chance for the mind to get to know the body, or perhaps, to reveal their unity.

The Scientific Attitude

The fact is that it's difficult to sell anything associated with the body in a mind-worshiping world. Perhaps that is why the credibility-starved sports establishment has so fervently embraced scientific methods. Exercise science is a legitimate major. Sports medicine is a recognized specialty. Athletes talk knowledgeably about fast-twitch muscle fiber percentage and VO2 max.

The lab-coats and test-tubes bring an aura of intellectual respectability to sport, but they objectify the athletic body more than ever. Now my body plays object not only to my mind, but also to scientists and technicians who regard it as an item to probe, measure, and examine.

Athletes have sold their souls to a scientific mindset interested only in matter. They take it as a compliment to be called "magnificent physical specimens," seeming to celebrate a kinship with laboratory rats. They regard a competitor with awe and call him a "wrestling machine." Do they aspire to be robots?

This development is not recent. John Hoberman identifies the 19th century invention of ergometers—machines that could quantitatively measure athletic performance—as the dawn of an era in which athletes themselves would be viewed as machines.[14]

Eventually the myth of the scientific techno-athlete would be immortalized in the movie *Rocky IV*, where superstar Dolf Lundgren plays a mysterious Russian boxer honed to athletic perfection by a team

---

13. This is the theme of a paper by R. Scott Kretchmar, whose thesis is parallel to mine here.
14. Hoberman (1992, 62–69).

of great minds. The athlete's own mind is not an issue; it's not even in the picture. He is pure body-object, created and controlled entirely by others.

Is treating our bodies as objects really the best path to excellence?

Thinking Activity: Are You a Dualist?

Question: Would you characterize yourself as more of a dualist or materialist in the way you think about your mind and body?

Observe: Take a clean sheet of paper and describe a moment you have experienced in sport where your mind and body seemed to function together in perfect harmony OR where your mind and body seemed at odds with each other. Try to give as many details as possible about how you felt at that moment.

Analyze: Now evaluate your essay to see how you used the word "I"—do you associate the "I" more with your body or your mind? Do you use the possessive pronouns "my" just for your body or for your mind also? Do the good or bad feelings about your performance originate in your body or in your mind? Which seems more important to you in sport?

Question Again: If you identify more with your mind than your body, is that based on external (social and cultural) input or more on internal observation? Next time you work out, see if you can distinguish your mind from your body in real experience.

2.2 Have Athletes Lost Their Minds?

The Myth of the Dumb Jock

It's not hard to see how athletes "lost their minds" in a dualistic world that has come to worship science and matter. It is the assumption of our culture and its philosophical heritage that thinking is superior to doing, the researcher superior to the runner. Society values physical activity insofar as it promotes health or yields financial rewards, but ultimately sports are something we should either "make money from" or "grow out of" as more pressing matters render us "too busy" to indulge the mind's physical support system. Imagine if people neglected their minds as they routinely neglect their bodies.

We do this not only because Plato and Descartes prioritized mind over body, but because we've since decided as a culture that excellence of mind is at best unrelated to and at worst mutually exclusive of excellence of body. This attitude may be traced to Darwin's theory of evolution in which intellect, not strength, distinguishes higher from lower life forms. Physical strength is routinely viewed as nature's recompense for a weak intellect.[15]

Our culture values mind over body and associates the athlete with body. No wonder the athlete has become little more than an object of study, profit or entertainment for other minds more worthy. As their bodies became the objects of scientific query, the mental dimension of athletic persons was first minimized and then ignored.

The dumb-jock myth has survived sport's scientific revolution intact because the mind associated with the science of human performance almost never belongs to the athlete. In the end, athletes' minds aren't considered worthy of those great physical specimens—even by the athletes themselves. We leave the big thinking up to some other person, some other place, or some other time.

Perhaps the athlete's best hope is the belief that the mind is just another material component of the body-machine. But prospects seem grim for an athlete-robot whose mind can be reduced to a programmable computer-brain. Notes rower Craig Lambert in *Mind over Water*:

> These reductive analogies exact a fearsome price from the human soul. If we believe our bodies to be machines and our brains to be computers, we will wonder why we do not function with mechanistic consistency. I should perform perfectly 100 percent of the time. Humanity becomes a case of defective technology. We feel flawed since we lack the reliability of the inanimate world; what is alive fails by comparison to that which is not.[16]

Ironically, it just may be computer scientists who inadvertently recover the athlete's mind. That is because the efforts to reproduce human intelligence in computers are teaching us much about the wonder and complexity of minds and thinking.

Philosophical Background:
Reductive Materialism: Mind = Brain

Perhaps Descartes and other dualists are just wrong about there being an immaterial mind. These days, people tend to look to science for answers about the nature of human beings and since science ob-

---

15. Darwin's effect on attitudes toward the body in general and athletes in particular is revealed and explored by Hoberman (1992, 33–61).

16. Lambert (1998, 138–139).

serves material things, the idea that our minds are in fact matter (brains) is gaining favor.

This view is called *reductive materialism* — "reductive" because mental phenomena are "reduced" to physical phenomena, and "materialism" because the underlying assumption is that whatever exists must be physical matter. The corresponding analogy might be a robot (material mind) driving a car (material body). An athlete's mind, on this view, is merely one component of an autonomous machine.

Neuropsychologists, brain researchers, and computer scientists aiming to wrest intelligence from silicon all tend to be materialists of one kind or another. Says computer guru Bill Gates:

> I don't think there's anything unique about human intelligence.... Eventually we'll be able to sequence the human genome and replicate how nature did intelligence in a carbon-based system.[17]

Mind-brain identity theory is among the most popular of materialist philosophies of mind. Its basic premise is that every mental state is identical (and reducible) to some physical state of the brain. Human minds function like computers, receiving external inputs (stimuli), which cause particular brain states and result in specific outputs (behavior).

Materialist philosophers, such as Paul Churchland, explain that scientific observation of human and other organisms leads logically to the thesis of mind-brain identity. So much of what we know about humans can be explained in purely physical terms, from our origin as fertilized eggs to the blueprint for development encoded in our DNA. Behaviors of simple creatures have been explained in terms of their neural structure; it's just a matter of time before neuroscience is capable of doing the same thing for us.[18]

Indeed, advances in neuroscience and computer technology suggest to many that the differences between human intelligence and computers may not be so great. On the other hand, while computerized machines may match or even exceed human ability to remember or calculate, the revelation of what computers *cannot* do is also giving us insight into the very special nature of the human mind.

How can materialism account for *qualia* or the "raw feel of things" that human beings experience? Even if I can program an electronic eye

---

17. Gates quoted in Issacson (1997, 47).
18. See, for example, Churchland (1981).

to distinguish one shade of red from another, can it ever be said to *experience* red in the same way that I do? It turns out that our minds do much more than gather, sort, and store information. Will a computer ever be creative or insightful? Could it feel jealousy or rage? Maybe its screen will get red like my face does, but the question of whether such physical events are identical with the mental ones is still open.

To Think or Not to Think?

The dumb jock myth, prefaced by Cartesian dualism, endorsed by Darwinsim, and rubber-stamped by reductive materialism is as much a theory of intelligence as it is a stereotype about athletes. The idea that muscularity and intellectual ability are inversely proportional in humanity is a hard one to shake, but it depends on a comically narrow definition of intelligence.

We tend to envision "thinking" as something done while sitting on a chair, perhaps crouched over with chin resting on fist, *a la* Rodin's sculpture *The Thinker*. Our conventional idea of intellectual activity emphasizes the collection, storage and recall of information, quick calculation and strategic planning.

Athletes are not known for this kind of mindwork. When sport requires such information processing, calculation, and strategizing it tends to be done by others. An entire committee of coaches and managers sits in a stadium skybox and does that kind of thinking for professional American football teams.

In fact, athletes have found that too much conventional thinking can interfere with their performance. "Not-thinking" is the secret to success in sport, according to many influenced by Eastern philosophies, such as basketball coach Phil Jackson and advocates of Taosports.[19] Says baseball guru Ray Knight, "Concentration is the ability to think about absolutely nothing when it's absolutely necessary."[20]

But is the kind of processing, planning and calculation found to be an obstacle to athletic performance a valid definition of intelligence? Athletes say that their ability to suspend such mental busywork results not in mindlessness, but a greater "mindfulness" — a more efficient use

---

19. See Jackson's (1995) book *Sacred Hoops*. For more on Taosports, see Huang and Lynch (1992).

20. Knight quoted in Jones (1997, 147).

of their mental capacity. Perhaps intelligence increases as conventional thinking decreases. Says Jackson:

> Basketball is a complex dance that requires shifting from one objective to another at lightning speed. To excel, you need to act with a clear mind and be totally focused on what everyone on the floor is doing... The secret is not thinking. That doesn't mean being stupid; it means quieting the endless jabbering of thoughts so that your body can do instinctively what it's been trained to do without the mind getting in the way.[21]

Intelligence Beyond Thinking

The question of just what intelligence is has been raised by efforts to reproduce it artificially. The information processing and calculation we've associated with "conventional thinking" are precisely the kinds of activities done so well by computers. But research is revealing that intelligence involves much more than our conventional idea of "thinking."

IBM has a computer that can defeat almost every human being at the game of chess, and machines capable of passing the "Turing Test" (see Thinking Activity) are practically reality. But even as computers can catch and surpass human beings in performing certain mental functions, it remains to be seen whether they will ever be *intelligent* as long as they lack insight, creativity, and independent ideas.

As part of his project to create a holistic view of persons, sport philosopher R. Scott Kretchmar distinguishes between "impressive" and "unimpressive" intelligence by evaluating human activity not in terms of whether it's active or sedentary, but in terms of insight and creativity.[22] Low intelligence activity tends to be constrained, repetitive, and lacking in creativity or insight. Freedom, unpredictability, inventiveness and the experience of meaning, on the other hand, characterize high intelligence activity.

Kretchmar observes that the characteristics that distinguish the intelligent practice of sedentary activities such as math and history can be applied to athletic activities such as basketball or gymnastics. Looked at in these terms, a "dumb-jock" is someone who plays without imagina-

---

21. Jackson (1995, 115–116).
22. Kretchmar (1994, 74–77).

tion or creativity. Likewise, the genius displayed in a Michael Jordan dunk may reflect the magnitude of intelligence exhibited in an Einstein theorem.

On this view, genius is something expressible through the body as well as the mind.

Thinking Activity: Athletic Turing Test
Question: Could a robot ever display athletic intelligence?
Observe: To determine whether a computer was in fact intelligent, Alan Turing devised a test in which an interrogator sets before a computer screen in one room and types in questions which are then answered by either (A) the computer to be tested for intelligence, or (B) another human being. If the interrogator can't distinguish between the computer and the human based on their answers, the computer is considered intelligent.
Now imagine a similar contest between a human athlete and a sophisticated humanoid robot (like the "Terminator" or "Bicentennial Man") Assume that by looking at them, you cannot tell the difference between the two. What sort of contest would you devise? What sort of feats would the robot have to perform to convince you it was athletically intelligent?
Analyze: How are the test and criteria for intelligence different from Turing's? Is athletic intelligence any different from conventional ideas of intelligence? How and why?
Question Again: What does this exercise tell you about your attitude toward athletic minds? If a robot can perform the physical functions of an athlete, does it need anything more to compete? Should robots be allowed to compete against human athletes in sport?

2.3 The Athlete's Embodied Self

The Experience of Embodiment

The distortion caused by viewing athletes through the prism of dualist philosophy is an obstacle to understanding because it doesn't cohere with our experience in sport. In the moment of challenge, at all moments in sport, athletes experience themselves *as embodied*. The "I" who shoots this free-throw is neither a disembodied mind nor a mindless body-machine. Sure, I can *focus* on my mind or on my body, but I can never *be* one without the presence of the other.

So philosophical athletes, in seeking to discover our selves at the moment of challenge, often take the approach of phenomenology. We ask the question "What am I?" not from an abstract, theoretical perspective; we ask it from the inside out. We begin by observing the phenomenon of our personal experience, which is always embodied, then proceed to analyze and evaluate it.

Philosophical Background:
Phenomenology: A Middle Path

Phenomenology represents a new and different approach to the mind-body problem. Phenomenologists reject both materialist and dualist positions because both assume that we have some privileged access to the truth about these things when in fact all we can know is the way we experience them.

Phenomenology grows out of the insight of famed German philosopher Immanuel Kant who distinguished objects and events in our experience (*phenomena*) from objects and events as they really are in themselves (*noumena*). His point was that we can never know *noumena* and should admit being limited to *phenomena*. Later philosophers including G.W.F. Hegel believed that deep examination of *phenomena* might lead to an understanding of *noumena* after all. The point, however, is that we must evaluate our experience in full awareness of its limitations.

The 20th century philosopher Maurice Merleau-Ponty criticized his countryman Descartes' dualism from a phenomenological perspective. In his *Phenomenology of Perception*, Merleau-Ponty charges that Descartes assumed our understanding of matters both internal and external to ourselves to be more transparent than it possibly could be. The thesis of separate body and mind, says Ponty, simply doesn't match up to our real experience. We never are *just* a body or *just* a mind. My body is not an object with "I" as the subject, I don't live inside my body and operate it like some fancy motorhome. Says Ponty:

> There are two senses, and two only, of the word 'exist': one exists as a thing or else one exists as a consciousness. The experience of our own body, on the other hand, reveals to us an ambiguous mode of existing. If I try to think of it as a cluster of third person processes — 'sight,' 'motility,' 'sexuality' — I observe that these 'functions' cannot be interrelated, and related to the external world, by causal connections, they are all obscurely drawn together and mutually implied in a unique drama. Therefore the body is not an object.[23]

23. Merleau-Ponty (1962, 198).

Furthermore, experience clearly shows my body to be more than a dubitable thought. Descartes' methodical thinking allowed him to separate his mind from his body the way a 3D spaceship may emerge from a computer-generated wallprint after I stare at it for hours. But these are illusions and in our real experience, say phenomenologists, the body and mind are experienced simultaneously as a unity:

> Whether it is a question of another's body or my own, I have no means of knowing the human body other than that of living it, which means taking up on my own account the drama which is being played out in it, and losing myself in it. I am my body, at least wholly to the extent that I possess experience, and yet at the same time my body is as it were a 'natural' subject, a provisional sketch of my total being. Thus experience of one's own body runs counter to the reflective procedure which detaches subject and object from each other, and which gives us only the thought about the body, or the body as an idea, and not the experience of the body or the body in reality.[24]

Phenomenology is less a position on the mind-body problem than it is an approach to the question of the nature of human beings that rejects the reductive claims of materialists and dualists alike. Whatever the metaphysical reality of minds and bodies, the attitude we take toward them will affect our behavior.

We can see how the dualistic beliefs of the western philosophical tradition affect those cultures' attitudes toward the relative worth of our bodies and minds. We value mental over physical labor. We demean nudity, sexuality, and body odors. We envision heaven as a place inhabited only by purified spirits. In contrast, the objectives of scientific and computer researchers tend to commit them to materialism, despite the varieties of human mental experience.

Ultimately, we must look inside in our drive to answer the question, "What am I?"

Phenomenology and the Sports Experience

Several philosophers of sport advocate phenomenology—and the unity of body and mind that it endorses—as the only way to answer

---

24. Merleau-Ponty (1962, 198–199).

the metaphysical question of the nature of persons.[25] While it is obvious that the dualistic tendency to value mind over body has harmed the enterprise of sport and physical education professionals, one should be careful not to make assumptions about what we can know.

There's a big difference between taking a phenomenological *approach* to the question of mind and body, and coming to the conclusion that the *phenomena* of our personal experience can lead us to truth about *noumena*, things as they are in-themselves. Even sport philosophers who identify Descartes as the mortal enemy of their profession get tangled up in dualistic language while attempting to denounce it.[26]

Perhaps in our western world it is as difficult to eradicate mind-body thought as it is to eliminate mind-body talk. Philosophical athletes must work to transcend all assumptions about mind and body in seeking to understand our selves through sport.

"If you are looking for the answers to the Big Questions about your soul," says runner/philosopher George Sheehan, "you'd best begin with the Little Answers about your body."[27] The sporting experience denies escape from either mind or body, so our reflection on that experience provides special insight into the connection between them (whether a real distinction exists or not).

To seek genuine answers to the *metaphysical* question of self, philosophical athletes must examine our sporting experience as free as possible from prejudice about souls, spirits, computers, and machines. When we do this, we will discover truths not just about minds and bodies but about our*selves*.

Integrating Mind and Body

In contrast to such sedentary activities as taking tests or watching TV in which we try to ignore our bodies, sport forces us to *listen to our bodies*. All athletes know the importance of this skill. They take their

---

25. For example, Meier (1979) and Kretchmar (1994).

26. For example, Paul Weiss (1969, 41). In the midst his famous essay advocating sport as a path accepting our bodies as ourselves, Weiss says, "Man uses his mind to dictate what the body is to do."

27. Sheehan (1978, 53).

pulses upon rising, gauge the tightness of their calf muscles, worry about every tingle in their throats. Even as they savor the exhaustion that follows a game well-played or a race well-run, even as they welcome the pain-numbing endorphins that miraculously quiet their bodies' screams midway through a hard effort, athletes neglect or ignore their bodies at their peril and they know it.

What most athletes don't know but philosophical athletes do know is just how much can be learned from listening to their bodies. Listen closely enough to your body and you might discover a window to your soul. The fact is that we can't effectively distance our bodies from ourselves, nor should we treat them as objects to be used and abused. Sport provides an opportunity to transcend the love-hate relationship so many of us have with our bodies.

Sport allows athletes' bodies to escape from being passive objects of social judgment and transforms them into active subjects seeking personal excellence. Since the criteria for success and failure in sport are clearly delineated, the emphasis is shifted from how your body looks to what it can do. A pass can be caught in American football with artistic elegance or lumbering awkwardness; what matters in sport is that it is caught. Even in such sports as diving or figure skating that are judged partly on aesthetic criteria, the score ultimately rests what your body does, not what it is (or how it looks).

The feminist goal to "take back our bodies" is achieved in sport (by both males and females) every day. As an athlete, I need not agree with Gabriel Marcel that "I am my body," any more than I must concede to Descartes that I'm essentially a thinking thing.[28] Nor must I view my mind as a computer or my body as a machine. But as a philosophical athlete I will experience myself as embodied and as a result I might at last welcome my body—complete with its limitations and imperfections—into my conception of myself.

Such body-acceptance is rare in our culture, but rewarded richly with the freedom to be oneself in every dimension. By refusing to separate my body from my self, by absorbing it into my "I"-subject and not letting it be an object for myself or anyone else, by seeing that bodily strength does not exclude intelligence but may enhance it, I take back my body, accept it into my self, and give myself permission to be *me*.

---

28. See Marcel (1952, 87–8).

Only a self that recognizes and incorporates both body and mind can experience the freedom of being what it really is. Fortunately, for the philosophical athlete, sport also provides a medium through which that authentic self can be expressed.

Thinking Activity: Psychosomatics
Question: Are body and mind characteristics linked?
Observe: Begin by identifying three basic body types (1) the stick-figure type tends to be all arms and legs, thinner, and taller or lighter in build. (2) The fireplug type tends to be solidly built and more heavily muscled with thicker arms and legs. (3) The Falstaff Type tends to be roundly built with shorter arms and legs. Place yourself into one of the categories and put someone you know well into each of the other two. List 3–5 mental characteristics for each person—introverted or extroverted, active or passive, socialite or loner. Now compare these mental qualities to those of other people with similar body types—do you see a pattern?
Analyze: Whether you see a pattern or not, what do you think it says about the connection of mind and body? Do you think people are happier when their personality matches their body type?
Question Again: What did you learn about your own attitudes toward mind and body in conducting this experiment? Were you skeptical or did you hope to find some connection? Are you happy with your personality? Your body type?

Chapter Review

Summary

For an athlete the mind-body problem is approached, like the question "Who am I?" from a unique perspective: it is *lived*. Athletes experience themselves as embodied and so the western belief in dualism, which associates the "I" with the mind, is circumvented by the sports experience. Unfortunately, the rise of science and the influence of reductive materialism have led many to view bodies as machines and intelligence as calculation. Such attitudes often leave body-conscious athletes caught in love-hate relationships with themselves.

To bridge the mind-body divide, philosophical athletes must embrace the mind-body *connection*. Following the phenomenological approach, we can refuse to view our bodies as objects or machines and resist the idea that others are more worthy to control them. We can expand our idea of intelligence beyond skills better suited to computers and embrace uniquely human qualities such as creativity and meaning—

expressing that intelligence within sport and without. Next time you work out, leave the walkman or magazine behind—try to restore the mind-body connection within the practice of sport.

Further Reading

Philosophy

Descartes, Rene. 1993. "Second Meditation." In *Meditations on First Philosophy*, translated by Donald A. Cress. Indianapolis: Hackett, 17–23. This is the philosophical classic that introduces Descartes' famous conclusion "I think, therefore I am." (although he doesn't say it in just those words here). It contains important material about the puzzle of discovering who we are and the problem of knowing our bodies.

Merleau-Ponty, Maurice. 1962. "The Body as Expression." In *The Phenomenology of Perception*, translated by Colin Smith. London: Routledge and Kegan Paul, 198–199. This brief selection denies the idea of the body as object in summing up the phenomenological perspective on the mind-body problem.

Spicker, Stuart F., ed. 1970. *The Philosophy of the Body: Rejections of Cartesian Dualism*. New York: Quadrangle/New York Times Book Co. This is a useful anthology of essays that challenge the notion of Cartesian dualism. It boasts an all-star lineup of authors including Spinoza, Kant, Dewey, Marcel, Sartre, Merleau-Ponty, and Bernard Williams.

Philosophy of Sport

Belaief, Lynne. 1977. "Meanings of the Body". In Vanderwerken and Wertz, ed., 414–434. This essay explores our stormy relationships with our bodies and celebrates sport as an area where authentic acceptance of our bodies into our identities is possible.

Meier, Klaus V. 1979. "Embodiment, Sport, and Meaning." In Gerber and Meier, ed. (1979), 192–99. Dense and complicated, this essay has the virtue of covering both Cartesian and phenomenological approaches to the mind-body problem within the context of sport.

Weiss, Paul. 1969. "The Challenge of the Body." In Gerber and Meier, ed. (1979), 188–191. A groundbreaking essay, referenced by Meier, in which Weiss describes the athlete's challenge as a harmonizing of mind and body. Weiss says, "Athletics is mind displayed in a body well-made."

Journalism and Literature

Reid, Elwood. 1998. "My Body, My Weapon, My Shame." In Littlefield, ed., 118–131. A first-person account of a young athlete's bodily self-sacrifice to

the sport of football, it is a simultaneously graphic and poignant account
the struggle to find oneself.

Chapter 3

Discovering Yourself as Free

Chapter Preview

Introduction:
The Experience of Freedom in Sport

> *What I'm about, really, is just being free to be who I am in my own country.*
>
> — Cathy Freeman, Olympic Gold Medalist

"Smith" is at the same time every athlete and no athlete at all. A fictional character in Alan Sillitoe's classic novella *The Loneliness of the Long Distance Runner,* he seems to embody the experience of freedom known to real athletes everywhere. Most of all, his story reveals that freedom in sport is paradoxical: born of contradiction and consecrated by deliberate choice.

You see, Smith is quite literally a prisoner, the inmate of a juvenile detention center run by a "pop-eyed potbellied governor" who expects Smith to win the cross-country nationals for his reform school. It's no surprise that Smith is willing to leave his warm bed before dawn for chilly runs though the countryside—anything to get outside the gates.

But Smith makes it clear that he's not looking for a chance to run away,

> because to abscond and then get caught is nothing but a mug's game, and I'm not falling for it. Cunning is what counts in this life, and even that you've got to use in the slyest way you can.[1]

On these morning runs, Smith escapes more than the prison. As he trots out of the doorway, he imagines that he is the first man on earth.

---

1. Sillitoe (1959, 7).

He transcends psychological as well as physical boundaries, letting his mind run as freely as his legs. He probes the limits of his inner-strength and endurance. He obeys only the voice within.

As a runner he is valued—and he values himself—for something at which he excels. He reaches beyond his troubled upbringing, his lowly social status, even his crime (a burglary). During the sweet morning moments of his daily run, Smith experiences freedom, even as the guards tail him from behind.

The biggest threat to Smith's freedom is the fact that the Governor wants to profit from *his* running. He wants Smith to win the race so he can display the trophy on his bookshelf and gloat in front of his governor-buddies. It's not the prison walls that limit Smith's freedom, it's the chance that he might lose his independent sense of self.

In the end, Smith takes back his freedom by exercising an outrageous choice. On the day of the championships, he assures the Governor he'll win and sure enough he enters the stadium well ahead of the other runners. But then he stops just before the finish line to the astonishment of the crowd:

> And I could hear the lords and ladies now from the grandstand, and could see them standing up to wave me in: "Run!" they were shouting in their posh voices. "Run!" But I was deaf, daft and blind, and stood where I was, still tasting the bark in my mouth and still blubbing like a baby, blubbing now out of gladness that I'd got them beat at last.[2]

The second-placed runner comes and crosses the line for the win. The embarrassed Governor punishes Smith with six months of hard labor. But Smith had asserted his freedom and independence by making a choice that only he could make and thereby emancipating himself from the physical, social, and psychological shackles of his life.

Fate or free will? Destiny or deliberation? Providence or possibility? The philosophical issue of freedom and determinism endures like no other. On the one hand, experience clearly suggests that we human beings have control and free choice in what we think and do. On the other, there are many reasons to believe that things are predetermined: logical reasons, theological reasons, scientific reasons.

The soothing song *Que Serà Serà* celebrates an acceptance of our human powerlessness in the face of overriding fate and, indeed, the be-

---

2. Sillitoe (1959, 45).

lief that things are out of our control can be soothing at times. But just how much freedom must we concede in order to make sense of the world? The stakes are high. If free will can't be justified, all praise, whether applause, admiration, or annual salary, becomes, in a sense, undeserved. Likewise all blame loses its rationale, whether it takes the form of a social snub, parking fine, or the electric chair.

Despite all the evidence against it — or perhaps because of it — freedom is among the most fundamental human desires. There's something pardoxical about sport and the feeling of freedom it can provide. When athletes compete in rule-governed contests, they may be subject to more restrictions and regulations than at any other time in their lives — yet they *feel* free.

The truth is that we humans are limited in many different ways — even by such simple things as space, time, and gravity. The moment of challenge is a place where our senses are heightened: our sense of aloneness, of embodiment, and of freedom. The uncertainty in the moment of challenge imbues it with a palpable air of possibility. For the philosophical athlete, sport can be an opportunity to experience the freedom so widely sought yet so rarely experienced.

Chapter Preview List

- Can sport transcend the limitations and boundaries of space, time, and gravity?
- How might athletes cultivate psychological freedom through sport?
- What is the role of choice in our experience of freedom?

3.1 Freedom from Physical Reality

Sport: An Escape from Limitations

Sometimes I think of sport as one of those inflatable jumping chambers they have at the county fair. You know, the kind you can rent for a five-year-old's birthday party. It starts out as a flat tangle of rubber-coated canvas, then inflates into a giant balloon-like castle or spaceship. The kids then go inside and jump around with abandon. They run as fast as they can and bounce off the soft vinyl window or leap high into the air and come down any which way they want. There's a sense of freedom inside that inflatable pleasure dome—an escape from the reality of scraped knees, hard concrete, and the authority of parents who must wait outside, bemused and impotent.

For the philosophical athlete, sport carves out a similar escape from the equally oppressive world of adulthood. It is a place where we can savor uncertainty in an otherwise predictable world. Sport takes back and manipulates such seemingly untouchable elements as space, time, and gravity. It also releases us—if only temporarily—from our social contract with the community, personal obligations, and duty to authority. In sport, we can rise above our pretensions about ourselves and the prejudgments of others based on race, gender, ethnicity or social standing.

There is even a softening of consequences. Winning and losing, as seriously as we take them, are ultimately symbolic. The race driver careening around a specially-designed speedway in a protective cocoon is actually safer than the teenager speeding down a country road. Ultimately we learn that this freedom in the arena of sport is *of our own creation*. It is by exercising personal choice that we manufacture the freedom we experience as athletes.

History suggests that sport was in fact manufactured as a way to escape the reality of war and experience human freedom in a relatively safe, if artificial, environment. Such was the conclusion of sport-philosopher Eleanor Metheny upon examining Patroclus' funeral games as recounted in Homer's *Iliad*.

In that epic poem, Achilles, Odysseus, Ajax, and others stage contests in such activities as running, throwing, and wrestling to honor their fallen comrade. The games are a celebration of the late Patroclus' skills and also a welcome diversion from the heavy burdens and harsh realities of war.

Although the contests tested skills used by warriors in battle, Metheny observes that the rule-governed games transformed the warriors' milieu into one where they were *free* to go all out. The javelin throwers were free to throw their weapons as far as they could; the runners were free to run as fast as they could. The rules of sport create an ideal world, says Metheny, a world where we can escape the demands and realities of our real existence and find the opportunity to truly be our best:

> These rules are paradoxical. They restrict in order to free. They impose restrictions on human behavior, and they limit human action; but within those restrictions they offer every man an opportunity to know the feeling of being wholly free to go all out—free to do his utmost—free to use himself fully in the performance of one self-chosen human action. [3]

Perhaps our need to experience freedom is most acute at those times when reality seems so oppressive: the inevitability of death, the unpredictability of war, the feeling that we are no more self-determined than leaves floating down a stream. Anyone who has experienced the phenomenon known as *deja-vu* is sometimes haunted by the possibility that events are fixed and inevitable.

Philosophical Background:
Hard Determinism

The strict belief that *everything* happens for a reason and therefore could not have happened other than it did is called *hard determinism*. For a hard determinist, there are no free actions, no random events, no such thing as free human choice. Different philosophers have believed this for different reasons. Aristotle, for example, believed that simple logic entailed determinism. Logically, a claim like "Italy will win the 1990 World Cup" is either true or false even if I make it in 1989. And if the statement "Italy will win the 1990 World Cup" was true in 1989, then it is inevitable or determined that Italy will win, despite the fact that we didn't *know* about it until it happened. Says Aristotle:

> It follows that nothing either is or is not happening, or will be or will not be, by chance or as chance has it, but everything of neces-

---

3. Metheny (1968, 235).

sity and not as chance has it (since either he who says or he who denies is saying what is true). For otherwise it might equally well happen or not happen, since what is as chance has it is no more thus than not thus, nor will it be. [4]

Those who believe that God knows the answers to all questions about future events can be classified as theological determinists. The traditional Judeo-Christian conception of God holds that He is omniscient (all-knowing), omnipotent (all-powerful), and omnibenevolent (all-loving). Taken together, these divine perfections suggest that this must be the "best of all possible worlds," or so said the 18th century philosopher G.W. Leibniz. [5] Think he's crazy? Think again. Could a being that is all-knowing, all-powerful, and all-good create *anything other* than the best world possible?

Of course, many theologians seek to attribute the world's apparent imperfections to us human beings and our roguish free wills, but the concept of free will is very difficult to reconcile with the doctrine of God's omniscience. Was Eve really free *not to take* the fruit, as long as God knew what she would do? As a result, much of religious philosophy from the 4th century onward is a fantastic wrestling match with just this issue. [6]

The rise of a scientific worldview has only strengthened the case for hard determinism. Systematic observation revealed that Nature itself works according to predictable laws, while the doctrines of materialism and complete physical causation revealed that the domino theory applies to much more than governments and game pieces. Even my turning of a book page is caused by hand movements caused by muscle contractions caused by nervous system activity, caused by certain stimuli, and so on.

Of course, any theory proposing long chains of causes needs to explain the mysterious finger that flicks the first domino. Theologians such as Thomas Aquinas propose God as this "unmoved mover." Science's search for a different answer has done little but raise more questions. The study of quantum physics, for example, revealed apparently random, uncaused, and undetermined movement among micro-particles.

---

4. Aristotle, *De Interpretatione*, 18b5–10.
5. See Leibniz ([1875] 1985, 378).
6. For a sampling, see Augustine's *City of God*, Boethius' *The Consolation of Philosophy*, and Aquinas' "The Five Ways" from the *Summa Theologica*.

The question of what such movements say about events in the macro-world—particularly the question of whether this provides enough "slop in system" to accommodate human free will—remains open.[7]

An Escape to Uncertainty

Given the logical, theological, and scientific evidence for hard determinism, it is perhaps predictable that we crave freedom and uncertainty. In fact, this might be among the reasons we cherish sport. The rules and boundaries of sport carve out an oasis from the predictability of everyday life—an oasis of uncertainty. Uncertainty is essential to the "ideal world" of sport. The moment before a kick-off, tip-off, or starting gun in any sports event is perhaps the most cherished moment in the contest. It is full of uncertainty about the game's eventual outcome and therefore pregnant with possibility, hope, and wondering. Says famed miler Sir Roger Bannister, "No athlete enters a race sure that he's going to win."[8]

Uncertainty is the secret of sport's success as "live television." Pre-recorded or even tape-delayed events haven't nearly the same appeal, and what appeal they do have seems to rise and fall with the fact of whether the viewer knows the outcome. Just ask NBC, whose tape-delayed broadcast of the 2000 Sydney Olympic got terrible ratings. "Don't tell me what happens!" insists the viewer of a pre-recorded event—like the viewer of any good drama. We humans seem to be fatally attracted to uncertain outcomes. Perhaps it's our ever-looming suspicion of hard determinism that makes us savor the uncertainty inherent in sport.

Uncertainty also attracts and drives the individual athlete. Unlike an actor who has read the script of the play, an athlete never knows how the drama of sport will unfold. Athletes train for weeks in predictable and methodical cycles, trying to tame an uncertainty about their eventual performance in competition—an uncertainty that by its very nature can never be eradicated.

Athletes know through all their calculated daily efforts—the 10,000 stair steps, the 200 sit-ups, the 80 mile training rides, the 4 sets

---

7. This question about causation isn't so modern as it may sound. For the ancient Epicureans, the quantum discovery would have come as no surprise. They predicted "swerves" among atomic particles as the explanation for free will and responsibility in a wholly material world. See Lucretius (1946, book II, paragraph 216ff).

8. Bannister quoted in Jones (1997, 157).

of 10 reps at 70% of max—that their performance at the moment of challenge will nevertheless be uncertain. Training prepares you to face with courage those moments of uncertainty in sport, moments which always conjoin the freedom to fail with the freedom to transcend who you are.

What we may not realize is that the uncertainty essential to sport is deliberately created by its rules. Sports themselves—games, races, contests, challenges—are basically sets of man-made rules. They designate the object of the endeavor, dictate the conditions under which it will be performed, and stipulate specific criteria to determine success or failure. A 100m sprint, for example, sets its object as determining the fastest sprinter, limits the space in which this will be determined to a flat surface 100 meters long by 1 meter wide, and defines the winner as the athlete whose shoulders first break an imaginary plane at the finish line.

As the athletes wait at the starting line, crouched in their blocks, they know all these rules and they know there will be a winner. Such secure knowledge provides room to breathe in the sweet air of uncertainty. Who will win? How will I run? How many steps will I take? Will I take the lead? Will I come from behind? Implicit in these uncertainties is freedom—the freedom to run as fast as I can, to be the best I can, to stumble and fall on the track.

Transcending Boundaries

The rules of sport also provide an escape from seemingly untouchable natural and physical laws. They manipulate space by creating boundaries: the walls of a hockey arena or ropes of a boxing ring that bounce contestants back into the contest, the paint or chalk lines delineating an area of play which, when violated by the ball or a player's foot, stop the game.

These boundaries not only contain the arena of sport, they deny the importance of everything outside them—diminishing or even rejecting its existence for the time being. Some sports boundaries, such as baseball's outfield walls or the shot-put's last measurement line are set up specifically to be transcended. Through sport we can limit the infinitude of space and through sport we can transcend those limits.

Time is in many ways the very source of determinism. It plods on inevitably, completely ignoring our need to slow or accelerate it. But the rules of sport somehow manipulate time, too, shrinking, stretching, and stopping it at will. Clock-controlled contests such as basketball or football seem to create a new type of time parallel to conventional time. Sport-philosopher Michael Novak calls it "sacred time" that transcends the secular.[9]

Sports time can be stopped and started at will by a referee's whistle or an athlete's mid-air hand gesture. It can be slowed beyond belief as the final two minutes of a game are scattered out along the distance of a conventional hour. Slow motion replay is just a media duplication of a sensation athletes have experienced since sport began. Losing a sense of "clock time" results from deep concentration and absorption in athletic activity—it's among the most frequently reported experiences of "being in the zone."[10]

Sports time is often split into incomprehensibly small fractions in the effort to distinguish winners from losers. Sprinters talk about hundredths of seconds as if they were weeks or even light-years. Rigid time that so unmercifully ends a game is also so malleable that referees may restore expired seconds to the game clock. In a way, they are reversing time—something contemplated and fantasized about for much of human history, but achieved only in sport and Superman movies.

Through all this slowing, splitting, expanding and reversing, sports time flies by faster than anything. Twelve hour Ironman triathlons are remembered by athletes as a blur of arms, feet, and wheels. People who could not sit through a 90 minute movie, can spend an entire Sunday afternoon completely absorbed by one game. In so many ways, sport liberates us from conventional time.

On a larger scale, some sports seem specifically designed to thwart the limitations imposed by nature. Scuba divers make habitable the underwater world. Skydivers fall freely through the native territory of birds, then escape the natural consequences of their folly with a parachute. Those who fly aircraft for sport, whether it be planes, gliders or parapentes, crave the sensation of freedom found by escaping our groundedness as land-born beings.

Even athletes performing on land often report feelings of weightlessness or soaring. Runners call it floating, basketball players seek "hang time," rock-climbers defy the logic of the earth and its cen-

---

9. Novak (1988, 126–131).
10. See Jackson and Csikszentmihalyi (1999, 73).

tripetal force.[11] Sport and its rules are like a special jumping chamber where the reality of hard determinism can only wait outside and peer in through the vinyl windows.

Thinking Activity: Who Knows?
Question: Are sports events contingent or determined?
Observe: Enact or imagine a turning point in some important sporting event—perhaps a crucial free-throw in a championship game. Designate someone to play the role of the athlete, someone else to play the coach, another to be statistician, others to be fans or teammates, and finally have someone be God. Describe the action up to a point just before the crucial moment, then "freeze the action."
Analyze: From each of the designated points of view, ask (a) whether the person knew what was going to happen and (b) how that fact affects their response to the moment. If God knows the outcome, could He be interested in the game? Compare the statistician's knowledge of the athlete's performance with the knowledge of the coach and the athlete's self-knowledge.
Question Again: What does this exercise demonstrate about the role of contingency in sport? Does it prove anything about the metaphysical reality of freedom or determinism?

3.2 Freedom from Psychological Limitations

Philosophical athletes adopting a phenomenological approach to self-understanding will be less concerned with the objective reality of determinism and more interested in their subjective experience. To us, the important thing is not whether events are truly determined, but whether we experience them that way.

Athletes know too well that the pressure they put on themselves to perform can be infinitely more stifling than any external threats or expectations. Some athletes learn to free themselves mentally from the hype surrounding a big competition. Remember that scene from the movie *Hoosiers* where the coach has his athletes measure the dimensions of the championship court to try and dispel their fears abut playing in a professional arena?

Likewise, an athlete can mentally free herself from anxieties about determinism. I am free so long as I believe myself to be. By the same token, however, my mind can be just as limiting a force as any external

---

11. For accounts of such sensations, see Murphy and White (1995, 7–20).

reality. How can I escape from the psychological limitations I place on myself?

Philosophical Background:
Psychological Determinism

A popular solution to the problem of human liberty is to concede the reality of physical determinism while revising the concept of free-will. The strict materialist Thomas Hobbes may have inspired this movement by defining human liberty simply as the lack of external restraint. Human beings are free, he said, in the same way a river is free to flow within its banks.[12] Such attempts to reconcile free will with physical determinism are called *psychological determinism* or compatibilism.

John Locke explained human liberty simply as the freedom to do what we desire. He illustrated his position by describing a man in a room who "freely" stays to converse with a long-lost friend, unaware that he is actually locked inside the room. His point is that freedom is really psychological. The man in the room *feels* free to leave, even while he is actually compelled to stay.

> Again, suppose a Man be carried, whilst fast asleep, into a Room, where is a Person he longs to see and speak with; and be there locked fast in, beyond his Power to get out: he awakes, and is glad to find himself in so desirable Company, which he stays willingly in, i.e. prefers his stay to going away. I ask, Is not this stay voluntary? I think, no Body will doubt it: and yet being locked fast in, 'tis evident he is not at liberty not to stay, he has not freedom to be gone. So that Liberty is not an Idea belonging to Volition, or preferring; but to the Person having the Power of doing, or forbearing to do, according as the Mind shall chuse or direct. [13]

Perhaps the most powerful compatibilist view came from the Scottish philosopher David Hume who argued that humans had liberty even while their actions were caused.[14] Hume's defense of liberty has its origin in his skeptical position on causation itself. He believed that causes had no special connection to effects other than the fact that they preceded them. So the constant conjunction of motives and actions is as

---

12. Hobbes (1651, 170–171).
13. Locke (1689a, Book II, 238).
14. Hume (1739, 399–418).

much causation as anything, and human freedom is simply our ability to act in accordance with our motives.

Compatabilists warn that those who require *uncaused* or indeterminate actions for human freedom better hope they don't get what they wish for, since such actions would be random and uncontrolled, like a muscle-spasm—hardly the ideal of human liberty.

Understanding Imagined Limitations

Space, time, and gravity are only abstract threats to our sense of freedom. For most of us, the psychological constraints we imagine for ourselves are much more oppressive than any real limitations. What we need to realize is that the limitations on freedom in our modern lives tend to come as much from within ourselves as from such external forces as Nature or God.

Those vague obligations we have—to read the paper, dress appropriately, wipe our feet at the door, appear busy at work, salute the flag, fill out the proper forms, laugh at friends' jokes, and signal before changing lanes—those vague obligations deflate our sense of freedom. We become willing prisoners of our everyday routines. We derive these limiting attitudes from our social and personal realities, what existentialist philosophers call "our facticity," in vast disproportion to any *real power* they have over us.

Fortunately for the philosophical athlete, the sports experience can provide perspective on and escape from these psychological limitations as well. Sport, as we have seen, is an escape from social concerns. No one berates Michael Jordan for hanging out his tongue on a drive to the basket, but he'd never get past the *maitre d'* doing the same thing in a restaurant. The important thing to learn is not that you should hang out your tongue in restaurants, but that obedience to such rules is a matter of choice and context.

Obedience becomes an overrated virtue once we lose sight of the reasons for it. As psychologist Stanley Milgram showed in his groundbreaking experiments on human behavior, ordinary people will torture and even kill innocents out of a vague sense of obedience to authority.[15] Milgram set up an experiment in which ordinary people were told by an authority figure to administer electric shocks to victims. Subjects were sur-

---

15. Milgram (1974).

prisingly willing to perform such torture and, even more fascinating, they would harshly devalue their victims after acting to harm them.

To what extent are we ourselves victims of our own obedience to authority? Do we devalue ourselves as a result?

Psychological Freedom in Sport

Just as obedience to civic law is rewarded with freedom from having to defend our castles and grow our own food, obedience to the rules of sport can be rewarded with moments of freedom from the mundane demands of our workaday lives. The same dynamic in the moment of challenge that yields a sense of individuality also has the power to release us from the social and personal obligations of everyday existence.

As a rule-abiding participant in sport, not only am I absolved from mundane obligations, I am largely released from consequences as well. Just as Homer's Greek warriors staged competitive games as a way to exercise their skills in isolation from the consequences of war, athletes can imbue their contests with life-or-death seriousness without ever risking their lives at all. Winning and losing, even when large amounts of cash are involved, are really of little consequence in "the real world."

No doubt the world cup soccer player who was murdered after scoring an own-goal in the tournament knew he had made a fatal error on the field. But everyone was shocked at his real-world fatality. Even so-called risk sports that flirt with danger and death work to minimize the reality of bodily harm.[16] Sport is an escape from real-world obligation and real-world consequences.

Being Judged by Actions

Sport-philosopher George Sheehan compares an athlete's sense of escape from the world to "a child in the corner playing with his blocks."[17] The authority of my coach or even of the referee is miniscule in comparison with the authority of the state, of the street, of social etiquette.

As an athlete I am judged by *what I do*, not who I am in a social sense. And while what I should do—that is, my athletic objective—is clearly defined for all to see, *how* I do it, how hard I try, even whether I attempt it is entirely up to me. The crowd knows that as well. So here

---

16. We'll explore the psychology of risk sports in chapter 5.
17. Sheehan (1978, 38).

on the free-throw line at my symbolic moment of challenge, not only do I sense and recognize my pure freedom—everyone around me must pause to recognize it as well.

Then they must judge me on *what I do* at the moment. My gender, my accent, or the pigment in my skin may color their judgment outside this chamber of freedom called sport. In the yearbook picture, at the job interview, on the country-club grounds, these social categories may define and limit my possibilities. But within the strictly-limited task at hand, on the rule-governed field of sport, such factors count only as much as I let them.

What matters now is just what I *do*. What matters is whether I am able—whether I choose to even try—to put this ball through that hoop. *I* am the only one who controls *that*, whatever external judgments anyone makes about me. In the moment of challenge, I am free.

Thinking Activity: Finding Our Freedom of Choice

Question Do you, as an athlete and a human being, acknowledge your freedom of choice?

Observe: Make a list of things in sport that you feel you have no choice about or control over. After each item, describe how you feel about your lack of choice in that area. For example, you may say that you have no choice about running stadium steps and you don't like that because they're boring and give you sore legs.

Analyze: Take a fresh look at things you said you have no choice or control over and evaluate whether this is strictly true. For some things, such as having to follow the coach's orders, you may have the option of quitting the team or the sport. These things are simply a price you pay to get something else you desire. Write down what would happen if you refused to pay that price. Which do you prefer—paying the price, or giving up on the larger desire? Go back and acknowledge the things you choose to do in order to achieve a higher goal. For example, write "I choose to run stadium steps because it's part of becoming a stronger athlete and earning my spot on this team."

Question Again: How do you feel about what you have written? Have you acknowledged all the reasons for the choices you make? Do you believe they are worth it?

3.3 Freedom Is a Matter of Choice

The Power of Choice

Philosophical athletes, upon observing their freedom at the moment of challenge, may come to learn that it is ultimately their own creation.

Choice is not the *result* of freedom, freedom is the result of exercised choice.

No one describes this phenomenon better than Algerian philosopher Albert Camus who finds a way for the mythical Sisyphus to be free and happy despite the complete determination of his environment and even his actions.[18]

In ancient Greek mythology, Sisyphus was condemned by the gods as his eternal punishment to roll a rock up the side of a mountain. Each time he completed his task, the rock would roll back to the bottom of the hill and Sisyphus would follow it down, only to begin the task anew. In this situation, where everything except his mind is strictly and spitefully controlled by tyrannical gods, Sisyphus finds freedom by exercising his free choice. Camus says he must *choose* to push the boulder. Just as Locke's man in the room is freed by the desire to do what he must, Sisyphus aligns his mind with what his body must do and so he finds freedom and happiness.

The liberating power of choice is present on many levels in the field of sport. As I stand at this free-throw line savoring my freedom (to succeed and also to fail) in this moment of challenge, I may realize that the path leading up to this place was one of constant choice. First of all, I chose to *participate*. In almost no context, outside the brooding wishes of an overbearing parent, is participation in sport mandatory for anything. We choose to play or not to play. We also choose to practice, to train, to drill — perhaps as a price to be paid for the privilege of playing in games — but as a price willingly paid in the context of the larger choice.

Philosophical Background: Self-Determinism

The fullness of freedom derived from choice is known as *self-determinism*. For many, it's not enough to simply say that free action has internal rather than external causes. The question remains, "Am I in control of my psychology?" Liberty, on this view, requires not just that I can *do* what I choose, but that I am able to *choose* what I choose — true freedom of choice.

After all, smokers may be free to light up while at the same time being enslaved by their addiction. Many smokers actually desire to lose

---

18. Camus (1955, 88–91).

their desire to smoke—this is what contemporary thinker Harry Frankfurt calls a second-order desire. True freedom seems to lie in our ability to act on such *desires to have desires*. It's my free choice to apply a nicotine patch as part of a stop-smoking program, even while the desire to smoke is not chosen.

The 18th century philosopher Thomas Reid perhaps summed it up best when he insisted that free actions must ultimately be caused by agents (i.e. the people who act) and not by other events.[19] Free actions are the result of human intentions—beliefs, wants, and desires we have about particular outcomes. This account puts the burden of proof on hard determinists who, to prove complete causation, must prove that human intentions are themselves caused. The best way to do that would be to reduce intentions to physical events, a major stumbling block for mind/brain identity theorists and artificial intelligence researchers alike.

Even if intentionality ultimately fails to provide metaphysical space for free-will, our *experience* of freedom remains strong. As with the mind-body issue, the phenomenological approach to the issue of freedom and determinism leads us to affirm our freedom. Philosopher Jean-Paul Sartre takes the ideal of human freedom to be a fundamental assumption of the good life.[20]

Acknowledging Choice

The freedom created by our choice to play sport is revealed by the fact that we can always withdraw it. I may abort a workout, skip a game, quit the team, or walk away from a sport altogether. In sport, no one *really* holds a gun to your head, except you.

Now, I know this freedom sounds strange. As athletes we train ourselves to forget that we have it. Quitting—even just a workout—seems anathema to what being an athlete is all about. This is as it should be. But too many athletes forget that they are involved in sport by choice, *their* choice.

According to Camus, the fact that we make an analogous choice to live each day is proven by the fact that we can always commit suicide.[21] Now Camus no more advocates suicide than George Sheehan advocates becoming a couch-potato. The point is that it is only by *ac-*

---

19. See, for example, Reid (1788, 259–66).
20. Sartre (1956, 439–441).
21. Camus (1955, 4).

knowledging the choice we make to play or to live that we can experience the true freedom that we have. To fail to acknowledge that we have a choice is to fail to take responsibility for the choices we make. All too often this is the first step toward the destruction of the athlete as a human being.

So here I am on this free-throw line by choice. Even the rules that define my success in this endeavor — putting a ball of a certain size and weight through a hoop of a certain diameter and height from a certain distance within a certain time — even those rules are chosen by me. They weren't *written* by me, but in choosing to participate in the sport of basketball, I choose to play by those rules.

Different sports have been concocted and refined to test almost every combination of skills imaginable. Philosophical athletes who seek to discover themselves in sport must also be willing to seek out sports that reveal and cultivate their selves. Physical realities of body type and constitution are a factor, but so are considerations of temperament, time availability, and team spirit. Too many athletes abdicate not just their choice to play, but also their choice of what to play to some other authority such as a parent, boyfriend, or peer pressure. You have the freedom to choose any sport you please; exercise it.

Expressing Freedom

The choices of what and whether I play express quite limited freedom in comparison to the choice of *how* I play. Even within the rules of a given sport there is room for movement, innovation, even revolution. Dick Fosbury may be the poster-child for this kind of athletic freedom. His choice to perform the high jump with a back-to-the-bar flop rather than the traditional stomach-down roll was such a bold expression of "the freedom of how" that it changed the sport forever.

Predictably, authorities were sufficiently startled to change the rules in an effort to ban the Fosbury flop. They did the same thing to cross-country skier Bill Koch, who mastered the skating technique thereby catapulting himself to the top of the world rankings (a place few Americans have occupied before or since). As Dr. Martin Luther King, Jr. said, "freedom is never voluntarily given by the oppressor; it has to be demanded by the oppressed."[22] Sport is certainly no different. But the freedom expressed by both Fosbury and Koch eventually prevailed.

---

22. King, Jr. (1963, 87).

Sport has great potential to satisfy our human thirst for freedom, but only as long as we understand how that freedom is manifest. By providing an oasis from the limitations of both nature and society, by helping us to realize how often "limitations" are really self-imposed, and by providing an opportunity to exercise acknowledged choice, the experience of sport can truly be an experience of freedom.

Thinking Activity: The Remote-Controlled Athlete
Question: When is my performance not truly my own?
Observe: In many sports, coaches communicate pre-designed plays to athletes performing on the court or field. Imagine that these communication devices became so sophisticated that the command was transferred directly to the athletes' brains, eliminating their choice to accept or reject it. Athletes' brains could be programmed on the fly by coaches operating a kind of remote control.
Analyze: How would you feel, as an athlete, if your decisions were controlled from the sideline? Is it really so different from accepting a play through hand signals?
Question Again: How many decisions do you actually allow others to make for you as an athlete? How many decisions must athletes make themselves in order to be considered free and autonomous?

Chapter Review

Summary

It's not an exaggeration to say: to be human is to seek freedom. Unfortunately, we humans encounter limitations in nature, society, and even within our own minds. Sport provides an opportunity to escape these limitations—if only figuratively and only for a moment. It manipulates the boundaries of time, space, and gravity. It battles the unwritten rules of society with clearly-defined rules of its own. And it showcases the power of choice to achieve the ideal of self-determination in the face of towering limitations. For the philosophical athlete, the experience of freedom in sport can cultivate an awareness of the freedom to be had throughout life. Sport is like an inflatable fun-house where we discover the freedom essential to being ourselves.

The problem with athletes is that so few of them acknowledge, much less exercise, the freedom inherent in the sport. Our rational understanding of hard determinism, whether guaranteed by logic, theology, or atomic causation, is a constant challenge to our undeniable experience of freedom. The rule-governed arena of sport provides a place where the experience of freedom can be heightened, even savored, at the wonderfully uncertain moment of challenge.

Sport is also an escape from the realm of psychological determinism in which actions are motivated by minds, but minds themselves may not be free. Social obligations, judgments, and consequences are suspended within the arena of sport insofar as the athlete allows them to be.

Ultimately, philosophical athletes must recognize our responsibility for this freedom by acknowledging the power of our personal choice. Sport requires choice at every level, from whether we play to how we play. This choice is the key to experiencing liberty and self-determinism in sport and the satisfaction, if only momentary, of our fundamental human desire for freedom.

Further Reading

Philosophy

Camus, Albert. 1955. "The Myth of Sisyphus." In *The Myth of Sisyphus and Other Writings*, translated by Justin O'Brien. New York: Vingate, 88–91. With Sisyphus, a figure condemned to eternally roll a boulder up a mountain, Camus paints a vivid image of the human capacity for mental freedom even in the face of physical compulsion. Sisyphus gains freedom by choosing his inevitable task; Camus concludes that we must imagine Sisyphus happy. This essay sends a good message about the importance of freedom, power of attitude, and the role of personal responsibility in happiness.

Morris, Herbert ed. 1961. *Freedom and Responsibility: Readings in Philosophy and Law.* Stanford, California: Stanford University Press. This is a collection of philosophical essays on free will, action, responsibility, intention and motive as well as legal issues such as negligence, liability, punishment and legal insanity. Authors range from Aristotle and Aquinas to J.L. Austin.

Philosophy of Sport

Metheny, Eleanor. 1968. "The Symbolic Power of Sport." Presented to the Eastern District Association for Heath, Physical Education and Recreation in Washington D. C., April 26, 1968. Reprinted in Gerber and Morgan, ed. (1979), 231–236. Metheny provides an eloquent account of the ironic way that sports rules create an arena for freedom with continual reference to Homer's Greeks and modern athletes.

Novak, Michael. 1988. "The Second Seal: Sacred Time." In *The Joy of Sports: End Zones, Bases, Baskets, Balls, and the Consecration of the American*

Spirit. Lanham, NY: Hamilton Press, 126–131. This pseudo-religious description of sport's ability to transform time is well-written and enjoyable.

Journalism and Literature

George Sheehan. 1978. "Understanding." In *Running and Being: The Total Experience.* Red Bank, NJ: Second Wind, 36–50. This is a first-person account of the runner-philosopher's disdain for conventional authority and appreciation for natural authority. It concludes with an acknowledgment of the freedom provided by the rules and laws of the universe.

Part Two

Taking Responsibility

Section Preview

Introduction:
"Choose Thyself"

> *All my life, and particularly in the last fifteen years, I've tried to develop a personal philosophy built on the belief that I cannot be free until I accept responsibility for what I do."*
> —Bill Russell, *Second Wind*

Days earlier, John Krakauer stood on the top of the world—literally. He had successfully climbed Mount Everest, realizing a lifelong dream. Having returned home safely, however, his thoughts were less of triumph than worry. In his best-selling book, *Into Thin Air,* Krakauer describes how he worried about his responsibility—to himself, to his family, to his climbing companions (some of whom died on the expedition), even to the sport itself. What kind of person devotes so much of his life to sport, maybe even risks his life for it, when there are bills to be paid, children to be fed, and books to be read? How can the joy of sport be reconciled with the grave seriousness of real life—and real death?

The experience of sport is characterized by play and joyful freedom, but freedom always comes with the weight of responsibility. Even while sport helps us to escape from the pressures of everyday life, we remain responsible for the choice to play, for how we play, even for how we *interpret* our play.

The phenomenological insight that consciousness is free brings with it the reality that we are at least partially responsible for how the world appears to us. That means our attitude is as big a responsibility as our actions, and our interpretation of key events may be even more important than the events themselves.

To revise a famous quote: "It's not whether you win or lose, it's how you view the game." In fact, sport is only possible as long as the contestants decide to *view* it as play. We create sport and attribute meaning to otherwise meaningless activities. Why else jump things you could go around, why flip on a balance beam…why flip at all?

We even create sports, like mountain climbing, in which participants purposely risk their lives. It's hard for many to see anything playful about that. But just as sport may be a metaphor for life, so it may be a way to confront death — to tap it on the forehead then run back to life — before the game is truly over. There's a sense in which risking life forces us to take responsibility for our lives.

Where there is freedom, there is responsibility. But responsibility also represents opportunity — the opportunity to make the most of our sporting experience. Just as we choose to make the sports experience meaningful, so we can choose to make our life experience meaningful. In that case, the choices and responsibilities we take on as athletes can become part and parcel of meaningful life-stories.

This is the mission of the philosophical athlete — should you choose to accept it: to take responsibility for making meaning in your life.

Section Preview List

- How do attitudes and perceptions affect the experience of sport? (Chapter 4)
- Does risking death help some athletes to appreciate life? (Chapter 5)
- What is the role of meaning in life and in sport? (Chapter 6)

Chapter 4

Responsibility for Actions and Attitudes

Chapter Preview

Introduction:
Mind Games

> *What happens in competition is sometimes controllable, sometimes not. How you choose to react to what happens is entirely within your control, and this provides an enormous source of power. Unfortunately, this power is often an untapped resource because athletes either do not recognize that they are free to choose how to respond or because they have learned ineffective responses.*
> —Jackson and Csikszentmihalyi, *Flow in Sports*

On one of those silly sports blooper shows, I once saw a curious dog race. The dogs leap out from their starting gates and begin to race around the track in pursuit of a fake rabbit that charges along the inside rail a few meters ahead of the dogs. Everything seems normal until the pack of dogs reaches turn one. Just then one of the dogs leaps over the rail and cuts across the infield to take a straight shot at the fake rabbit. But cutting the corner, he catches up to the rabbit and leaps in the air to try and bite it.

Of course, the dog was disqualified from the race.

At the same time, what he did made perfect sense. If the objective is to catch the rabbit, why run around that silly track? I think the dog has since retired from racing and settled into a life of hunting. He never could understand the racing gig anyway—which begs the question: how can *we*?

The dog only fails as a racer because he doesn't do what we expect him to—and what we expect him to do makes no sense on its own. All sports share this nonsensical nature—it's what makes them "play," what cordons them off from the serious, practical pursuits of everyday life. Even some practical pursuits, such as tree cutting, become sport when made part of a lumberjack contest. The activity hasn't changed, just our attitude toward it. Now it is done for fun, to see who is best, or maybe even to win the prize. But it isn't done because it *has to be done* and that makes all the difference in the world.

In some ways, the freedom and playfulness characteristic of sport seem opposed to the concept of responsibility. The image of sport as a playful escape from the realities of life appears to contradict the idea that we are inevitably responsible for everything we do and see as athletes. What the dog racing example shows is that sport is only possible to the extent that we voluntarily accept its absurd demands. From the seed of our playful attitudes grows every joy and sorrow, every win, loss, and bad break that we experience within the world of sport.

This puzzling fact about freedom and responsibility in sport reflects a philosophical insight into the nature of our human experience. Even things outside of our control become what our minds make of them. You didn't create the rain, but you did forget your umbrella. You didn't call the questionable foul, but you did choose to scream at the referee. You expect justice when it benefits you, but you interpret the flat tire that took your opponent out of the race as a deserved piece of good luck.

There's nothing inherently wrong with interpreting events as you see them as long as you take responsibility for your choice to do so. The saying, "It's just a game." reflects an attitude that can be chosen or rejected. Philosophical athletes should remember that our attitude toward life is as much within our control as our attitude toward sport.

Chapter Preview List

- Why is the freedom to fail central to our conception of sport?
- How can your attitude change losses into gains?
- To what extent is "who you are" a matter of choice?

4.1 Athletic Free Agency: Responsibility for Action

Freedom in the Sports Experience

I know what you're thinking. Mention "free agency" to most athletes and they think of contract negotiations in major professional sports. But athletic free agency, understood philosophically, runs much deeper than that. It has to do with the freedom to act of our own volition that is experienced so intensely in sport.

Free agency affects issues of praise, blame, and general responsibility. Can you imagine sport without reason for applause? Or boos? Or personal bests? Can you imagine sport where every victory, every play, every head-fake was inevitable and determined from time immemorial?

That may already be the case if hard determinism is metaphysically true, but it's sure not the way we *experience* sport. In fact, sport's appeal may largely derive from its ability to point out free-agency and to impose responsibility, putting humans briefly in control of a too-predictable world.

Philosophical Background: Determinism's Threat to Free-Will

"The Devil made me do it!" How old is this defense? How laughable? How implausible? Our earlier discussion of freedom and determinism raised a very serious question about the possibility of human freedom, a question in which there is a lot at stake. Unless we humans act freely, on some level, it is very hard to make sense of blame and punishment. After all, if the Devil really did make me do it, if I'm no better than a remote-controlled robot, how can I be truly *responsible* for my actions?

Of course I can be punished for missing practice or committing a foul, but do I deserve my punishment if I am not a *free agent* (i.e. a person acting of my own volition)?[1] If hard determinism is true, then it

---

1. Obviously this question is very important for the criminal justice system. Legendary lawyer Clarence Darrow was famous for the "determinism defense"; he defended admitted murderers Leopold and Loeb by arguing that the boys never had control over their lives.

seems as though tennis champion Monica Seles is no more deserving of praise than the scoundrel who attacked her with a knife at courtside is deserving of blame.

Our commonsense intuitions about winning, losing, and moral responsibility reveal an underlying assumption of human *free will* (the idea that we voluntarily choose at least some of our actions). But can our concepts of free will and responsibility be defended? And, if we do have free will and responsibility, just how far does it extend?

Free will is a problem for all three forms of hard determinism examined in the last chapter. If I couldn't act otherwise than I did, my action wasn't free, but determined by circumstances out of my control. On the other hand, if human actions are entirely undetermined, then they occur by pure chance—like a lottery. What occurs by pure chance must be outside my control, so I'm still not a free agent. Either it was determined that I would make the free-throw or it happened entirely by chance—in either case, I am not responsible for it.

Christian philosophers have had a passionate stake in the issue of free will and responsibility. Since God's nature as all-powerful and all-knowing suggests theological determinism, Christians struggle to explain human responsibility for sin.[2] Likewise, the scientific doctrine of causal determinism is a threat to free will and responsibility since actions and events are compelled by the causal chains that precede them.

Self-determinists, from the ancient Greek skeptic Carneades to the 18th century Scot Thomas Reid sought to solve the problem of human responsibility by distinguishing self-causation from the natural causation observed in the physical world.[3] By positing the human will as an uncaused agent, they salvaged the concept of human free-agency and its attendant responsibility.

---

2. The fourth-century theologian Pelagius observed that such traditional doctrines as original sin, grace, divine foreknowledge, and omnipotence led to the unjust consequence that humans were held morally responsible on judgment day for things outside of their control. Since Pelagius believed God to be absolutely just, he pushed to reconcile human responsibility with these doctrines.

3. Carneades was probably the first to suggest that something could be "uncaused" without being random as logical determinists suppose. Reid's ([1788] 1969, 259–73) view of free-agency holds that we can deliberate and choose among real sets of possible options because we have power over our own wills. Reid's idea of causation is somewhat unconventional, but he defends it by pointing out that humans originally derived their concept of causation from the awareness of themselves as agents.

The Nature of the Test

Athletic free agency is an integral part of sport's most basic element: the test. In northern Italy there's a 33-kilometer climb that boasts 48 numbered switchbacks and grades surpassing 12%. This windswept mountain pass is called the Stelvio and as I pedal towards it up the quiet alpine valley, I go from being a simple cycle-tourist to a true athlete participating in a real sport.

The reason? The test. Once I face the climb, cycling is no longer a matter of pedaling from point A to point B. The mountain provides a challenge that I will either pass or fail—and I'm not sure which. This uncertainty is essential to the test because it creates a tension that can only be resolved by my voluntary physical action.

There's no way to resolve the question of whether I can ride up the mountain except by turning the pedals of my own free will. If my husband drives behind me with a cattle-prod the whole way, I would still wonder whether I could have made the climb on my own. Notice that I need no starting gun, no official time, not even a competitor in order to face my test.

In distinguishing 'tests' from 'contests', sport-philosopher R. Scott Krechmar observes that the presence of opponents may enrich or complicate a sporting challenge, but they are not essential to it.[4] All I need is a particular problem to solve—every sport proposes its own unique set —plus specific criteria to determine whether I have solved it successfully. On the Stelvio, the problem is the climb and the criteria for success require that I reach the top by pedaling a bike under my own power.

The Purpose of the Test

The first purpose of the test with its starkly defined criteria is to generate uncertainty as to whether the goal can be accomplished. This is why the 9,000 foot high Stelvio is a good test, but a 50-foot high driveway is not. Both the possibility of failure *and* the possibility of success have to be present to create tension. The possibility of failure begets the freedom to succeed and my responsibility for the outcome of the test.

It's the tension in sport, like the tension in drama, that determines the quality of the experience. The task can neither be too hard nor too easy. That's why athletes attempt to climb Everest but don't bother try-

---

4. Krechmar (1975, 39).

ing to snowboard back down. No doubt the presence of a goalie, opposing team, and large noisy crowd *heighten* the tension involved in shooting a puck into a net. But it all reduces down to *my personal* uncertainty about *my personal* ability to make the shot.

Now a big part of the attractiveness of the sporting test is the knowledge that it will be resolved—definitively—within the sporting task. And the connection between the test and the issue of free-agency is that this tension will be resolved—and can only be resolved—by the deliberate and voluntary action of the person who undertakes it.

If a test is passed just by chance, or something outside the athlete's control, then it hasn't been a true test. If some magic wind blows me up the hill, if a marathon course was two miles short, if the rim I dunked through isn't regulation height, then the question I asked has not been answered, the test has not been passed, and the tension is not resolved. To feel satisfied, I need to defeat my opponent fair and square—even when that opponent is a mountain. Furthermore I can't take responsibility for either success or failure unless I acted as a free agent in facing my sporting test.

Thinking Activity: Control Freaks
Question: What is and isn't within your control in sport?
Observe: Nerves are part of sport, but there's no sense in worrying about things you can't control. Make a list of 4–5 things you tend to worry or get nervous about before competition.
Analyze: Go back over the list and write a "C" by everything that's within your control (e.g. fitness) and "NC" by everything that's out of your control (e.g. weather). Write "PC" next to things partially under your control (e.g. a teammate's performance), then specify which part of that thing you have some control over (e.g. the teammate's morale).
Next, for every item on your list, ask yourself what you can do about it and remind yourself what you have done about it. For fitness, you can train and you have trained—so remind yourself. For weather, you can prepare by bringing the proper clothing and equipment. The teammate you can encourage; make a special effort to put in a good word.
Question Again: What do you really have to be nervous about before competition? Uncertainty is part of sports' beauty.

4.2 Adopting a Stance on Sport: Responsibility for Perception

Keeping Perspective

Having established that free-agency and responsibility for action are essential to our conception of sport, a question arises about the scope of athletic responsibility. It turns out that athletes are responsible not only for our actions but also for our perceptions: for how sport *looks* to us.

Think about the basketball player who disagrees with the referee's calls, becomes frustrated, and plays poorly. After the game, he might say, "the ref made us lose," when it was in fact his poor play. Whether the calls were bad or not, the player chose to perceive them as grossly unfair. This perception *did* hurt the team, but it is a perception for which the player (and not the referee) is responsible.

In fact, if you think about it, sport is actually made possible by the athlete's free choice to view the event in a particular (and quite unusual) way. Just as children create worlds of "make-believe" in which bedrooms become spaceships and colanders become helmets, athletes create a world of sport by perceiving contrived tasks as important challenges to be met. This specific mode of perception is what sport-philosopher Bernard Suits describes as *"lusory attitude."*[5] Our ability to see an activity as a game is just what makes it a game.

Imagine that a rational alien lands on earth and stumbles over to a stadium where runners are competing in the 400m high-hurdles. Without adopting the relevant athletic mode of perception, how could the alien make sense of the scene? There are people running around, very quickly, in a circle—trying very hard to get back to where they started. What's more, someone has set up silly artificial barriers that the runners insist on leaping over despite the fact that they're obviously in a hurry and could easily run around the barriers—or better—cut across the entire field. If they're so anxious to return to where they started, why do they run away in the first place?!

The whole scene would seem ridiculous to an alien and only makes sense to us because we choose to suspend our everyday reason and adopt a particular attitude.

---

5. Suits (1973, 8).

The hurdles on the track are metaphorically reflected in all sports, which set up artificial barriers and constraints that the participant must face for no reason understandable outside the sport itself. Suits actually defines game-playing as, "the voluntary attempt to overcome unnecessary obstacles."[6]

Philosophical Background:
Responsibility for Thought and Perception

Suits' insight about sport owes much to the 20th century philosophical movement called *phenomenology* which expanded the concept of human free will and responsibility beyond action and into the realm of perception and selfhood.

Immanuel Kant's distinction between the way things are and the way they appear to us inspired philosopher-psychologist Franz Brentano to focus on the concept of *intentionality*, the mind's ability to take intellectual and emotional stands toward the objects it thinks about.[7] So, for example, when I think about Jackie Joyner-Kersee I not only conjure up her image in my mind but I adopt a particular attitude toward it—one of admiration for her strength and courage. Edmund Husserl expanded on Brentano's insight to conclude that we affect how the world "shows up" for us in our experience.[8]

The insights of Brentano and Husserl expanded the amount of our personal experience that we "create" and are therefore responsible for. So not only is there an important distinction between, for example, the actual outside temperature as objectively measured by a thermometer and my personal experience of shivering cold, there is also an important sense in which I create (and am therefore responsible for) much of my own experience.

I can stand shivering on the shore under six layers of clothing and watch nearly naked members of the polar-bear club plunge into freezing water off an ice-covered pier. To be sure the cold is not all in my mind, but it's somehow interpreted differently in my experience than it is in the polar bear swimmers' experience.

Combining their affirmation of human choice and freedom with Husserl's insight about how we affect our perceptions, some existential-

---

6. Suits (1973, 11).
7. Brentano ([1874] 1960, 50–52).
8. Husserl ([1929] 1960, 118–128).

ist philosophers concluded that we are actually *responsible* for our perceptions. As with the classic example of seeing the glass half-full or half-empty, how we interpret the raw data of perception reveals something important about us as individuals. A pessimist, for example, sees the glass as half empty. An optimist sees the glass as half-full.

According to the existentialists, these general attitudes toward life, like the specific attitudes that affect our perceptions, are also a matter of choice. This is sometimes called "taking a stand on the world," and the particular stance we take is ultimately up to us. I choose to see the glass half-empty because I choose a pessimistic stance toward the world by choosing to interpret events around me in a negative way. It's no use to say that these choices are predetermined—even if the actual events that inspire them are—because the attitude I adopt toward these events is always mine to accept or change.[9] Jean-Paul Sartre uses the personal example of World War II in which he participated as soldier, prisoner, and part of the resistance. He says, "If I am mobilized in a war, this war is *my* war...For lack of getting out of it, I have *chosen* it."[10]

Sartre explains that even avoidance of the issue is a choice. He must take full responsibility for the war because he freely chose not only how the war would appear in the phenomena of his perception, but also whether to live and have the perception at all. Just as the runner chooses to make her race exist, Sartre has actually chosen (by living) to make the war exist. After that he still chooses to accept or resist it. He must take responsibility for the world, for his attitude, and even for who he is. Says Sartre:

> ...man being condemned to be free carries the weight of the whole world on his shoulders; he is responsible for the world and for himself as a way of being. We are taking the word "responsibility" in its ordinary sense as "consciousness (of) being the incontestable author of an event or of an object."[11]

Particular Perspectives

Athletes, too, are responsible for what they perceive because they themselves condition how the world shows up for them. Just as athletes

---

9. Allowing, of course, for certain mental illnesses or brain-chemical imbalances.
10. Sartre (1956, 554), emphasis the author's.
11. Sartre (1956, 553).

choose to perceive sport's unnecessary obstacles as important tasks to be accomplished, so too their perception of their performance and the role of sport in life is colored by their specific knowledge and experience. We each view the world from an individualized perspective.

For example, while watching an unfamiliar sport on television, I'll often be at a loss to explain the expert commentator's reaction. Gymnastics expert Bart Conner can gasp in horror at some parallel-bar move that looks perfectly fine to me. What you know, to a large extent, determines what you see.

Our perceptions are guided largely by knowledge and expertise, as in the linebacker's ability to interpret the scrambling players as a particular passing play, or a race-car driver's ability to estimate the size of the slipstream of the car in front of him.

On top of that, however, our perspectives are linked to chosen attitudes. Athletes of similar expertise and experience may vary wildly in their attitude toward competition. For every 'go-to player' yelling "Just give me the damn ball!" there are three so nervous they're throwing-up in the locker room before the game.

What many athletes don't realize is that they *choose* to be one kind of player or another. Even being passive—deciding not to choose—is a kind of choice. Competition, and sport in general, exposes human beings to their *possibilities*—the real freedom of choice that permeates their lives.[12]

Choosing to Care

Freedom of choice is not always welcome because it is accompanied by the burden of responsibility—responsibility for the paths we choose and responsibility for those we don't. There may be no bigger regret that letting golden opportunities pass: the person you should have married, the stock you should have bought. We'll do almost anything to shirk responsibility for them. Excuses abound and are met with sympathetic nods.

Sport, on the other hand, puts us face to face with a myriad of distinct possibilities, then clearly holds us accountable (as winners or losers) for the choices we make. Given the emphasis on choice and responsibility in sport, it's no wonder so many people avoid participation.

---

12. This is the theme of Esposito (1974).

Even some "athletes" avoid competition.[13] In cycling, I recall the phenomenon of the "winter racers"—strong riders who took pride in training alongside top athletes in the off-season, but were nowhere around when springtime came and starting guns were fired for actual races. The point is that we *choose* whether we see hurdles, races, and competition in general as something inviting or something to dread.

Furthermore, how we react to competition once we're entered is also a matter of choice: the stand we choose to take on sport. As philosopher Martin Heidegger says about human beings in general, athletes attribute meaning to sport through the chosen phenomenon of "care." The skill of hitting projectiles with carved pieces of wood is just about useless from a practical point of view. But in the sport of baseball, it means a lot—and all because we've collectively chosen to care.

Since sport is an artificial construct, meaningless in and of itself, the stakes of winning and losing are ultimately symbolic—unlike the challenges faced in "real life." We *choose* to make an issue of sport. So we are *responsible* for how big an issue we make of it. The seriousness that we bring to sport is entirely of our own volition.

That's not to say that we shouldn't care, after all, "because it's only a game." First, we should recognize the root cause of our seriousness. Often it derives from extrinsic factors such as the money, glory, or admiration to be won. This criticism is often levied on modern sports, and not without justification. Many pro and college athletes report that their sports "become just a job," devoid of playful joy and any sense of freedom.

Others consciously adopt a mercenary approach, making all sports decisions on the basis of personal wealth. What's funny is that these players often lose their desire to play. As their bank accounts expand so do their problems. They find out very quickly that sports can bring money, but money can't buy happiness. Like two-sport millionaire superstar Deion Sanders, they often end up disillusioned and still searching for answers.

But it's not the fault of the money, or the coach, or the team—it's the fault of the attitude the athlete chose to adopt. Many professional players who earn their living from sport are not beyond ignoring its attendant awards. Former pro basketball player Bill Bradley says he often played just for the "pure pleasure" of it:

---

13. For more on the phenomenon of competition avoidance, see Kretchmar (1994, 216).

In plenty of games, I played simply for the joy of it, shooting and passing without thinking about points. I forgot the score, and sometimes I would go through a whole quarter without looking at the scoreboard.[14]

Most athletes aren't even in a position to reap external rewards, but either way the seriousness we bring to the game—and the effect it has on our play—is entirely up to us. We are responsible for it.

Thinking Activity: Who Cares About Sport?
Question: Why do you care about sport?
Observe: Write down the reasons your sport is important to you. Include the benefits you're receiving now as well as those you hope to receive in the future.
Analyze: Go back to your list with a fresh perspective and ask yourself why the things you've written down are important. For example, if you said you want to earn the respect of your father or a professional contract, explain why these things are important to you as a person.
Question Again: Now, assume that you fail in sport. Ask yourself if your ultimate goals can be achieved in another way. Does this exercise change your perspective on the seriousness and importance of sport in your life?

4.3 Adopting a Stance on Oneself: Responsibility for Self

Choosing Your Athletic Self

One good reason to value sport and take it seriously is the opportunity it provides to learn about ourselves. And you guessed it; this too is a matter of choice. We are ultimately responsible for the stance we take on ourselves, the way we interpret events, and the kind of athletes we become.

Our interpretation of ourselves as athletes is symbiotic with our perception of sport itself. Indeed the specific type of sports we choose, the positions we choose to play, and the *way* we play those positions all say something about how we see ourselves in the world.[15]

---

14. Bradley (1998, 5).

15. Contemporary sport-philosopher Drew Hyland (1990, 71–77) believes our sport-choices offer useful insight into an athlete's psychology. Kretchmar (1994, 217) says that our sporting experience, and the choices we make within it, can remind us of our personal orientation toward life

These reflections are visible on many levels. American sportswriter Adam Gopink was puzzled by the Europeans' love for the game of Soccer. To his eyes, it was failed entertainment—a capricious and unsatisfying sport in which enormous amounts of effort were wasted on 0–0 draws. By the end of the 1998 World Cup, however, Gopink learned to see the game reflected in the Europeans' view of life:

> Soccer was not meant to be enjoyed. It was meant to be experienced. The World Cup is a festival of fate—man accepting his hard circumstances, the near certainty of failure. There is, after all, something familiar about a contest in which nobody wins and nobody posts a goal. Nil-nil is the score of life.[16]

The significance of our perspective on life runs even deeper. Beyond the choice of sport, there is the choice of position. The taste for guts and glory exemplified by the goal-scoring striker contrasts meaningfully with the personality and worldview of the reliable but nearly unnoticed sweeper.

Nevertheless, the freedom and choice to play either position—to *be* either sort of player—is open. One thing philosophical athletes should remember is that they are responsible for who they are in sport.

Philosophical Background: Responsibility for Ourselves and Our World

Responsibility for self is a central characteristic of existential philosophy. Beyond being responsible for our actions, intentions, and environment we are also responsible for how we *interpret* ourselves within that environment. Perhaps the best expression of the interdependence of self and environment comes from German philosopher Martin Heidegger. His description of human beings as *Dasein*, literally "being there," derives from the philosophy that we are best understood in terms of our care and concern for objects in our world.[17]

Heidegger's concept of "Being-in-the-world" shows how our worldly situations affect who we are. First of all, environment limits our choices within a context; I cannot be a point-guard while herding a flock of sheep. But I can be a destructive rather than a benign sheepherder by driving my flock to trample the farmer's garden. So who I am, even

---

16. Gopink (1998), 37.
17. See, for example, Heidegger (1962, 235–241).

within a limiting context, is largely up to me. My selfhood is not determined by my environment, but rather by the way I choose to react to it.

Self-interpretation within a particular context expands quickly to the concept of self-interpretation in general or what might be called "taking a stand on oneself." Sartre and some of the other existentialists believe that we ultimately can transcend our "facticity"—the real-world situation into which we are "thrown." Whether I find my self in the darkness of prison or bathed in sunlight on a warm sandy beach, I ultimately choose the self I will be. After all, the sunbather may be imprisoned by debt or some psychological limitation, while the inmate freely wanders the expanse of his consciousness.

We adopt stances not only toward the world but also toward our selves and our personal lives. In the words of Sartre, "We are condemned to be free."[18] With that freedom comes the "nausea" of responsibility, but also the opportunity to actually create ourselves through our freely-chosen actions and attitudes. Belief in determinism, from an existentialist point of view, is a reprehensible attempt at self-deception. Whatever the metaphysical reality concerning the determination of events, an honest examination of consciousness will reveal the freedom to actually create ourselves as well as the responsibility for who we have become.

Choosing Your Reactions

Mental training programs for sport, such as the one described in Kay Porter and Judy Foster's *The Mental Athlete*, start by encouraging athletes to accept responsibility. Porter and Foster say that athletes alone are responsible for their level of readiness, reaction to events, and positive or negative frame of mind. Successful athletes, they say,

> ...understand that the attitude they bring to their performance is their choice and that it will either help them win or defeat them.[19]

The bottom line is that we and we alone are responsible for the level of our performance. We may not be responsible for our genetic profile, any more than we're responsible for a fan throwing a tin can that hits us on the head. But we are responsible for *our reaction* to these things. We are responsible for our level of readiness and for our

---

18. Sartre (1956, 439).
19. Porter and Foster (1986, 9).

positive or negative frame of mind as we prepare to perform. Say Porter and Foster:

> We can choose to learn from a less than perfect performance or event and go forward, using it to our advantage, or we can choose to become upset and tense. So often we defeat ourselves by adopting a negative attitude. We are totally free to see ourselves as important, competent, talented, and unique or as incompetent, unworthy, untalented and second best.[20]

Testament to the phenomenon of disparity between perception and reality is Shulman and Bowen's discovery of the extent to which female college athletes underestimate their academic ability (as measured by SAT scores) while male college athletes overestimate it.[21] The goal for all athletes is to accurately estimate potential, then to realize it.

Our perceptions of ourselves and our performances are a matter of choice. Athletes make the choice to blame others for their failures or to feel badly about a defeat. Indeed what we make of our sporting experience—victories and defeats—perhaps says the most about who we have chosen to be.

Choosing a Life-Story

It's not only important how I react in the short term to such events as a defeat-causing hamstring pull or a victory-inducing second wind. It also matters how I interpret the meaning of these events within my larger "life story."

The salient point once again is that we create and hence are responsible for our interpretation of the sporting experience. What can you make of a disappointing loss? You can choose to see it as a learning opportunity, a reminder of personal imperfection, an affirmation of life's unpredictability.

Porter and Foster pose a series of questions to help athletes self-diagnose problems with event-interpretation:

> Think of the last big event you participated in that meant a lot to you. When the big play came to you or when the outcome depended totally on you, did you pull it off or did you lose your concen-

---

20. Porter and Foster (1986, 7).
21. Shulman and Bowen's (2001, 134–5).

tration and choke? If you did succeed, what was your feeling? Relief? Joy? Elation? If you did not succeed, were you filled with self-hate, strong, sharp anger with yourself for days or weeks? Or did you feel disappointed and dissatisfied for a few hours and then go on with life?[22]

A useful tactic for dealing with troubling sports events is to think about how you will fit that event into your life's story. No athlete is successful all the time; the great ones learn to transform "failures" into stepping stones to success by viewing them as learning opportunities.

How we interpret events in sport and life speaks volumes, not just about who we are, but who we have chosen to be.

Thinking Activity: Sports Time Machine
Question: Would knowledge of the future affect my attitude?
Observe: Every athlete gets nervous the night before a big game. Imagine that you could enter a time machine and skip ahead past tomorrow's game to view its results in the next day's newspaper.
Analyze: Would your knowledge of the future eliminate the nervousness you feel the night before? Would your reaction be different depending on whether your team was about to win or lose? Would it change your motivation and attitude? Even if you knew the outcome of your game, wouldn't your attitude about it still be a free choice? You could choose to ignore the "knowledge" or to let it affect how your feel. As a learning opportunity, a win is no better a loss.
Question Again: In the end, does it matter whether events are in fact determined—as long as we can choose our reactions to them?

Chapter Review

Summary

The philosophical athlete is focused on the self. Responsibility for our actions, for our perceptions, and for our interpretations are welcomed as natural consequences of free-will and, most important, as opportunities to learn. The philosophical athlete approaches sport—and life—with an attitude of wonder, an eagerness to learn, and a love of wisdom. Above all there must be an awareness of the power and scope of our choice.

---

22. Porter and Foster (1986, 8).

The awareness that we can control so many aspects of our existence can be daunting and terrifying, but it's definitely superior to the deterministic alternative. Imagine if our lives were like video-taped movies — or worse, video-taped sporting events — that could be fast forwarded into a fixed and unchangeable future. While acknowledging that metaphysical determinism *may* be the case, philosophical athletes revel in the experience of freedom in sport, flexing their volition in the face of possibility, and enjoying the drama they create in their lives.

Further Reading

Philosophy

Chisholm, Roderick, ed. 1960. *Realism and the Background of Phenomenology.* New York: Ridgeview Publishing Company. This is a useful collection of seminal essays on the topic, including important work from Brentano and Husserl.

Reid, Thomas. [1788] 1969. *Essays on the Active Powers of Man.* Cambridge, MA: M.I.T. Press. A classic of western philosophy, this book recounts Reid's liberal views on free-agency.

Sartre, Jean-Paul. 1956. "Freedom and Responsibility." In *Being and Nothingness,* translated by Hazel E. Barnes. New York: The Philosophical Library, Inc., 553–556. This brief but powerfully-written account of human freedom is a must-read for the philosophical athlete.

Philosophy of Sport

Esposito, Joseph L. 1974. "Play and Possibility." Originally appeared in *Philosophy Today,* XVIII: 137–146. Reprinted in Morgan and Meier, ed. (1995), 114–119. This important essay in the philosophy of sport celebrates the power of possibility as experienced in competition.

Porter, Kay and Foster, Judy. 1986. *The Mental Athlete.* New York: Ballantine Books. This is a straightforward guidebook to mental training for athletes in every sport. It covers a variety of techniques and includes such activities as goal-setting charts, affirmations, and guided visualizations.

Journalism and Literature

Gopink, Adam. 1998. "Endgame." Originally appeared in *The New Yorker.* Reprinted in Ford, ed., 29–38. This beautifully written essay is the confession of an American sports fan who attends the 1998 World Cup and learns to appreciate soccer not as a spectacle or as entertainment, but as a metaphor for life.

Chapter 5

Taking Responsibility for Life and Death

Chapter Preview

Introduction:
Risking, Losing, Dying

> *Within the edgy terms they set up, the risky sports provide an area in which you must take complete responsibility for your own life; that is, they provide precisely the occasions for choice and responsibility that never quite arrive in clear, recognizable form in the routine world. However trivial the context—who, finally, cares about a piece of rock, or a big wave, or a racing record that will be broken next year?—the element of risk can turn a weekend hobby into a small-scale model for living, a life within a life*
>
> —A. Alvarez, "I Like to Risk My Life"

Your mother was right. Sports are risky, even dangerous. As soon as you enter the arena of sport you risk failure, pain, injury, embarrassment, losing, even death. Every athlete experiences and must overcome 31 flavors of fear. However, the scariest thing about sport is not facing what might be, but dealing with what is. It's not about who you think you are, but who you really are. It's not about facing death, it's about becoming aware of life. What we risk in sport is losing the illusion and finding the truth about ourselves and our lives.

The mythical story of Oedipus Rex laments man's mortality—the fact that we all must die. But more important, it reminds us of our inability to *know* ourselves truly. Though Oedipus cleverly plots his life to avoid the prophecy that he would kill his father and marry his mother, a blind "seer" reveals to him that his dreamlike life is, in reality, his nightmarish fate. He has killed his father and married his mother without ever realizing it. The tragedy reminds us of our mortal limitations; not only in the sense that we all inevitably die, but also that our understanding of ourselves and of the world around us is always imperfect.

Sport, too, involves confrontation with our limitations, from the constant risk of failure to the actual risk of death. Despite zealous attempts to banish losing from the vocabulary of athletics, no competitor's experience is completely free from failure. The claim that "Winning is the only thing" is logically impossible. Winning cannot be separated from losing in sport—for every winner of every game there must also be a loser.

In sport, losing is often seen as a metaphor for death. Of course, this "death" is almost always followed by the possibility of rebirth in another contest. Smart athletes turn losing into something beneficial—an opportunity to improve and to learn about oneself. Says coaching legend Joe Paterno:

> I think you profit more from getting a licking because it makes you zero in on the things you didn't do well. There's a tendency when you win to overlook some of the things you didn't do well. I've always said to my squad, you're never as good as you think you are when you win and you're never as bad as you think you are when you lose.[1]

Sometimes death in sport is not metaphorical but real. In fact, some risk-sports seem to seek out death. But a closer look reveals that the goal isn't death at all. The confrontation with death enhances the experience of life. Philosopher and mountaineer A. Alvarez explains that the appeal of risk sports lies not in the thrill of fear, but rather in the fact that

> intentional, planned risk demands all the qualities most valuable in life: intelligence, skill, intuition, subtlety, control. These are precisely the qualities the good artist brings to his work, and they are also those called upon in the lonely, risky sports.[2]

Alvarez' insight about risking death in sport reflects the philosophical discovery of how awareness of mortality affects our attitude toward

---

1. Joe Paterno, quoted in Packer and Lazenby (1998, 290).
2. Alvarez (1967, 204).

life. Indeed, awareness of death seems to be distinctive of humans. Plants, animals, and insects all die but, as the French philosopher Voltaire noted, "The human species is the only one which knows it will die, and it knows this through experience."[3]

We also know from experience that death is an issue surrounded by much myth and mystery. It ranges from being an unspoken taboo subject to a virtual obsession, and either status reveals its importance to us as human beings.

Chapter Preview List

- Can sport help us to confront our own mortality?
- Is losing really a form of metaphorical death?
- Do athletes in risk sports really seek death?

---

3. Voltaire quoted in Edwards, ed. (1967, vol. I, 307).

5.1 Risking in Sport

Facing Up to Fear, Mortality, and Imperfection

Everyone has heard of risk-sports: sky-diving, bungee-jumping, street-luge, rock-climbing. The made-for-TV *X-Games* seem to worship danger as the central component of sport. What everyone does not realize, though, is that all sports are risk sports in their own way. There's always something on the line: failure, loss, or disillusionment.

Look up 'risk' in *Roget's Thesaurus* and you find three key synonyms: 'chance,' 'danger,' and 'invest.' This is telling, because in sport we take chances with our egos (self-conception) and our reputations (others' perceptions of us). We face physical and psychological danger. And we do this as part of an investment in our selves. That is, we willingly accept certain risks in sport as necessary conditions for the improvement we seek as persons.

And it is scary. Not every athlete consciously calculates the relevant risks and applies them against some predicted rate of return. But every athlete feels fear. In the brilliant non-fiction book *Friday Night Lights,* the high-school football player Ivory Christian feels this fear so acutely he spends every pre-game retching into the locker-room toilet. Fear is essential to sport, because risk is necessary for success.[4]

Philosophical Background:
Fallibility, Mortality, and Immortality

The ancient injunction "Know Thyself" carried with it a tacit admonishment to those who thought themselves gods. A false sense of knowledge, power, or invincibility is often the downfall of great human beings. Croesus, King of Lydia, consulted the oracle at Delphi asking whether he should go to war. The divine response was that if he went to war, he would destroy a great kingdom. Confidently, he went to war. The great kingdom he destroyed was his own.[5]

The tragic fault of *hubris* or excessive pride so important in classical drama is but one dimension of the human reluctance to admit our

---

4. For more on fear in sport see Kahn (1959).
5. See Herodotus (1954, 32).

own mortality. The imperfections that distinguish us from gods encompass our failure to know just as much as our failure to live forever.

Perhaps this is why Socrates—who humbly interpreted his status as "wisest of men" as a reward for admitting his ignorance[6]—said that philosophy is the study of death.[7] Philosophy demands that we constantly acknowledge our ignorance, our fallibility, and our mortality.

Socrates faced his own death with a surreal sense of calm. Having eschewed several opportunities to avoid execution (each of which would have compromised his integrity), he willingly drank the hemlock. He even bathed beforehand to spare servants from having to wash his corpse. Socrates took comfort in the fact that in life, he cared above all for his soul, which, he believed, would be judged fairly and favorably in the afterlife. He did not fear a confrontation with the truth about himself—because he had always risked security to pursue wisdom.[8]

Risking Illusion

Risk is part of the sporting test and it's part of sports' appeal. In order to jump, you must risk falling. In order to perform, you must risk choking. In order to win, you must risk losing. In order to be a hero, you must risk appearing the fool. But the most frightening thing about sport is its power to unveil reality. In order to know the truth, you must be willing to sacrifice your most comforting illusions.

Here's where Socrates comes in. His amazing courage in the face of death is all based on his admission of imperfect knowledge. He said he did not know what death was; he had no illusions that it was painful, no illusions that it was bliss.[9] By admitting that he did not know, he freed himself to discover the truth.

Athletes, like philosophers, must admit their imperfections in order to discover the truth—that is they must risk dispelling any illusions of

---

6. See Plato, *Apology* 23ab: "But the truth of the matter, gentlemen, is pretty certainly this, that real wisdom is the property of God, and this oracle is his way of telling us that human wisdom has little or no value. It seems to me that he is not referring literally to Socrates, but has merely taken my name as an example, as if he would say to us, The wisest of you men is he who has realized, like Socrates, that in respect of wisdom he is really worthless."

7. See Plato, *Phaedo* 64a.

8. These events are recounted in Plato's *Apology, Crito,* and *Phaedo.*

9. Plato, *Apology,* 40b–41e.

perfection by putting themselves on the line one more time. Most of us know how much courage it takes just to go out and try to do better than the last time.

Can you imagine the courage it takes when your past performances are perfect to risk failure the next time you compete? At the 2000 Olympics in Sydney, 400m world record holder Michael Johnson had a lot more to lose than to gain. He brought a perfect record of gold medals and a huge undefeated streak to the starting line in Sydney. But he didn't lament the risks. He said the risks were what made it interesting.

The whole concept of the "Achilles' heel" shows that no athlete is invincible. Remember that the great runner Achilles was finally killed in battle when an arrow found his one vulnerable part. The trick for most of us is to find and protect our own "Achilles' heels" before competitors can exploit them. But to do that we must first admit that we have such weaknesses, risking damage to our egos, our delicate self-esteem.

If we think about it for a moment, however, philosophical athletes will realize that what's really risked is an illusion. I believe I can beat my rival in a race, but on race day the rival wins. I feel bad, I get down on myself, I lament who I am. But this makes no sense. What I learned is that I'm not the person I believed would win the race. I lament that I'm not who I thought I was. But my goal is to find who I truly am! I haven't lost anything but an illusion about myself. What I've gained is a truth about myself—a starting point for improvement. I've discovered one of my "Achilles' heels," so now I can go about protecting it.

Heroism and Immortality

Sometimes it seems as though athletes focus less on admitting their imperfections and mortality than they do on achieving immortality. In fact, modern talk about "immortal heroes" almost always turns to athletes whose youthful vigor and flawless performances become etched in the public consciousness—for a long time, if not all time.

The connection between great athletic performances and immortality probably goes back to ancient Greek athletic festivals which were designed to honor the gods by staging a spectacle of mortals whose athletic deeds would approximate the perfection of divinity. Even today, an athlete who approaches perfection may be reverently referred to as a "god."

It's worth noting, however, that heroic or immortal athletes are "awarded" their status not by gods, nor themselves, nor even other athletes, but by the masses of ordinary people who witness their deeds with amazement. Philosopher Karl Jaspers analyzes sports heroism as "the venturesome doings of individuals [that] show forth what is unattainable by the masses."[10] It's part of the nature of sport that athletes rise above the limitations of ordinary people, and it's clear that some reach lofty heights unimaginable even to other athletes.

Typically, however, these athletes' perfection is apparent to everyone but themselves. The limitations faced by "most people" are largely self-imposed; they choose comfortable illusions rather than facing their fear and pursuing the truth. The athlete reaches "immortal" perfection precisely by admitting *imperfection*, risking failure, and recognizing weaknesses.

In fact, it may be that the pain, suffering, and fear we face in sport are the source of our improvement. American philosopher William James says that experiences demanding extraordinary effort destroy our customary inhibitions, after which "ranges of new energy are set free, and life seems cast upon a higher plane of power."[11]

So heroism and immortality in sport have less to do with transcending our personal limitations than they do with underestimating our abilities. Therefore, the biggest obstacle to discovering what we're capable of is our aversion to risk, specifically the risk of admitting imperfection and opening ourselves to the discovery and refinement of truth about ourselves.

Necessary Risk

Unfortunately, outside of sport, the general tendency is to minimize or even eliminate risk altogether. A. Alvarez, a transplanted European rock-climber, observed that risky activity is considered "un-American."[12] Almost anyone who played actively in the 1980's can remember the legal war on risky-behavior that took as casualties the trampolines, skateboard parks, and go-cart tracks of days past. Fees for bike races, lift-tickets, and sports licenses rose precipitously in step with the premiums for liability insurance.

There's something profoundly frustrating about being protected from yourself. I understand why they put straightjackets on mental pa-

---

10. Jaspers (1957, 118).
11. James (1902, 283).
12. Alvarez (1967, 203).

tients and mittens on babies with sharp little fingernails but I'm a (relatively) clear-headed adult and it seems that my ability to recognize a risk should entitle me to take it.

Frustration over *paternalistic* limitations (i.e. those imposed upon me for my own protection) might derive from a basic human desire to encounter risk. Theories about our propensity to take risks range from a Freudian death wish driven by subconscious feelings of guilt to the existence of a "thrill-seeking" gene. It seems reasonable that we humans might harbor some feature designed to help us survive in the risky environment of our Neanderthal ancestors.[13] There's no question that for most of us living with the soft comforts of a modern industrialized world, natural risks are muted and hard to come by.

Philosopher Johan Huizinga noted that in the modern world, play is taken more seriously than ever while work acquires more and more play-elements.[14] Maybe all those people investing their savings in the stock market or launching new e-businesses have learned to satisfy their appetite for risk outside of sport. But which risk is healthier? The payoff of self-knowledge gained in sport is at least as valuable as any financial gain. Sporting risk may allow us to face up to the truth about ourselves.

Thinking Activity: Risk and Fear in Sport
Question: What should we fear in sport?
Observe: Make a list of things you fear or get nervous about before a competition. Likely candidates are losing, physical injury, disappointing family or friends.
Analyze: For each item on your list, assume that your worst fear comes true, then analyze what the consequences will be. For example, imagine that you lose a big game; what will happen? Write out a chain of consequences covering how your life might change. Is there any way it may change for the better? If death is a consequence of failure, imagine its effect on people you care about. Next, assume that you are successful in your endeavor and write out a chain of consequences—good and bad—from your success.
Question Again: Comparing the lists, ask yourself whether both scenarios (success and failure) can be part of a meaningful life. If the answer is yes, the risk may be worth taking. If the answer is no, perhaps it is not.

---

13. See Greenfield (1999, 32).
14. Huizinga (1949, 199 f.).

5.2 Losing: A Metaphor for Death

Sport Viewed as a Microcosm of Life

Some people view sport as a microcosm of life. It is limited in time and space just as we are. The new season or the start of the game is viewed like a birth, in which each athlete is created equal in the eyes of the rules, and the future is puffed full of expectation and possibility. In sport we face struggles just as we do in life. We encounter pain, doubt, hope and elation. We feel the urgency of a ticking clock, every second is hoarded and savored especially in our waning moments — sometimes marked by a "two-minute warning."

We sense the weight of our limitations, our personal smallness in the face of a towering mountain, winding marathon course, or interminable last yard needed for a touchdown. We know from the start there will be losers — in a zero-sum game we can't all be winners. And when the loss comes, we compare it to death: "They were *killed*," "He *died* out there," "We lost in *sudden death* overtime."

It's funny, but so many of the things we try to divert ourselves from in life — risk, pain, failure, death — are confronted head-on in sport. Or are they?

Philosophical Background:
Diverting Our Attention from Death

Some philosophers regard the stories about heaven, hell, and the immortality of the soul as irrational attempts to allay our already irrational fear of death. A better strategy might be to simply think about something else. This seems to be the message of the 17th century philosopher Baruch Spinoza, who declared:

> A free man thinks of death least of all things; and his wisdom is a meditation not of death but of life.[15]

Spinoza's contemporary, Blaise Pascal, noted that diversion is precisely the tactic most of us take in dealing with our fear of death. In *Pensées,* he says that

---

15. Śpinoza ([1677] 1955, 232).

death is easier to bear without thinking of it....As men are not able to fight against death, misery, ignorance, they have taken into their heads, in order to be happy, not to think of them at all.[16]

Pascal does not view these diversions as healthy. Immortality is not achieved by ignoring one's mortality any more than wisdom is achieved by ignoring one's ignorance. Diversions that console us from our miseries are even greater miseries in that they prevent us from truly reflecting on ourselves.[17]

In the 20th century, Martin Heidegger would build on Pascal's insight, reinterpreting his "diversions" as a kind of social conspiracy to avoid facing up to our mortality.[18] Did you ever notice how in social conversation, death is something of a taboo subject? We even avoid the word, preferring less final terms such as "passed on" or "gone away." Heidegger sees these social conventions as a denial of our natural anxiety about death. We escape from that anxiety into the realm of society (what Heidegger calls the "they") which provides a "constant tranquilization about death."[19] The "they" work together to "level off" their fear of death into a vague concern about something that happens to other people.

Heidegger thinks that indulging in diversion from death by "absorbing ourselves in the they" is nothing short of dangerous. In his view, we must face up to our mortality as individuals in order to be true to ourselves and achieve the good—or what he calls "authentic"—life.

Why? If we start imagining that we'll live forever, or if we discount our lives in the hopes of some superior afterlife, we lose the sense of urgency needed to "*Carpe diem!*"—seize the day—and make the most of our lives now. That's why denial of death is "tranquilizing;" it lulls us into inaction. Heidegger's authentic person should not mope and brood about death since that is a waste of precious time. Awareness of death heightens our sense of life and inspires us to savor it, just as we savor the last chocolate in the box knowing there are no more.

Heidegger calls this attitude "anticipation" of death and he believes that it reveals existence as an authentic concern. In facing up to death as individuals (which is the only way we can face up to it since we fear not

---

16. Pascal ([1662] 1966, 168).

17. Pascal ([1662] 1966, 171).

18. Heidegger's discussion of death is primarily found in *Being and Time*, (1962, 279–312).

19. Heidegger (1962, 298).

death in general, but our own personal death), we acknowledge something real about ourselves as individuals: our lives are finite and may end at any time.

This realization then conditions the way we live our lives, but in a healthier way than beliefs about immortality or an afterlife do because this belief is something true about us now. It allows us to see ourselves as we are and inspires us to take advantage of the real possibilities available in our lives. As Heidegger says, death is just the "possibility of the impossibility of any existence at all."[20]

Avoiding Losing; Avoiding Death

Heidegger and his sympathizers said an awareness of death frees us to find meaning in life. You would think that the awareness of loss in sport would provide a similar kind of liberation. An awareness that our life-clock is ticking down, just as game-clocks do, should remind us to make something of ourselves while the making is good.

But it doesn't seem to work that way. Athletes, at least stereotypical athletes in the major stick and ball sports, seem prepared to waste all of their lives outside the stadium or arena. For them, it seems that sport *is* life, and that final buzzer signifying the end of the game, that sense of death that accompanies a loss, those are just part of sport. Life, for these athletes, is nothing more than waiting for the next game to start.

To be sure, our failure to learn from the metaphorical connections between sport and life is due mostly to a lack of philosophical reflection. A closer look reveals something more, however. Just as society disdains and diverts itself from the reality of death, much of modern sport tries to cast aside losing: "Winning isn't everything," goes the athlete's mantra, "it's the only thing."

But winning only exists on the flip-side of losing, and almost never does the losing belong exclusively to others. Every athletic success is built on some kind of defeat. It's hard even to imagine what an athletic career devoid of failure and disappointment could be like.

But to hear some people talk, you'd never believe it. Coaches routinely demand "nothing less than victory." Parents threaten to dock a kid's allowance if his T-ball team loses another game. Athletes declare that they hate nothing more in life than losing.

---

20. Heidegger (1962, 307).

You can go through life hoping never to get HIV by avoiding situations that risk infection. But you can't go through sport avoiding situations that risk losing. Sport just is a situation that risks losing; therefore vain attempts to deny defeat only damage sport itself.

College football teams try to insure a perfect record by scheduling games with "pansy" opponents who have almost no chance of beating them. Parents and coaches keep kids away from certain positions or even entire sports when they don't think success can be assured. More often athletes themselves, having been bombarded with the message that losing is abhorrent, quit competing in sport because their self-esteem can't stand to risk another loss.

Finally, there's the phenomenon of playing not-to-lose. Athletes who won't give themselves permission to fail perform so conservatively that they destroy any chance to truly excel. Runner and philosopher George Sheehan recalls a marathon he ran conservatively with shame and disgust:

> I had chosen the middle way, the way of the lukewarm. And afterward, when there were awards for almost everybody, I didn't wait around. I wanted no memento of that race.[21]

Choosing Our Response to Losing

All this aversion to loss in sport becomes particularly repugnant to philosophical athletes once they realize that fear of loss is really just a fear of truth. Losing, furthermore, is in fact crucially different from death in that it's almost always followed by another opportunity to play. It's like the feeling you get as the roller-coaster train pulls into the station—you're disappointed that the ride is over but you know you can ride again—the track is just a loop after all.

If we've learned one thing about life from the existentialist philosophers, it's that we *choose* how things look to us; we're responsible for our interpretations of events. It stands to reason, then, that we *choose* our response to losing—and great athletes almost always view losing as a great opportunity to learn and improve. Even the legendary wrestler Dan Gable—who experienced fewer losses than almost any athlete in history—acknowledges the educational opportunity defeat can provide:

---

21. Sheehan (1978,193).

You know, a loss every once in a while will straighten you up. You know, that's okay, so long as you don't get used to losing. It'll get you back going in the right direction." [22]

Ironically, winning may be more of a "death" than losing. As sport-philosopher Paul Weiss observes, defeated athletes learn more about themselves than victorious ones because they discover their limits and identify the weaknesses that led to their downfall.[23] Winning athletes aren't so sure what they can do to improve next time. This may explain why some athletes and coaches seem to act like they lost even when they won; they remain as self-critical as possible, trying to ferret out all their mistakes and vowing not to repeat them the next time.

Some athletes actually fear being the best. Defending champions, world-record holders, undefeated teams all know that it's harder it stay on top than it is to get there. 100-meter sprint champion Maurice Greene is fond of saying that when you're #1, you have to train like you're #2. Seem strange? Think about it. The cyclist who won the Tour de France last year can do little more than repeat the same training program this year, while the challenger's hunger to win will be fed by knowledge of where he needs to improve.

All this is not to say that athletes should dread winning. They shouldn't. But neither should they dread losing. Instead, they should choose to respond to winning *and* losing in constructive ways.

Sport-philosopher Kathy Ermler says athletes often choose to view failure as a tragedy. They helplessly lament their failures like Shakespeare's Hamlet or Sophocles' Oedipus. It's true that failures in sport reveal athletic weaknesses that resemble the "tragic flaws" causing protagonists' downfalls in classical drama.[24] But an athlete, unlike Oedipus, has a chance to fix the flaw.

An athlete's capacity to use past failures as a road map to future success is described as a "comic response" by Ermler. Whatever the dramatic parallels, it's clear that losing in sports is simply what the athlete chooses to make of it, and given the rebirth and renewal metaphorically reflected in sport, an athlete can make much of a loss indeed.

---

22. Gable quoted in Packer and Lazenby (1998, 249).
23. Weiss (1969, 188).
24. See Ermler (1982, 762).

Death Is the End of Striving

When I ask my students to reflect on what they most value in life, the idea of having goals—something to strive for—recurs repeatedly. When I ask what they would do once the goals are achieved, they always say they would set new ones. It seems that ultimately it is the *process* of striving—the journey and not the destination—that is the reward.

If this is true, then loss in sport is nothing like real death. Losing a game or race or match just suspends the striving until the next workout. Each metaphoric death in sport is accompanied by almost infinite rebirths. Even when competitive sport ends for some people other goals are adopted to replicate the athletic dynamic.

Good athletes—even top athletes—always attempt to improve. Sport, like life, is imbued with possibility. But real death, unlike sporting loss, is precisely the end of possibility. How, then, do we explain those athletes who flirt with death—and sometimes experience it—in sport?

Thinking Activity: Winning and Losing
Question: What is losing?
Observe: Attempt to define losing in sport, starting with the analytical definition for your sport (i.e. scoring fewer points, crossing the finish line second or later etc.) Then write a paragraph how you feel when you lose.
Analyze: Notice the gap between what losing is and how we feel about it. Why does something so objectively insignificant mean so much to us? Try to get to the bottom of why you interpreting your losses as you do. What makes you feel the way you do? What kinds of personal concerns does it reveal? Write down a few of the personal concerns reflected in your attitude about losing.
Question Again: Does you attitude about losing make your life better or worse? In the long run, are you harmed or benefited as a person from these losses? If losses only harm you, should you continue the sport? Can a change in attitude turn athletic losses into personal benefits?

5.3 Dying

Death and Sport

In many sports, the possibility of death is more than metaphorical. Some sports are specifically designed to flirt with death—to make us conscious of its nearness and put the job of survival in our own hands.

Says extreme skier Wendy Fisher, "I always have death in the back of my mind."[25]

Nevertheless, it would be wrong to say that "extreme" athletes—or any other athletes—actually have a death wish. When an avalanche killed famed adventure climber Alex Lowe in 1999, the public registered little surprise, but fellow mountaineers were shocked and daunted. Even B.A.S.E. jumpers, whose sport of parachuting off such fixed objects as buildings, bridges, and cliffs is statistically the most dangerous in the world, say they don't want to flirt with death.[26] These reactions show that real death is *not* an accepted part of sport at all— even risk sports where fatal crashes are relatively common.

Sport-philosopher Howard Slusher argues that the function of risk sports is to allow a kind of "false bravado in the face of death."[27] Athletes talk casually about risking death: "I thought I was going to die out there." "He almost killed me." "One mistake and you're dead." But when death really occurs it casts a heavy spell over the sport and makes us wonder what we're doing.

I was at the Tour de France the day Fabio Casartelli died after crashing on a routine descent. As news of his death spread among the crowd, a pall of silence settled over us. No one knew what to say. That morning, every cyclist and fan would have casually told you that they knew fatal crashes were an ever-present possibility in the sport. But that afternoon, when it really happened, we were all shocked and dismayed—we never *really* expected it at all.

When death touches sport, it makes you wonder what the point of it all could possibly be. It seems to unmask the apparent importance of sport, to reveal it as a manufactured game we take far too seriously. No matter the amount of salaries and prize money, death always seems too high a price to pay for sport.

From a statistical point of view, the chances of being hurt or killed in a car crash or robbery may be greater than in sport. But the fact that sport is gratuitous—an unnecessary add-on to life—can make its risks seem unjustifiable, especially when someone dies.

On the other hand, philosophical reflection reveals that death is in fact inevitable. If I die tomorrow from being hit by a car while riding my bike, it's really just a matter of a life-event that was coming anyway

25. Fisher quoted in Greenfield (1999, 31).
26. Greenfield (1999, 34).
27. Slusher (1967, 752).

showing up much sooner than expected. When doctors say, "Don't worry, he's not going to die," it's misleading. We're all going to die, and we seldom know how or when. Dying while active in the arena of sport may actually be preferable to dying from what George Sheehan calls the most dangerous game of all: being a passive spectator.[28]

Freedom and Suicide

In *Being and Nothingness,* Jean-Paul Sartre disputes Heidegger's claim that we can anticipate our own deaths.[29] Although death seems like an inevitability—perhaps the one inevitability we must accept in life, Sartre observes that an individual's particular death is as random and contingent as anything else. Perhaps this is why we can never quite accept it.

Sartre admits that if all deaths were the result of old age or of scheduled executions, it might make sense to anticipate death. But the fact that sudden death is always a possibility, that it could occur in an infinite number of possible scenarios, means I can't ever *imagine* my own particular death, much less anticipate it. So I experience death as an overhanging possibility, the "always possible nihilation of my possibles."[30] Think of it like a game of musical chairs: you know the music will stop but you never know when or where you'll be when it does.

One solution to this overhanging uncertainty about death may be to stop the music yourself. Suicide. Albert Camus says that suicide is the only real philosophical problem. His reasoning is that we must say "yes" or "no" to life before we do anything else. Since life is absurd, we cannot hope for betterment or to understand its meaning. We either have to accept it in all its absurdity or exercise our freedom to reject it through suicide:

> Judging whether life is or is not worth living amounts to answering the fundamental question of philosophy.[31]

A third option, neither accepting nor rejecting and just going with the flow, isn't living at all. Camus is trying to emphasize our freedom.

---

28. Sheehan (1975, 194).
29. For the discussion of death and criticism of Heidegger, see Sartre (1956, 531–548).
30. Sartre (1956, 531).
31. Camus (1955, 3).

The possibility of suicide shows that living is a matter of choice: my choice. Suicide is usually a bad choice since it amounts to nothing more than a confession "that life is too much for you" because you can't make sense of it. But why do we need to make sense of life?

Suicide is like fast-forwarding your life to an end that was coming anyway. Why not make something of that last bit of tape? We express our freedom, our power, our humanity, not by just passively accepting life, but by actively, consciously choosing *it*. The point, for Camus finally, is *to live*.

Risk Sports: Attempts to Control Death

If death is not a natural part of sport, why do so many sports — extreme sports in particular — intentionally flirt with life's boundaries? Perhaps it's still that lack of risk in our modern lives and the insatiable drive to know ourselves — just taken to a new extreme. Says adventure racer Johathan Senk,

> Our society is so surgically sterile. It's almost like our socialization just desensitizes us. Every time I'm out doing this I'm searching my soul. It's the Lewis and Clark gene, to venture out, to find what your limitations are.[32]

Perhaps the point of risk-sports, too, is ultimately to live. The whole idea of "pushing the envelope" suggests the exploration of limits, and it's clear that it is. What we might not realize is that "the envelope" looks different from the inside and the outside. What risk-athletes see as a calculated tension between their well-honed skills and the particular challenge selected may look to spectators like warmed-over suicide. In reality, the tension between risk and skill in extreme sports is just a replication of the tension inherent in conventional sporting challenges.

It is fair to say, however, that risk-athletes view death in unconventional ways. Some deal with the danger of death by adopting a selective fatalism. My husband Larry, an ex-professional motorcycle racer, believes that "when your number's up, your number's up." It doesn't matter whether you're sitting on the couch at home or rappelling off the

---

32. Senk quoted in Greenfield (1999, 33).

face of Yosemite's El Capitan Rock, your time of death is pre-deter-mined.

"So why did you wear all that safety equipment then?" I once re-joindered, thinking I'd called his bluff.

"Oh, so you don't get so seriously hurt," he replied. "Your time of death may be determined, but it's your fault if you crash and get banged-up."

As sport-philosopher Drew Hyland observes, sporting risks are al-most always taken against a background of trust: trust in your skills to meet the challenge, trust in your competitors to abide by norms, trust in your equipment to perform as it should.[33]

The central focus is, of course, the trust athletes must have in them-selves. By allowing death to be the consequence of my athletic mistakes, risk sports put me in control of my own destiny. They make death seem like a matter of choice — a more visceral version of Camus' question about suicide. They turn the great human inevitability into a seemingly controllable possibility. Risk sports, in this sense, are all about freedom and control.

In addition, because the stakes are so high in risk sports, they de-mand a level of heightened concentration unattainable in ordinary activ-ities. Race-car driver Jimmy Vasser explains,

> At 230 M.P.H. a race car has your undivided attention. Instincts tell you when to back off. You have to take it to the edge, and you flirt with the edge. And the car will tell you. If you ignore it and try to take it to another level, that's when you're likely to crash.[34]

Athletes sometimes describe this state of concentration as a particu-larly acute sense of feeling alive, but it may better be called an en-counter with reality. Just as conventional athletics allows us to escape from the world by getting into the game, the concentration demanded by risk sports has the effect of melting the rest of the world away and allowing athletes to focus attention on themselves as they really are.

Building on Heidegger's claim that awareness of death is necessary for human authenticity, Slusher points out that we are most authentic

---

33. Hyland (1990, 135–138).
34. Vasser quoted in Greenfield (1999, 35).

when close to death.[35] There certainly is no room for pretense or putting on airs—risk sports demand our most basic life skills: courage, intelligence, and self-control.

Being Alive vs. Merely Living

The control demanded by risk sports produces a great sense of freedom. Analytically, it makes sense. If death is the end of our possibilities, and as the existentialists have said, possibility is essential to freedom, then, making death a possibility that's within my control rather than an inevitability that's entirely outside my control is a kind of ultimate creation of freedom.

If you add to that phenomenon the importance of freedom to quality of life (discussed above), you can see what these athletes who consciously flirt with death are really after: life itself. They want to experience not just living but *being*, feeling alive—knowing something about your limits and therefore something more about your self as an individual. Alvarez describes risk-sports as a "sharp close-up of your life, in which all the essentials are concentrated and defined."[36] The fascination, he says, is keeping the risk in complete control and taking responsibility, quite literally, for your life.

Athletes already know the difference between playing to win and playing "not to lose." Philosophical athletes can learn to live life with the same gusto, instead of just living "not to die."

Thinking Activity: Death in Sport
Question: Does the experience of death change our outlook on sport?
Observe: Think about a time when you directly or indirectly experienced death in the context of sport. Perhaps you personally faced death or were present when someone else died or was fatally injured. What kind of thoughts went through your mind? Did the event continue or stop? How did others around you react?
Analyze: Did this experience in any way alter your perception of the event or of sport itself? Did it make sport seem trivial or more important than ever? Did the event change your whole outlook on life?
Question Again: How should we respond to death in sport?

---

35. Slusher, (1967, 754).
36. Alvarez (1967, 205).

Chapter Review

Summary

Given what we've said already about self-knowledge, freedom, and responsibility in sport, extreme or risk sports seem not to be so different after all. And, as we saw above, all sports incorporate some form of risk while no sport—no matter what its level of rhetorical bravado—truly accepts death as part of the game.

The risk inherent in sport and the fear it generates are both connected to truth and the special opportunity available to philosophical athletes to discover it in sport. We all buy in, to one degree or another, to the comfortable illusions of society—Heidegger's "they." And certainly those who remain within that illusion, who believe whatever they want about themselves, who minimize the mental and physical risks of life—surely they are in some sense 'alive'. But are they truly living?

The risk in sport can be as frightening as the truth it allows us to find. But philosophical athletes should recognize its worth. "Risk can turn a weekend hobby into a small-scale model for living," says Alvarez, "a life within a life."[37] It can also help the athlete to distinguish mere living from truly being alive. "If you don't assume a certain amount of risk," says paraglider Wade Ellet, "you're missing a certain amount of life."[38]

Further Reading

Philosophy

Camus, Albert. 1955. "Absurdity and Suicide." In *The Myth of Sisyphus and Other Essays,* translated by Justin O'Brien. New York: Vingate, 3–8. This is a provocative exhortation to gain freedom by reappropriating the inevitability of death through awareness of the option of suicide. Camus advocates *choosing* life.
Choron, Jacques. 1963. *Death and Western Thought.* New York: MacMillan. This concise and comprehensive overview of death in western thought includes Socratic, Christian, and existentialist accounts.

37. Alvarez (1967, 205).
38. Ellet quoted in Greenfield (1999, 36).

Philosophy of Sport

Alvarez, A. 1967. "I Like to Risk my Life." *The Saturday Evening Post*, September 9, 10–12. Reprinted in Gerber, ed. (1972), 203–205. In many ways the definitive thinker on risk-sports, Alvarez draws on his personal experience as a mountain climber to communicate the meaning behind sporting risk.

Leonard, George. 1974. "Risking, Dying." In *The Ultimate Athlete: Revisioning Sports, Physical Education, and the Body*. New York: Viking, 216–228. Leonard argues that the rising of popularity of risk-sports can be attributed to the minimization of risk in everyday life since World War II. He offers many good examples that remain relevant today.

Sheehan, George. 1978. "Losing," In *Running and Being: The Total Experience*. Red Bank, NJ: Second Wind, 189–200. Connects the roles of losing, pain, and death in a celebration of life as a reflection of sport.

Journalism and Literature

Greenfield, Karl Taro. 1999. "Life On The Edge." *Time*, September 6, 29–36. An insightful look into the psychology of risk-taking in our modern world. Speculates on the existence of a "risk gene" that drives our dissatisfaction with the safety of civilized life.

Housmann, A.E. 1967. "To an Athlete Dying Young." In *The Collected Poems of A.E. Housman*. Reprinted in Battista, ed, 319. This wistful look at the early death of a young runner is among the greatest poems of all time.

Chapter 6

Taking Responsibility for Values and Meaning

Chapter Preview

Introduction:
Finding Meaning in the Athletic Life

> *"It's ironic, I used to ride my bike to make a living. Now I just want to live so that I can ride."*
>
> —Lance Armstrong

When cyclist Lance Armstrong started coughing one morning in the Fall of 1996, he initially wrote it off as just another after-effect of his strenuous training program. Then he saw the blood spattered in his bathroom sink, and at that moment he was transformed from a tough professional athlete to a vulnerable man rushing to save his own life.

He was coughing up blood because testicular cancer, relatively common among men his age, had spread to his lungs and to his brain. The cancerous testicle was removed immediately and he underwent brain surgery shortly thereafter. Aggressive chemotherapy was administered to shrink the tumors in his lungs. Almost overnight, the central question in Lance's life was not whether he could win the Tour de France, it wasn't even whether he'd return to the sport. The question at this point was: would Lance live or die?

In 1999 Lance Armstrong did win the Tour de France, and the victory meant more to him and to others around the world than it seemed like a bike race ever could. The meaning came, first, from the fact that he had stared death in the face and survived the grueling treatments. But it also grew out of some serious soul-searching about the purpose of his life and the values that would shape it. Finally, the victory had meaning for Lance—became a goal for Lance—precisely because it meant so much to others. It gave hope to thousands with cancer around the world.

It seems strange to say, but Lance Armstrong is fully willing to admit that cancer gave renewed meaning to his sport and to his life, and in this way, it helped him to win.

Much has been written about the meaning—and meaninglessness—of sport. Much less has been written about the role sport can play in a meaningful life. The difference is important to the philosophical athlete because the search for meaning seems central to our human condition.

Some would say philosophy is all about searching for the meaning of life, but relatively little philosophy has been written on that topic. Many people look to religion when asking this question. Those unconvinced by religious answers often end up with a negative, even pessimistic view of meaning. But others relish the opportunity to take responsibility for finding their own meanings in life. Whether personally created or divinely imposed, however, we choose how meaning functions in our life. Personal meaning is a matter of choice and, therefore, responsibility.

Can sport play a role in our own searches for meaning? Can it help us to identify, define, and pursue a meaningful life? The fact is that sport plays an important part in many athletes' personal searches for meaning, but we aren't aware of it because athletes in the public eye get questioned about statistics and strategies—not the meaning of life.

Cancer survivor and cycling champion Lance Armstrong provides a dramatic example of sport's role in a meaningful life. But any athlete can search for meaning in life by looking at the big picture, deciding what matters, and becoming the instrument of his or her own worthwhile design.

Chapter Preview List

- What role can sport play in a meaningful life?
- Are values a matter of choice?
- Can goals be a road-map for a meaningful life?

6.1 Getting the Big Picture

Confronting Finitude in Sport

As we saw in the last chapter, it is essential that philosophical athletes confront their imperfection and mortality. None of us hopes to have to confront it the way Lance Armstrong did. But acknowledging our limits and the finitude of our lives is an essential first step in the search for meaning. To truly come to terms with life, a follower of the philosopher Heidegger might say, we must first acknowledge the fact that we will die.

By applying a Heideggarian framework to his own experience on the Princeton basketball team, sport-philosopher Drew Hyland discovered that finitude *makes meaning possible* in sports and in life.[1] Imagine a basketball game, bike race, or golf course that never ends. How would you decide who won? What would be the point of being ahead or behind?

The boundaries of space and time give sport the possibility of meaning something: fields end, trails end, games end, seasons end, careers end. We care about what happens between these boundaries only as long as the boundaries are there.

So too with life; acknowledging the fact that our lives will end gives us a chance to envision the big picture, i.e. our lives as a whole.[2] Most young athletes never think about getting slow or growing old, much less dying. They look at their lives with blinders that restrict their view to a season or two in the past and a season or two in the future. Many athletes look to a future Olympic Games as if they represented the end of all time. We have no plans beyond that and no plans before it should we get injured or paralyzed in a car crash.

But looking at your life in short segments of time is like running a marathon one mile at a time. It may help you to focus and feel better in the short term, but ignoring the final 6 miles of the race (where most marathoners "hit the wall") only makes them harder—if not impossible. The good marathon runner keeps the whole race in mind and runs each mile for what it is: part of something larger with more overall meaning.

---

1. See Hyland (1972).
2. Baier (1994) agrees.

Philosophical athletes should use the same "big-picture" strategy so useful in sport to improve our approach to our lives. It can give us a sense of where we are in life and help us to deal with inevitable crises of meaning.

Philosophical Background: The Crisis of Meaning

"What's the point?" "Is my life worthwhile?" "Does it even matter?" Questions about the worth and meaning of life may be seen as the beginning of intellectual maturity, or as the beginning-of-the-end of human sanity. Nevertheless, there comes a time in most lives when we ask ourselves about meaning.

When the famed Russian writer Leo Tolstoy suffered his own crisis, he wrote about it.[3] Tolstoy's crisis, like most crises of meaning, revolved around three major issues: a heightened awareness of death, feelings of insignificance, and questions about self-worth.

The fact that Tolstoy enjoyed such artistic, material, and social success makes his crisis all the more interesting. He had everything most of us say that we want: a loving family, artistic fame, material wealth, a rich education, and a thriving group of similarly successful friends. So why the crisis?

For Tolstoy, as for many others, it began with an awareness of impending death—a sudden realization that the life-clock is ticking and time is running out. Questions about meaning started as a trickle for Tolstoy, but steadily increased until they washed out all other concerns. Like a chess player facing an impossibly complex move, Tolstoy glanced over to the ticking clock and realized the puzzle of life may never be solved.

The issue of mortality applied not only to himself, but also to the friends and family he held so dear. They too were mortal and therefore no more significant or worthwhile than himself. Even his work now seemed trivial. *War and Peace* would guarantee his fame forever, but it couldn't prevent its author's death; after all, those who grant fame are themselves doomed to die.

Tolstoy came to see art as a mere reflection of life's absurdity. It could no better answer the all-important questions about meaning than the analytical eye of science could. Well, science *could* answer such questions as "Who am I?" But the declaration that he was a temporal, accidental conglomeration of particles only deepened Tolstoy's crisis.

---

3. Tolstoy (1994).

The author noted that many of his friends escaped from these concerns by exploiting their wealth and enjoying pleasures of the flesh. But Tolstoy found that these "drops of honey" lost their sweetness as the ticking of his clock reached a deafening pitch.

> The former deception of the pleasures of life, which stifled the terror of the dragon, no longer deceives me. No matter how much one should say to me, "You cannot understand the meaning of life, do not think, live!" I am unable to do so, because I have been doing it too long before. Now I cannot help seeing day and night, which run and lead me up to death. I see that alone, because that alone is the truth. Everything else is a lie.[4]

In his autobiography, *Bad as I Wanna Be,* basketball star Dennis Rodman describes a crisis of meaning that reflects Tolstoy's almost perfectly: Rodman's crisis nearly led to suicide. In April of 1993 he found himself sitting in his car in a dark parking lot, deciding whether to kill himself.

Like Tolstoy, Rodman knew that he had everything he was supposed to wish for in life. He was highly skilled and wildly popular as a player. He had fame, a Ferrari, and a rags-to-riches story. Explains Rodman:

> From the outside, I had everything I could want. From the inside I had nothing but an empty soul and a gun on my lap.[5]

Tolstoy eventually recognizes that his questions about meaning point toward the infinite and can't be answered by finite means. He leaves behind matter and reason, turning toward infinite faith in God.

But religious answers don't work for everyone. Critics such as Kurt Baier contend that the religious ideal of eternal life engenders a negative attitude toward life on earth.[6] Whether the ideal world of heaven exists or not, it seems unfair to judge the value of our terrestrial lives against that standard—and it would be downright irresponsible to squander this life in hope of something better.

Rodman finds his answer by simply acknowledging a worldly choice:

> Did I want to be like almost everyone else in the NBA and be used and treated as a product for other people's profit and enjoyment?

---

4. Tolstoy (1994, 391–392).
5. Rodman (1996, 2).
6. See Baier (1994, 386).

Or did I want to be my own person, be true to myself and let the person inside me be free to do what he wanted to do, no matter what anybody else said or thought?[7]

Anyone who has seen him knows he chose the latter. Whatever you think of his lifestyle (or hairstyle), you should now understand why he resists your criticism. By facing his death, coming to terms with his values, and choosing his own path Rodman discovered freedom and meaning. He says, "It was like I came out from under the water and took a deep breath."[8]

"Athletic Angst"

Angst is a term used by existentialist philosophers to describe the sense of urgency that emerges from our awareness of finitude. "Athletic Angst" is a term coined by Drew Hyland to describe the parallel sense of urgency we often feel as athletes. Every athlete knows what it feels like to play the final minutes or seconds of a game, to dig deep in the homestretch, or to make the last crucial shot of a contest. This is "athletic angst" at its most intense.

But athletes also know "athletic angst" on a different level: the role of each day's training as part of the build-up toward a distant event, the importance of a single victory in the season-long pursuit of a championship, or the significance of achieving a state-level victory in the career-long progression of goals. Each event in our athletic lives—each measly repetition with that dumbbell—derives meaning from its role in the big athletic picture. By the same token, sport itself derives meaning from its role in the big picture of a meaningful human life.

Nazi concentration camp survivor Victor Frankl came to believe that the search for meaning is the primary motivation in our lives. He says that a certain amount of tension in life is normal and healthy. Self-help gurus fall all over themselves trying to eliminate tension and stress in life, but the problem isn't the tension itself—it's tension and stress suffered for no reason: *suffering devoid of meaning.*[9]

Frankl describes healthy tension as existing between two poles: the pole of where and who we are at the moment and the opposite pole of

7. Rodman (1996, 9).
8. Rodman (1996, 9).
9. Frankl, (1959, 126–128).

where and who we want to be in the future. Isn't this just the kind of tension essential to being an athlete: honest recognition of where you are today tempered by the belief in what you want to achieve tomorrow?

This angst or tension is what allows us to endure suffering. Frankl parrots Nietzsche's comment that if we understand the why we can bear almost any how. He says that survivors of the concentration camp found meaning in their suffering by believing in some future purpose for themselves.

Athletes too accept painful training and even injuries as prices for achieving their goals. But there's still something wrong with comparing concentration camps and training camps. How can an athlete's life gain the sense of meaning Frankl describes?

Athletes in Search of Meaning

Like many inhabitants of this modern world, athletes tend to live in what Frankl calls an "existential vacuum" characterized by widespread lack of care and concern about their lives. The vacuum is caused by the fact that we reject both instinct and tradition as guides for our action. That is not a bad thing in itself, since instinct and tradition can be very unreliable guides. The problem is that instead of guiding *ourselves* toward meaning, most of us just conform to the will of the masses or submit to the authority of others.

This is especially true of athletes. How much of what you do as an athlete is (1) because other athletes do the same thing, or (2) because a parent or coach told you to do it? These reasons may be characteristic of a modern athlete's life, but they are fatal to the search for a *meaningful* life because individuals must find their meanings individually—even such unique characters as Dennis Rodman.

Frankl is very adamant on this point: meanings are unique to each individual. No psychologist, philosopher or guru can tell you what your meaning is, you must discover it for yourself. Notice that this remains true whether you accept the religious argument that God gives our lives meaning and purpose, or you believe that meanings are personally created. In either case, becoming conscious of what our meanings are is ultimately an individual task.

Athletes who become conscious of a personal sense of meaning can tap into a deep and lasting motivational drive. Meaning-motivation is stronger and more constructive than motives such as money, pleasing others, or avoiding punishment. A philosophical athlete such as Drew

Hyland uses sport to learn lessons about the nature and possibilities of life. Examined with a philosophical eye, Hyland's basketball experience *reveals* to him something meaningful about life in general. Sport can help us to envision our own "big picture"—but sport is not the picture itself; it must be examined in context.

Of course there's a risk you'll discover that your sport has nothing to do with meaning. In his first year back from cancer treatment, Lance Armstrong dropped out of a wet and gloomy pre-season race in Europe. He flew home to Texas and contemplated his future in pro cycling. Was the pain and suffering any longer worth it? He'd already beaten cancer; what was the point of winning a bike race? It wasn't until cycling assumed its proper role in Lance's life picture—as a means toward meaning rather than a means toward a paycheck—that he uncovered the motivation to continue and excel.

According to Frankl, man can endure almost anything except the lack of meaning. Athletic angst is a training ground for the urgency of real life. Philosophical athletes don't dedicate their lives to sport, they dedicate their sport to the pursuit of meaningful lives.

Thinking Activity: My Obituary
Question: What is your vision of a happy and meaningful life?
Observe: Since questions of meaning involve an acknowledgment of mortality, begin by imagining that your life is over. Write your own obituary from a third-person point of view. State the date, time, and circumstances of your death. Describe at least 3 significant events that (you hope) will have taken place and explain why those events are important to you.
Analyze: Looking back at what you wrote about your life, what would you say are your key values? How do the events you chose as important reflect those key values?
Question Again: What have you done lately to reflect the values you derived from your obituary?

6.2 Deciding What Matters: Purpose and Worth

Is the Athletic Life Worthwhile?

Lance Armstrong's autobiography is entitled *It's Not About the Bike*. He chose that title as an indirect way of affirming his true values—the values uncovered during his battle with cancer that now guide his meaningful life. Lance now describes himself as "cancer-survivor, husband, father, son, human being."[10] His status as a pro bike racer—among his sport's greatest athletes—is only part of his identity. Cycling is just a means for expressing what he really cares about.

Decisions about the worth of a thing or "value judgments" are always made against a set of standards. For example, a $5 bill is valuable if you're looking to buy some coffee, but it's worthless for pulling a pickle from a jar. Likewise, judgments about the worth of a life (or a life activity such as sport) must be made against a set of values—an individual's considered view about what is important in life.

What many people don't realize is that these value-standards are chosen and prioritized by individuals—whether we do it consciously or not.[11] Even the *nihilist*, who says nothing in life is truly valuable, chooses the standard that places low value on life itself.[12]

You may wonder about your own set of values and you should. Where did they come from? Why do you hold them? Could you justify them to others, if challenged?

Values are important because they condition not only our judgments, but our actions. As the old saying goes, "you can learn a lot about people by watching them play a game." In sport as in life, how we act reflects what we value. Contrast the soccer player who keeps the ball and performs a spectacular maneuver for a risky shot with the player who passes off to a teammate with a more direct line on the goal. Our actions reveal what we care about—often more clearly than our words do.

Watch what you do with an open mind some day. Ask yourself why you did what you did and where that value came from. Sometimes when we reflect on our actions, we discover values that we didn't think we had. Other times when we try to act on values we don't truly believe, we find ourselves lacking in motivation; remember Lance in that first rainy race. As philosophical athletes, we must learn to evaluate our values—an essential step in the search for meaning.

---

10. Armstrong (2000, cover).

11. Kretchmar (1994, 5).

12. Arthur Schopenhauer, a 19th century German philosopher heavily influenced by Buddhism, is a famous *nihilist*. For Schopenhauer, life is a road of suffering that culminates, quite literally, at a dead-end. If we could choose not to live, we would. Schopenhauer viewed happiness itself as a negative concept, something we tend to notice only once it's gone, as with health, youth, and freedom. Truly happy people are very few and far between and their happiness is almost always fleeting: no sooner do we achieve it than it's gone. See Schopenhauer (1883).

Philosophical Background:
Values

The negative view that human lives have no preordained purpose and no great significance brings up the question of whether *anything* should be valued in life. For all our striving and struggle, the goals that we achieve come to seem rather small and unsatisfying when viewed against any big picture of the world. There doesn't seem to be an over-all plan for the world and what plans we humans make are often dashed without reason or justice. A promising doctor is struck down by cancer. A young philanthropist is murdered by the very people she's try-ing to help.

Kurt Baier notices an important misunderstanding in such negative views of life's meaning. Human life in general may not have the great significance and particular purpose ordained by God in the Christian view, but this does not preclude meaning and purpose from being found within *individual* lives. Even if life itself has no given significance or purpose, *my life* can.[13]

According to Baier, the foundation of this hope for individual meaning can be found in our logical understanding of value judgments. To ask of something, "Is it worthwhile?" is to assume some set of crite-ria or standards. Religious negativity toward terrestrial life, for exam-ple, can be blamed on the tendency to compare it to the unrealistic stan-dard of heaven. More positive judgments can be made about life when the standard adopted is more realistic—such as my life in comparison to the lives lived by great people in history, or even just people I know and admire.

Once we realize that we choose our own standards for making value judgments, the possibilities for finding meaning in life increase dramatically. Conflicts about the value of a given activity, such as com-peting in motocross, are considered against the background of other things I might do with that time. Judgments are made against standards I adopt about just what is and is not important.

What's to keep this self-designed system from dissolving into stan-dards by which anything—even suicide—could be judged valuable? Nothing, except my responsibility to subject my standards to criticism from other rational people. Such criticism would probably rule out sui-cide on the basis that death—an admitted unknown—can not be com-

---

13. Baier (1994, 386–388).

pared to life in a fair value-judgment. No matter how much I'm suffering now, I have no way of knowing whether death would be better or worse.

This was one of the many realizations made by Viktor Frankl as he suffered incredible atrocities in the concentration camp. Knowing that you have a future and learning to discover meaning even in suffering were keys to survival in Frankl's analysis.[14] Yes, life is limited. But what makes us think it should last forever? Length is not the sole criterion of worth.[15] Frankl views life as an opportunity to find meaning. The whole concept of an opportunity is by nature limited; if life never ends, the urge to find meaning could be delayed forever.

Taking Account of Your Values

To say that you value something is to say that you think it's good, but there are many ways that a thing can be good. Some important categories are intrinsic vs. extrinsic values and subjective vs. objective values. Consider an athlete who says she values her sport of tennis. The first question is whether she values tennis intrinsically, i.e. for its own sake, or extrinsically, as a means to something else. Maybe she values the sheer pleasure of playing. Maybe she sees tennis as a way to make money. Probably it's some combination of both.

Consciously or unconsciously, however, she has prioritized the intrinsic or extrinsic value and that priority will become manifest in her action. Imagine that one day she finds that although she's winning a lot of prize-money, the grueling training and travel of the professional circuit has drained all the pleasure from tennis. Will she stay or will she go? If she prioritizes the intrinsic value of tennis (the pleasure) she'll leave, if she prioritizes the extrinsic value (the winnings) she'll stay.

Of course her decision, if made in real life, may not be so simple. Perhaps her earnings pay for a sister's medical bills or her athletic success serves as inspiration to underprivileged girls in her neighborhood. In this case, tennis may just be a means to a greater, more meaningful end.

Here we get into the dynamics of the subjective vs. objective value of things. 'Subjective' means from your own point of view, so what is

---

14. Frankl (1959, 126–136).

15. Although it is plausible a happy meaningful life might benefit from an increase in length, there is no guarantee that a long life will in fact be meaningful. Thanks to my colleague Tom Gilbert for pointing this out.

good subjectively = what seems good to me. Often this reduces to what seems to be good *for* me as well. But they're not identical. Quitting the pro tour might be good *for* our tennis player because she could regain the pleasure of playing she values. But her playing is also valuable to others: her sister for one, and the girls she inspires. So there seems to be some "objective" value that reaches beyond her purely personal concerns.

Now many of the things we value individually are good objectively, i.e. peace or justice. But ultimately they become *our* values only because *we care about them.* So, if our tennis player keeps on for the good of her sister and the underprivileged girls, she does so because *she* cares about them, maybe even more than she cares about her own pleasure. Actions and the values that motivate them always come back to what the individual *chooses* to care about.

Evaluating Your Values

Once we understand how values motivate our actions and acknowledge that they're freely chosen, we realize that we're responsible for them and had better take inventory. Where do your values come from? Most people answer this question (quite accurately): "my parents."

The journalist asks: "Why did you refuse to participate in the point shaving?"

The athlete replies: "I was raised to be honest."

No doubt such inherited values are sincerely held, but should they be accepted without question? Parents generally love their children and therefore tend to give advice they sincerely believe will benefit them. But what if you were raised not to swim with people of different color? Would these adopted values truly be yours? Should they be?

Authority figures are another popular source of values: "Coach said I should play on the injured heel," says the athlete. But your values should reflect what YOU care about and that isn't always the same as what your coach, teacher, or anyone else cares about. Too often what we care about is *approval* from others—so much so that we sacrifice our own personal values to please them.

For example, we follow our peers. "Everybody fakes an injury to try and get a foul shot—it's common practice," says the soccer player. If everybody jumped off a cliff, would you do it too? Seriously, our friends and teammates—even society in general—greatly influence our values as well as the values of others we trust. But remember values are ultimately a matter of personal choice. If my values are just inherited from someone else without question, I still chose to accept them that way and therefore I'm responsible for the result.

So how should I evaluate my athletic and personal values? The answer won't be a surprise: you evaluate them in terms of meaning. This is not a trick answer, but it does need a little explaining. First of all athletic values are not separate from life values. Sport, like everything else you do, should aim toward that big picture of a meaningful and worthwhile life—a picture with one set of core values as its guide.

Kretchmar sets up useful criteria for ranking sports values.[16] He says we should (1) prefer intrinsic to extrinsic values, (2) focus on satisfaction rather than mere pleasure, and (3) aim for coherence. In a nutshell, the point is that things good in themselves, such as knowledge and happiness, are to be valued over things that are mere means to such ends, such as schooling or wealth. Likewise satisfaction, such as the pleasure arising from a job well done, is to be sought over simple pleasures such as those derived from chocolate. Finally we should aim for satisfactory experiences that fit together to build a coherent life story, rather than momentary pleasures that fade into the past.

We can apply these criteria to Lance Armstrong's life. After the cancer, he came to value the hope and courage he relied upon for recovery above such extrinsic things as money and fame. Whereas before he may have used hope and courage as means toward the end of cycling riches and glory, he now uses his money and notoriety as means to promote the intrinsic values of hope and courage among cancer victims. Specifically, he sponsors a foundation for cancer research.

The satisfaction derived from achievements that require work, pain and sacrifice, such as winning the Tour de France, is sweeter than the pleasure of hanging by the pool in the sun. And returning to dominate the sport that turned its back on him before makes more sense in a life-story that includes a dramatic comeback from death than retreating to a mountain cabin would.

Kretchmar says that "meaning seems more often to bring along excellence than vice versa."[17] This makes sense since motivation comes from things we genuinely care about. Frankl's story shows that even the

---

16. See Kretchmar (1994, 126–133).
17. Kretchmar (1994, 132).

greatest hardship and suffering can be endured for the sake of meaning. Lance Armstrong is living testament to such truths in athletics.

> **Thinking Activity: Evaluating Values**
> **Question:** Which are your strongest and most important values?
> **Observe:** Begin by making a list of things and accomplishments you care about in life. The list can include objects, people, and degrees or awards.
> **Analyze:** Go over your list decide whether the item is intrinsically valuable (i.e. worthwhile in itself) or extrinsically valuable (i.e. worthwhile as a means to something else.) Replace all extrinsic values with the intrinsic value toward which they aim until you list has only intrinsic values.
> **Question Again:** Do these intrinsic values actually guide your actions in life? Do extrinsic concerns such as money or popularity sometimes get in the way of your ultimate intrinsic goals such as happiness?

6.3 Mapping Out a Meaningful Future

Setting Goals for the Future

If values provide the roadmap to a life of meaning, carefully planning your route should be the next step. Athletes are legendary goal-setters. It is said that cyclist Greg LeMond sat down at his kitchen table as a teenager and wrote on a yellow legal pad a list of the races he wanted to win. It included junior and senior world championships, the Olympic road race, and the Tour de France. It even specified the years he expected to accomplish each goal.

Amazingly, LeMond achieved almost everything on the list. He was deprived of his chance for the gold-medal, however, by the 1980 US Olympic boycott. Few of us ever reach all our goals, and even fewer have a chance at accomplishments on the order of LeMond's. The important thing, however, is to *set* goals that are carefully selected as part of a coherent life-plan that is meaningful to you. Being future-oriented, in life as well as in sport, is an essential step toward living a meaningful life.

Philosophical Background:
Creating a Meaningful Life

Existentialist philosopher Jean-Paul Sartre viewed life as a work of art made by each individual. He agreed with Frankl that the question of meaning must be asked by each person individually. It is answered by choosing projects each of us judges to be significant and having the possibility to work on these projects.

Sartre distinguishes man as a being for whom "existence precedes essence."[18]—that is, unlike this chair or desk which is made for a particular purpose, human beings get to choose their own purpose or essence:

> What do we mean by saying that existence precedes essence? We mean that man, first of all, exists, encounters himself, surges up in the world—and, defines himself afterwards. If man as the existentialist sees him is not definable, it is because to begin with he is nothing. He will not be anything until later, and then he will be what he makes of himself.[19]

Sartre's insight opens up great opportunities to achieve a sense of worth and meaning, but it also saddles us with the awesome *responsibility* of making our own lives meaningful.

There's tension between what's worthwhile to me personally and what's worthwhile to mankind. We don't all have the generosity of Mother Teresa, but most of us recognize an obligation to something beyond ourselves. Sartre explains that in choosing for myself, I choose for all human beings because I am saying something about what a human being should be. As we saw earlier, freedom always comes with responsibility. I may be free to create my own meaning and purpose in life, but I must also be judge and jury.

Almost everyone undergoes a crisis of meaning in their lives, whatever their material circumstances or religious beliefs. Easy answers are as problematic as negative or nihilist views. Ultimately the responsibility for meaning falls back on the individual. It turns out that holding yourself to some standard—and holding your standards up to some criticism—can ultimately be a liberating and satisfying experience. As Sartre concludes,

> I am thus responsible for myself and for all men, and I am creating a certain image of man as I would have him to be. In fashioning myself I fashion man.[20]

---

18. Sartre thinks this idea is characteristic of existentialism. See his essay "The Humanism of Existentialism" in Kaufman, (1975, 222–311).

19. Sartre in Kaufman (1975, 290).

20. Sartre in Kaufman (1975, 292).

Getting Beyond Yourself

To be sure it is *your* future and *your* values that should direct the goals you set out to achieve, but part of selecting meaningful goals involves getting beyond yourself. Although we judge the value of things from a personal perspective, reflection on our values tends to take us beyond selfish concerns.

Frankl emphasizes that the true meaning of life is to be found in the world and not in ourselves:

> The more one forgets himself — by giving himself to a cause to serve or another person to love — the more human he is and the more he actualizes himself.[21]

Indeed the whole concept of significance hinges on finding meaning beyond an individual's finite existence. Lance Armstrong found his cause in the fight against cancer. Many find meaning in love for their children and family. The religious focus on God is another mode of transcendence.

So too the philosophical athlete seeks self-transcendence within sport. Team sports seem to be the paradigm here, but even while competing against others we are experiencing something *with* them. Remember the "com" in competition just means "with." Hyland found his experience in basketball to be a special experience of "authentic being-with-others."[22] That is, sport was a place where he could truly be himself while he was interacting with others. We have already seen the contrast between who we really are and the persona or mask we present to other people. Sport allows us to get beyond the self while still being authentically ourselves.

Creating Your Life Story

A meaningful life, like a meaningful movie, tells a dramatic story. There is a beginning, a middle, and an end and the events fall together in a way that makes sense. The whole thing heads somewhere and says something important. For the philosophical athlete, setting future goals is akin to writing an outline for your life story.

You want a story that means something, has a point and a premise. To an extent you are after something universal. Greek drama and

---

21. Frankl (1959, 133).
22. Hyland (1972, 93).

Shakespeare plays tell specific stories about specific people, but contain a universal message—something true at all times everywhere. *Romeo and Juliet* and *West Side Story* tell the same story at different places and times. The message is universal; we see ourselves in the characters and that's central to their appeal.

So too the drama of sport contains some universal message. Though conditioned by the values of the societies that create it,[23] sport can provide a universal drama of its own. Wrote George Santayana about sports, "The whole soul is stirred by a spectacle that represents the basis of its life."[24] Philosophical athletes must take their understanding of drama as played in sport and apply it to the plan they make for their own life stories. Like Shakespeare, you are the actor as well as the playwright and so your story should be recognizably your own—even while filling its universal paradigm.

How do I come to find my own life story? I may begin by thinking about other life-stories that I find inspiring or admirable. Then I should be sure that this is the kind of life I want to live. I should be aware of obstacles, pitfalls, and the general costs (to health and family) of ambitious goals. Finally, I should never regard my life story as something fixed. It's an ongoing drama that I live every day.

Thinking Activity: Goal-Setting
Question: Can Goals be configured into a plot for a meaningful life?
Observe: Most athletes are used to setting sports goals; they should learn to set life goals as well. Begin with the top three values you derived from the last exercise, then decide on lifetime goals that reflect those values in the short (1–5 years), medium (5–15 years), and long (15–25 years) terms. Make a chart reflecting each period of your life and a goal for each key value.
Analyze: Can this chart be interpreted as a coherent life plan? Are the goals realistic and simultaneously accomplishable—or are you planning to be a pro-athlete while studying full-time at medical school? Have you set the bar too low to be a challenge? What kind of personality will it take to achieve your goals?
Question Again: What have you done in the recent past that reflects the values you've chosen? If you haven't done much, you should ask yourself if this really is one of your values at all.

---

23. This is the theme of Felshin (1972).
24. Santayana (1972, 233).

Chapter Review

Summary: Life as a Work of Art

It was the stark reality of a Nazi concentration camp—an experience more crushing than any defeat in sport—that led psychologist Vickor Frankl to conclude that *meaning* is the central motivation in human life. R. Scott Kretchmar reflects Frankl's insight in his philosophy of sport, noting that sports and games are "wellsprings of meaning [that] provide special life-opportunities for meaning-seeking creatures like us."[25]

Philosophical athletes—having encountered ourselves in the moment of challenge, having confronted the mystery of our mind-body connection, and having encountered the terror of our own freedom—now set about creating ourselves and our lives through sport. Self-creation begins with acceptance of responsibility—for our actions, our perceptions, and even the stand we take on ourselves. There comes next the confrontation with death—figuratively, as the admission of mortal imperfection, metaphorically as the experience of losing in sport, and literally in the risks of extreme sport. Finally we come to meaning, the question spawned by the acknowledgment of death. We learn to view such limitations like the boundaries of a canvas on which we will paint the story of our lives. Values and objectives guide our paintbrushes, as even suffering becomes beautiful within the masterpiece of a self-directed and meaningful life.

Further Reading

Philosophy

Frankl, Viktor E. 1959. *Man's Search for Meaning*. New York: Beacon Press. This is a gripping first-person account of how meaning meant survival in a Nazi concentration camp. Frankl, a psychiatrist trained in existential philosophy, eventually developed a meaning-based psychotherapy.

Schopenhauer, Arthur. 1883. *The World as Will and Idea*. Translated by R.B. Haldane and J. Kemp. London: Trubner. Schopenhauer represents the classic nihilist approach to the issue. His claim that life has no meaning is heavily influenced by Buddhist thought.

---

25. Kretchmar (1994, 216).

Tolstoy, Leo. 1905. *My Confession.* Translated by Leo Wiener. London: MJ Dent. This is the classic essay in the field. Beautifully written and personal, this short piece concludes with an affirmation of faith.

Philosophy of Sport

Hyland, Drew. 1972. "Athletic Angst: Reflections on the Philosophical Relevance of Play." In Gerber, ed. (1972), 87–94. Only Hyland could apply Heideggerian theory so artfully to his experience in college basketball. One of the first and best articles in sport-philosophy.

Journalism and Literature

Armstrong, Lance. 2000. *It's Not About the Bike.* New York: Putnam. More than your typical athlete autobiography, Lance shares the details of his battle with testicular cancer and its transforming effect on both his athletic career and outlook on life.
Rodman, Dennis with Tim Keown. 1996. *Bad as I Wanna Be.* New York: Delacorte Press. This is a surprisingly thoughtful tale from the notorious bad boy of professional sports. Clearly written for the fan-market, the book nevertheless contains some interesting reflections on individuality and meaning in life.

Part Three

Showing Respect

Section Preview

Introduction:
The Ethics of Performance-Enhancement

> *A number of elite athletes were asked if, hypothetically, they would be willing to take a special pill that would guarantee them an Olympic gold medal even if they knew this pill would kill them within a year. Over 50 percent of the athletes surveyed said yes.*
> —Dr. Robert Voy, *Drugs, Sport and Politics*

What would you do?

Baseball's homerun king, Mark McGwire, was calmly giving interviews at his locker when a reporter spotted something that would turn his world upside down. It was a bottle of supplements containing androstenedione, a performance-enhancing substance.

Immediately, the athlete's ethics were questioned.

This was not a case of some sneaky mad-scientist trying to chemically coax superhuman performance from a scrawny weakling. McGwire had long been an elite player and the substance was neither illegal under Major League Baseball's rules nor hard to find; you could buy it over-the-counter at most shopping malls in the country. He was certainly not the only athlete taking androstenedione, just the most famous. McGwire even denied that he'd gained any benefit from it at all.

Still, his ethics were questioned.

Some might say that the only thing McGwire did wrong was let the reporter see the bottle. In their eyes, "sports ethics" is an oxymoron; drugs, violence, and widespread cheating are just facts of life in modern sport.

Ethics, however, concern not so much *what is*, but rather what *ought to be*. Accepting the way things are without question is not prac-

139

tical realism, it's lazy-mindedness. Those unwilling to critically examine reality are condemned to watch as it changes for the worse. Ethics is about making principled decisions on the basis of examination and thought. It is less about what exactly you do and more about being aware of why you do it. There are many ethical traditions and many rationales for actions. But when tolerance for others' positions breaks down into indifference about the reasons behind actions (others' and your own), ethical anarchy reigns. The crucial difference between ethical and unethical action, ultimately, is thought.

Of all the ethical decisions an athlete must make, those involving methods of performance-enhancement are among the most gut-wrenching and personal. After all, improving performance is the name of the game in sport, but everything you do, from drinking Gatorade to injecting anabolic steroids, is subject to question. It's not enough to simply label particular substances (aspirin good, growth hormone bad) since new products arrive regularly and each must be considered individually. Rules and laws are inadequate as guides, since they change independently of availability. Even the issue of harmfulness depends more on *how* something is used than whether its used; vitamins can be toxic in large doses while steroids can be administered safely under a doctor's care.

Still this is an ethical issue since the decision to use performance enhancers is always a choice. Drug-abusing athletes are notorious for saying that they had no option. A pro cyclist once claimed it was either use drugs or go back to being a house-painter. Since he was among the 10 best of thousands of professionals it is hard to take that ultimatum seriously. But even if it were true, an ethical house-painter may have a chance at happiness that the doped cyclist doesn't. Athletes may justify doping in their minds with such stories, but the reality is that there is always a choice. Sport is a voluntary activity; you can compete at a lower level, quit entirely, or choose another sport. Performance enhancement is always a choice for which the athlete must take responsibility.

Ethics and Self-Respect

Ethical responsibility in sport focuses on three main issues: self-respect, respect for others, and respect for the sport itself. How do we get from ethics to respect? If ethics requires thoughtfulness, and being thoughtful reflects concern, concern is manifest in respect. When you are thoughtful and care about something, you respect it—including when that something is yourself. Self-respect involves individual concern for happiness, based on a thoughtful view of a meaningful life. It means living up to the standards you set for yourself and being the kind of person you want to be. Since sport requires so many decisions about personal conduct, it is an excellent place to develop and exercise ethical self-respect.

Doped athletes imperil self-respect by giving up the opportunity to become the person they want to be. Although drugs might help me to achieve an important victory, they simultaneously prevent me from accomplishing my real, meaningful goals. For a self-respecting athlete, goals correspond to personal values. The issue is less winning than *being a winner*, less the medal itself than being the kind of person who could win the medal cleanly. The real goal is developing virtues that lead to a thriving, happy life.

It is possible, even probable, that some forms of performance enhancement can contribute to virtue and happiness. For example, weight-training might enhance discipline. But it's hard to justify things like drugs using these criteria. I can see the value in carefully following and improving by means of a swimming program, but carefully following and improving by means of a pill-taking program? Is the ability to respond to chemical stimulation something athletes should pursue and be rewarded for?[1]

Ethics and Respect for Others

Moral character is also expressed by respect for others. Athletes who seek truth and self-understanding in sport should recognize their responsibility to help others achieve similar goals — at least as far as this is prescribed by their roles as teammate, competitor, or coach. Doped athletes fail to respect their competitors by misrepresenting the challenge they provide as the performance of a clean athlete. We count on competitors to provide a measure for our skills, but when they're doped the measure is distorted.

Drug use in sport is so rife with deception, it's almost impossible to know the truth. Athletes cope by naively choosing what they want to believe. Losing athletes who are clean believe that everyone in their sport uses drugs except them; this provides a convenient excuse for their failure. Athletes who are doped, winning or losing, believe that everyone else also dopes. This creates the illusion that the playing field

---

1. This objection to drug use in sport is presented by Simon (1991, 84–89).

is level and thereby allows the doped winner to enjoy victory psychologically. Doped losers see sports as a pharmacological arms race and simply wonder what the other athletes are using.

Winning athletes who are clean believe either that no-one dopes, or that doping doesn't work. It's all they can do. Lance Armstrong says that in order to compete, he has to believe his rivals are clean.[2] Dopers, meanwhile, don't believe that clean winners exist. Of course none of these beliefs is really accurate. Some athletes dope, others don't. Who knows just what the proportions are? In sport and beyond, we depend on others' honesty to help find truth. Respect for others demands an understanding of relationships and the obligations implied by them.

Ethics and Respect for the Game

Finally, there is the question of respect for sport itself. The attitude adopted toward the rules, conventions, and ideals of a chosen sport reflects an athlete's understanding and concern for a valued practice and the community that engages in it. Respect for the game isn't a matter of mindlessly following the rules and traditions of a sport. Some rules, such as the designated-hitter rule in baseball, may be in conflict with the higher ideals of the sport. Respect for the game means understanding those ideals and critically examining the rules and actions of participants in terms of that understanding.

There certainly is a sense in which performance-enhancement may show lack of respect for a sport. To get past the question of breaking rules, imagine that all drugs were legalized in your sport. Some sports, like body-building, have all but admitted near-universal drug use. Think of the sponsorship potential of multi-billion dollar pharmaceutical companies competing for the best athletes and teams.[3] In the meantime, ask yourself whether this picture of openly drugged athletes bothers you. Is it still a sport you want to participate in? Is it still the same sport?

Eventually, Mark McGwire stopped taking androstenedione—perhaps for the sake of PR, perhaps for the sake of respect. Meanwhile, the manufacturer makes millions selling the substance to ambitious athletes. Philosophical athletes know the moral of the story: we need to develop ethical theories to guide our decisions on and off the field. The truth is

---

2. *Velo Club* television broadcast, July 1999, France 2 television.
3. I'll take up the legalization debate in chapter 9.

that sports don't build character, people do—by *thoughtful* engagement in activities such as sport.

Section Preview List

- Can there be self-respect in a victory without virtue? (Chapter 7)
- What is an athlete's duty to competitors, teammates, and coaches? (Chapter 8)
- Do athletes have an obligation to their sports? (Chapter 9)

Chapter 7

Showing Respect for Your Self

Chapter Preview

Introduction:
Victory and Virtue in Sports

> *Respect is an attitude of positive evaluation, a recognition of something, some reality that merits understanding and attentiveness. To respect something is to value and treat it as worthy in its own right. To respect something, I have to overcome my inclination to be selfish, my inclination to see the thing only in terms of my own needs and interests.*
> —Clifford and Feezell, *Coaching for Character*

Ethics is about respect and respect is about caring. But it seems like the thing cared most about in sport is winning; not the self, or others, or the game. In this modern world athletic excellence is often prized over moral excellence. "Moral victory" is just a nice way to say "lose." Furthermore, many think that sports ethics is a casualty of our modern emphasis on winning, that athletic excellence comes only at the cost of moral excellence. There's truth in what they say, but it needn't be that way.

The ancient Greeks had a single word for human excellence, moral, athletic or otherwise. *Areté* was conceived as a kind of health that infused mind, body and spirit. It could be manifest in sport, philosophy, art or science. In fact, they believed the gods enjoyed watching Olympic competition precisely for the *areté* displayed by the athletes. Victors were crowned with wreaths from sacred trees, exalted for their godlike qualities, and revered at home as civic ideals of virtue.

Could it be that we still associate winning with virtue? Images of champion athletes adorn inspirational posters meant to define such virtues as 'courage' and 'persistence.' People compare Michael Jordan

145

to a god, use him as an example of human excellence, and accept his opinion on shoes, sports drinks, and telephone companies. Even today, being a winner goes beyond scoring the most points or crossing the line first. We view winning as the manifestation of certain virtues inherent in the athlete in a given performance.

This is confirmed by the fact that when virtue is manifest by an athlete or team in an analytic loss, we describe the performance in terms of victory nonetheless; it is a "moral victory," a "personal victory," or some such qualified win. Likewise, when an analytic win is achieved without the accompanying manifestation of virtue, we try to disassociate the performance from victory by calling it a "tainted win" or a "win-on-paper."

Nevertheless, this weak association of moral excellence with athletic prowess is constantly challenged. There are just too many bad apples to support that old yarn about how sport builds character. This is not a recent insight. Attempts to fix races and ingest performance-enhancing substances were also common at the ancient Olympics. But even if it's painfully clear that success in sports is possible—perhaps easier—without good ethics, that doesn't mean that moral and athletic excellence can't go hand in hand. If we remember that virtue gives winning its value in the first place, athletic excellence can forge a path for moral excellence. It's a matter of priority and respect for oneself. For philosophical athletes, *being* a winner means more than just winning.

What ancient Greeks called *areté*, medieval monks called virtue, and modern parents call character can be summed up as "the disposition to do the right thing for the right reasons." Virtue ethics is distinctive among moral theories in that it determines what's right in terms of the good person and the good life. Virtue is envisioned as a kind of skill, learned and honed through a painstaking process of education and practice.

Plato conceived of virtue as the health of the soul, understood crudely as the harmonious function of head, heart and gut. This idea is based on a *tripartite theory of the soul*—his belief that human beings have three competing forces within them: the rational or wisdom-loving part (*logistikon*), the spirited or honor-loving part *(thymoeides)* and the appetitive or pleasure-loving part (*epithymetikon*). The trick to virtue is getting all three to work together with reason in the lead. The head determines the proper goal, the heart summons willpower, and the gut provides that burning desire.[1]

---

1. See Plato, *Republic* 441e–444e.

Athletes are great candidates for virtue-ethics because they're already goal-oriented, motivated, and disciplined: they know what they want in their heads, have the heart to go after it, and have the discipline to avoid gut-level temptations. Athletes are at their best—indeed they achieve excellence—when all three qualities come together and work as a team.

The hardest thing for modern thinkers to get used to with virtue-ethics is the idea that virtue and excellence are the same. We're used to thinking of virtue in terms of personal sacrifice rather than personal happiness. But being a good person need not be exclusive of being a good athlete. The idea behind virtue-ethics is that the *benefits* of athletics—like those of careers, family, or faith—come from being a good person first. As Socrates says,

> Wealth does not bring about excellence, but excellence makes wealth and everything else good for men, both individually and collectively.[2]

For the philosophical athlete, virtue gives victory its value in sport—and it gives sport its value in life.

Chapter Preview List

- In what sense is athletic success "all in your head?"
- What do we mean when we say an athlete has "heart?"
- What does it mean to have "guts" in sport?

---

2. Plato. *Apology*, 30b.

7.1 Getting Clear About Goals (Head)

Philosophical Background:
Starting Point: The Good Life

Aristotle, who was educated at Plato's Academy, adopted and re-fined virtue-ethics into a practical system that focuses on a rational idea of happiness, an individual's unique function, and conditioning the will though habituation.[3]

Aristotle began with the insight that every human action aims at some good. Most things are *instrumental goods*—good insofar as they lead to other goods. For example, I work to earn money, which is used to buy an airplane ticket, which is used to fly to Italy, where I can relax among vineyards. An *intrinsic good* is something sought for its own sake and Aristotle thought all humans would agree that happiness is the final good at which all our action aims.[4]

Eudaimonia, Aristotle's word for happiness, denotes something much broader than the beer-and-potato-chip pleasure you might imag-ine. Pleasure is a key part of it, but a better translation might be some-thing like "human flourishing." When we aim at happiness in virtue ethics, we must summon a complex picture of the good and successful life, from start to finish, with all its ups and downs.

This isn't as easy as it sounds. To get an idea of the kind of life you want to lead, you must develop a conception of the kind of person you want to be. Your dreams must be tempered by an honest assessment of the person you are, and the unavoidable limitations of temporal, finan-cial and personal resources. Sure you'd like to be a Nobel Laureate, but would you really be happy living the life required? What's your defini-tion of excellence anyway? Some criteria are needed.

---

3. Variations on this theme were espoused by the later Greco-Roman schools of thought known as the Epicureans, Stoics, and Skeptics. Preserved in libraries at Alexan-dria and Bagdadh, Aristotle's writings persisted to influence the Jewish thinker Mai-monides, the Islamic scholar Averroës, and countless Christians—most notably St. Thomas Aquinas. Traces of Aristotle's thought can also be seen in the ideas of such con-temporary ethicists as Alisdair MacIntyre. For an excellent account of virtue-ethics in the ancient world, see Annas (1993).

4. For more on Aristotle's conception of happiness, see *Nicomachean Ethics*, 1094a1102a.

What Do You Want to Achieve?

For the philosophical athlete, personal ethics begin in the head with a well thought out conception of happiness—a clear idea of what you want in life. This conception of happiness can be understood in terms of goals. For athletes, this is usually no problem. We all have specific goals, often organized into a realistic progression. Overarching goals don't vary much; usually athletes aim for an Olympic gold medal, professional contract, or status as a popular icon.

Not until our goals become clear in our heads, however, do they have the chance to mobilize our hearts. According to sports psychologists Susan Jackson and Mihaly Csikszentmihalyi, "goals harness psychic energy and direct it toward the desired outcome."[5] So be specific about what you want to achieve. Imagine yourself bowing to receive your gold medal, signing your name at the bottom of the contact, or being crowded by a herd of autograph-seekers.

As a young athlete I had a recurring mental newsreel of me thrusting my bike across the finish line of the Olympic gold medal race and raising my arms victoriously in the air, bathed by applause and cheering. Indulging in such fantasies is a favorite—and important—pastime of athletes everywhere. But to turn goals into a foundation for virtue-ethics we must reflect on *why* we think these things will make us happy. What is it about the achievement of a particular goal that makes it part of a good life?

Often what we're after in our athletic dreams seem to be instrumental rather than final goods. That is, we seem to be pursuing means to happiness rather than happiness itself. Athletes crave the adulation of the crowd and recognition from their peers, parents, and coaches. But why? Why should we care so much about the opinions of others?[6] Is their friendship genuine or superficial? Would they help you out in a jam?

Maybe it's better to have power over others, to acquire the physical strength that they respect and even fear. But strength can intimidate people we'd like to be close to. Is it really central to a happy life? Money is good for buying things; even Aristotle recognizes the need for a modicum of wealth in the good life. But there are too many unhappy rich people to believe that money can buy happiness or anything even close.

---

5. Jackson and Csikszentmihalyi (1999, 87).
6. A paraphrase of Socrates' statement to Crito in Plato, *Crito*, 44c.

Who Do You Want to Be?

When I reflected on my own athletic goals, I realized that it wasn't so much about what I wanted to achieve but rather *who* I wanted to be. I wanted to be the kind of person who was capable of winning gold. I was really after the virtues I believed were necessary for that goal—the courage, the strength, the perseverance, the intelligence, the independence, the creativity. It wasn't enough just to be capable of winning or even to win—I was after a certain package of attributes that I believed gold medallists to have.

Reflection showed me that the medal itself wouldn't bring happiness. I was aware of several gold-medallists that I wouldn't want to emulate at all. On some level I knew that athletic success could be achieved without the virtues I was after—some champions used drugs, others exploited teammates or family connections, others just had sour or arrogant personalities. My goal was not just to win a medal, but also to be an Olympian in the idealized virtuous sense.

Many athletes have dreams similar to mine about who they want to be. Often we start with a specific role model, but eventually we develop a personalized ideal of our own selves. "I don't want to be the next Jeremy McGrath," says the young motocross racer, "I want to be the first Brock Sellards." Again, to fit the goal into a system of virtue-ethics, we have to get clear on why we think that being a certain type of person will lead to happiness.

Idolizing sports heroes ignores your (and their) individuality. A better way to approach happiness is to reflect on who you want to be in light of what you already know about *yourself.* Are you trying to be a better you or someone else completely? Start with your body. Athletes can adapt to many challenges; people survive cancer and go on to win the Tour de France. But some aspects of physical reality, such as height, can't be changed.

Great athletes accept and creatively overcome these shortcomings (literally in the case of the diminutive basketball star Mugsy Bogues). Others try to compensate chemically, using anabolic steroids or growth hormones. Forget the legality and risks for a moment, and ask yourself whether you really want to be that kind of person. Few of us are born with the exact physical traits we desire. The question of the goals we have as athletes, however, is inextricably tied up with the kinds of means we're willing to accept.

Often what we admire about star athletes is their lifestyle. It seems like a dream to be paid for playing a game, to travel in private jets and stay in luxury hotels, greeted at every port by adoring fans. But the skill of professional athletes comes with a mandatory side-order of physical pain including exhaustion, injuries, illness, and for some, an early death.

Lyle Alzado had a glamorous career in the NFL, but it crash-landed quickly when his body finally succumbed to the chemical and physical abuse he endured to reach the top. When Lyle's ritual steroid and growth hormone abuse apparently led to a premature cancerous demise, the biggest surprise for many was that *he* didn't expect it. The superstar life didn't seem worth the physical price he eventually paid.[7]

In fact, the travel and celebrity of top athletes often conceals a grossly unbalanced life in which education, lasting career skills, and family life are compromised. Things we take for granted such as privacy and job security are all but absent from the pro athlete's lifestyle. As Aristotle said, we need to think about the big picture of life, with all its checks and balances, all its ups and downs, to get a clear vision of what may constitute happiness for us.

Setting and Revising Goals

Just as with winning, I think that we glamorize the lives of champion athletes out of admiration for the virtues we think make their success possible. Being excellent at what you do and making money from what you love are goals that can be achieved in any number of fields besides sport.

What's satisfying is to profit from virtues, rather than from luck or even talent. Don't we admire the millionaire entrepreneur more than the millionaire lottery winner? Isn't the love and approval of a close friend more satisfying than the admiration of an autograph-seeker or groupie? Wouldn't you rather achieve victory through hard work and perseverance, without the help of drugs? Deciding *what* you want to achieve is connected to deciding *the kind of person* you want to be, and that depends on a package of virtues and attributes that dictate acceptable means to your goals.

Your actions paint a picture of yourself, they express *who* you are. In order to guide those actions, each individual must find a personal formula for happiness that takes into consideration an entire life in length

---

7. For an inside account of Alzado's demise, see Huizenga (1994, 282–310).

Thinking Activity: Role Models
Question: What should we admire in athletic role models?
Observe: Think of an athletic role model—either one of your own or one popular with many young people. Ask yourself what makes this role-model special. Then list several of the qualities admired in this person.
Analyze: Compare your own qualities with those of your role model. Are there any qualities the role model has that you can't achieve (i.e. height)? Of the qualities you wish to emulate, did your role model pay a price for any of them that you are not willing to pay (i.e. did the person develop skills by long hours of practice). Are any of the qualities applicable to other endeavors besides sport (i.e. courage, discipline, perseverance).
Question Again: Does admiration of this role model prevent an honest analysis of your own idea of the good life?

---

and breadth. Sport must find its place among other areas of importance such as education, career, and family. Furthermore, no area of endeavor should be discarded after a certain age; retirement from competitive sport is no more an excuse to abandon physical activity than college graduation is an excuse to abandon the life of the mind.

This personalized vision of the good life need not be fixed. Goals and ideas can change as time and reflection help us to learn more about ourselves and the elements of our happiness. It seems natural as one ages and gains a broader view of the world that the desire for an Olympic gold medal might transform into the desire for a Nobel prize. However, it is always essential to virtue ethics that our life plans can be rationally defended and justified to others whom we admire and trust.

Appropriate goals are individual, realistic and achievable, but nevertheless challenging. The point of goal-setting is to improve as a person, to develop the virtues needed for a good life. By focusing on virtues rather than the specific goal, we will be prepared to make good decisions when sport requires an unforeseen sacrifice of education, health, or family. Virtues are adaptable whereas specific goals are not. I can still show the discipline I developed on the running track after a debilitating injury or an unexpected child changes the trajectory of my athletic career.

Philosophical athletes should set specific goals and priorities for life, just as we already do for sport. We should examine how well the goals reflect our personalized ideas of happiness, connecting the specific achievement desired with a particular set of virtues or attributes.

For philosophical athletes, the real goal is a good life and the virtues that make it possible as developed in sport. Getting a clear idea in your head about who you want to become is the first step toward a meaningful life as a philosophical athlete.

7.2 Motivation (Heart)

Who I Am vs. Who I Want to Be

The best-conceived vision of happiness and the most laudable and realistic goals mean nothing without the motivation to put these ideas into action. This is the job of the spirited part of the soul, or in more familiar terms: heart. Motivation comes from concern; what you care about you'll do.

This phenomenon is everywhere in athletics. When you really care about a particular game or contest you become hyper-motivated, ready to give everything you've got in pursuit of victory. I always enjoy the racquetball game more when I play so hard that I have trouble walking back up the stairs to the locker room afterward. Knowing that I marshaled all my forces for that game has its own satisfaction, whether I actually won or not.

Good athletes can take the will to win a particular point, and stretch it out over an entire game. Once they become convinced of the link between victories in competition and their daily training sessions, the motivation spreads even further. The best athletes understand that glorious victories are built on a foundation of repetitive and mundane training tasks. That's how they can carry game-day motivation over into challenges of training, diet, and recovery.

Willpower comes from clarity of purpose: getting your goals straight in your head. Philosophical athletes can expand the formula beyond sports and gain the motivation to act rightly, when we add life-goals to athletic objectives in a cradle-to-grave picture of the good life. The trick is to *care* about yourself, to respect the person you are and want to become.

The feeling of *care* is also a good barometer of the *authenticity* of your goals. We all experience moments of weak motivation, during the long bus ride to the next competition or standing on the doorstep before going out to train in the rain. In those moments we can marshal our willpower by focusing on our goals. The person I want to be is willing to train in the rain.

In my very first bike race overseas, the sky turned black and a heavy cold rain turned the road into a sooty river. I remember actually delighting in the inclement conditions, "This is European racing," I thought to myself, "just like the pictures in the magazines." Of course the delight quickly faded when I lost sensation in my feet, but the opportunity to transcend *who I had been,* and to move a step closer to *who I wanted to be,* was rightly met with joy and enthusiasm. It showed I cared about my goals.

At other times the motivation simply isn't there—no matter how hard we focus on our goals. Overtraining and exhaustion are physiological causes of this, but the lack of motivation may also signal a lack of authentic care. I once tried to motivate myself by going after money rather than victory in a bike race. There are cash prizes on particular laps, but the energy expended chasing them usually kills you for the final sprint. People in America always seem to understand and support you when money is your aim. But I never felt satisfied as a mercenary athlete. I discovered that, deep down, I cared more about victory than prizes.

You have to ask yourself honestly why you are pursuing a particular goal, understand its role in your happiness, and be ready to give it up when you really don't care. Concern can be a guide to your unique athletic and ethical profile.

Philosophical Background:
The Nature of Concern

It seems as though theories of happiness are as different as individuals—and in some sense that's true—but virtue ethics need not collapse into the *relativistic* view that there are no universal standards or criteria for evaluation. Aristotle reasoned that the excellence of all things is found in their unique function—for example, the virtue of a knife is to be sharp. Since reason separates humans from the rest of the animals, our excellence (and happiness) must lie in the exercise of reason.[8]

The requirement that our personal theories of happiness must be rationally defensible provides virtue-ethics with a crucial degree of universality and objectivity.[9] It's what keeps serial killers from claiming that their lifestyles are aimed at happiness and virtue; such an idea of happiness can't be rationally defended. Reason also keeps virtue-ethics from

8. For more on man's function see Aristotle, *Nicomachean Ethics* 1097b–1098a
9. See Annas (1993, 445).

collapsing into *egoism*—the view that I should be ethically concerned only with myself. As Aristotle noticed, humans are also social animals; it therefore makes sense that our idea of the good life must take into consideration the well being of others and the environment we depend on.

In categorizing humans as rational animals, Aristotle also made use of the paradigm of nature. He was a great practitioner of the physical sciences and believed that nature exhibited a plan and order with which human beings should live in harmony. He even viewed our communities as large organisms that thrive only when each citizen plays a particular role. A deep respect for nature complements rationality as a standard for evaluating our theories of happiness. Notably, it allows us to distinguish "natural" goals from merely conventional ones. Do I want to become a schoolteacher because it's what I'm naturally suited to do, or is it merely a convention in my society for a woman like me to seek that career?

Of course, social conventions get confused with natural capacities all the time, and Aristotle's own deliberations often fall into that trap— especially when it comes to gender-roles and slavery. The point, however, is that by having an objective standard to couple with rationality, virtue ethics is able to transcend and even criticize social convention. After all, if I set my goals according to what's expected of me rather than according to my independently derived and reflected-upon wishes, there's little chance that I will achieve true happiness. A guide to this is gauging my own concern for my goals.

Self-Policing

Since discipline and motivation depend ultimately on self-respect, athletes should declare independence from convention and authority in setting the parameters of their goals. No penalty devised by a coach, referee, or governing board could be harsher than the loss of self-respect. Just as our personalized vision of happiness can push us to train on cold rainy mornings, that same vision should motivate us to act rightly. Like bodily health, health of the soul depends on action.

You're a much better policeman of your own ethical behavior than any external law-enforcer could ever be. In fact, some rules may be unethical and you'll need a strong sense of moral responsibility to oppose them. We all look into the past and see the folly of racial segregation, but who among us would have recognized the injustice then? How many unjust rules and laws are we overlooking today?

Often rules are more lenient than personal ethics. I constantly hear athletes defend their use of performance-enhancing substances on the grounds that (for now, at least) they're legal. In 1984, the U.S. cycling team engaged in a performance-enhancing practice known as "blood-boosting." Several weeks before the Olympics, a unit of blood was removed from each rider, then centrifuged and frozen for storage. Just before the event, after the riders' red blood cell count had rebounded naturally, the stored blood cells were reinjected, raising the riders' hematocrit (i.e. the density of oxygen-carrying red blood cells) and therefore, their performance level. The cyclists won an unprecedented number of medals, none of which were revoked after the scandal broke. At the time, blood-boosting was not against any rules — but just about everyone including the cyclists admitted it was unethical.[10]

I know of at least one athlete who refused to engage in the practice. According to him, this angered the coaches so much he nearly lost his place on the team. He won no medal, but he retained his self-respect despite lenient rules and overbearing coaches.

We've already seen the importance of taking responsibility in our lives (section 2). Athletes must police themselves ethically. We face many tollbooths on the road to athletic success where a price to continue must be paid. Many athletes give up their education or forgo personal relationships and family life in order to pursue their dreams. In basing our ethics on a complete vision of happiness, we commit ourselves to accepting truths about who we are. We must distinguish external appearances from internal reality. It's not enough to fulfill the image of standing on the Olympic podium of your dreams, you have to be the person you hoped to be on the inside, too.

Trouble-Shooting

Ironically, few athletes are as honest with themselves as their sports are with them. They become so enamored with their goals that they forget the importance of process. Since virtues give most of our goals their meaning, however, it makes no sense to compromise your virtue in order to reach the goals; it deprives them of their meaning. Focusing too much on

---

10. For a detailed account of the scandal see Prouty (1988, 121–171).

instrumental goods such as money, glory, or medals threatens to damage our ultimate end: happiness. The patience, planning, and endurance required for athletic success should be applied to the longest race of all: life.

Athletes who sacrifice the future to take what they can get now are making a mental mistake. If I hold a baseball in my hand and compare it to the moon, both objects might appear to be the same size. Rewards closer in time are difficult to pass up in favor of bigger rewards down the road. How many collegiate players have lost eligibility and huge professional contracts to have a few hundred dollars right now? This is a mental mistake, and the heart is only too ready to go along with it.

Athletes love to make exceptions for themselves from the general rules. "Sure, I know faking a foul is wrong but everybody is doing it." Almost every athlete who takes drugs is convinced that everyone else is doing it. It's self-deception and self-indulgence—a refusal to let your head run the show, and a surreptitious victory by the gut in pursuit of immediate gratification. The problem with making one exception is that it conditions you to make more. You have to train your heart to feel the right things. Once you have, pursuing the head's roadmap won't be such a big deal.

Thinking Activity: Rules and Ethics
Question: Should rules ever be broken?
Observe: Civil rights activists used civil disobedience, the open and public breaking of an unjust law with a willingness to accept the penalty, to battle segregation. Martin Luther King Jr. said that one criterion for determining an unjust law was the degradation of human personality. Imagine a rule in sport (past, present, or future) that you think may be unjust.
Analyze: Isolate the reason you think this rule is unjust and say how you think its repeal would make your sport better. For example, in some leagues, female beach volleyball players are required to play in bikinis. The rule makes the sport appealing to male fans and pleases the sponsors, but some say that it degrades athletes by treating them as sex-objects.
Question Again: Would you have the courage to fight such a rule even if it conflicted with your professional interests? Why or why not?

7.3 Discipline and Desire (Gut)

As everybody knows, the appetitive or pleasure-seeking part of our souls can be as strong a leader to action as the head—oftentimes stronger. It is popular to describe gut feelings as containing their own brand of wisdom. "On a gut-level I knew that this job was all wrong for me." But more often the gut is responsible for overriding wisdom and leading us down paths we regret later.

Our appetites tempt us to eat and drink what we know we should not. Sex drives motivate all sorts of troublesome behavior from over-spending on clothes and fancy cars to turbulent relationships that end in agony. Then there's plain laziness — against which every athlete must fight — as it leads us to such short-cuts as performance enhancing drugs. We all know hearts are fickle; motivation can swing either way. Getting our hearts to follow our minds rather than our guts is called discipline.

Philosophical Background:
Putting Virtue to Action

We often hear that doing good is its own reward; in virtue-ethics that may be true in more ways than one. Aristotle believed that we could condition our souls to do the right thing, just as we condition our bodies to hard training. Athletes already know how this process works. At the beginning of a training program there is resistance and pain, but with time the body comes to desire its workouts.

It all begins with setting priorities and acting on them. Once I understand that performing well in my job as a postman is key to my personal happiness, I become motivated, even enthusiastic about doing it. Aristotle described the process of turning theory into action as a *practical syllogism*. You begin with a universal good, apply it to the particular situation at hand, and derive a *maxim* or personal call to action.[11]

For example, combine the *universal idea*, "Health is part of happiness," with the application or *middle term*, "This carrot is healthy," and you yield the maxim for action: "Eat this carrot." Of course this example is grossly oversimplified, but the practical syllogism illustrates a way to connect theory and practice that is easy to understand and use.

Even with the tool of the practical syllogism, the biggest obstacle to a virtuous life remains choosing the right thing to do. We often confuse happiness with pleasure and end up choosing the wrong things. Heroin, for example, may provide an incredibly pleasurable sensation, but that pleasure is outweighed by the cost of the agonizing desire for more and the destruction of all meaningful aspects of a good life.

---

11. See, for example, *Nicomachean Ethics*, 1141b.

One tool Aristotle proposes for discerning proper actions and attitudes is *the doctrine of the mean*.[12] By 'mean' he means the midpoint between excess and deficiency. The virtue of courage, for example, would be found at the midpoint between the excess of recklessness and the deficiency of cowardice. The doctrine is more a rule of thumb that doesn't work for everything. Still it reflects the ancient wisdom inscribed on Apollo's temple at Delphi, "Nothing in Excess," as well as the Buddha's "middle path."

Getting the right idea about what to do is only half the battle, however. Actually doing it requires the heart and gut to follow along with the head. Aristotle believed we could train ourselves to follow through with our ideas through habituation. For example, you make community service a requirement for college students and pretty soon they acquire a habit that continues on well past graduation.

Of course, we can be habituated to do almost anything (good or evil), so it's crucial that the project begins with a carefully constructed big-picture of happiness. That picture must be constantly questioned and evaluated using such standards as reason and the paradigm of nature. From there we can select useful goals and activities, gaining the will and enthusiasm for our personal project through the actual exercise of virtuous action.

Conscience Responds to Training

Training the body and training the soul are similar. At first, behaving ethically can be a bit of a struggle. The gut isn't interested in our long-term plans for happiness; it wants to be reclining on the couch in front of the tube. But if the gut follows the mind and heart often enough it comes to derive pleasure from doing the right thing and eventually starts to seek it out.

A popular name for this phenomenon is strength of character. When people say "sports builds character" this is often what they have in mind — training of the soul to forgo immediate gratification in favor of long-term goals. The truth, however, is that sports don't build character, athletes build character by constantly acting according to their heads.

Strength of character just like strength of body is achieved through training and practice, by constantly testing ourselves. The more often we do the right thing, the more disposed we become to doing it again.

---

12. For more on Aristotle's doctrine of the mean see *Niomachean Ethics*, 1106a–1109b.

Former NBA star and U.S. senator Bill Bradley compares this process to tempering steel. The challenges and trials we face in sport prepare us for the challenges and trials we face in life; they help us to achieve a kind of resilience. Says Bradley,

> Each life blow no longer shatters us like a hammer hitting brick; rather it makes us stronger. It tempers us, like a hammer hitting metal.[13]

Courage and Conscience

With all this talk about steel and strength, however, it's important to remember that the soul can be just as easily conditioned to do the wrong thing as to do the right thing. Just as there is a thin line between genius and madness, so there is not much distance between courage and callousness.

The reality of modern sports is that moral callousness is widespread and infectious.[14] In many places there's a culture of reinforcement for winning at any cost. An athlete who worries about taking some drug, harming a competitor, or deceiving an official is quickly reassured that it's OK—maybe even expected—if it helps the team. Having the "guts" to do whatever it takes to win is considered a central virtue.

But think about it for a minute. What does it mean to have "guts"? A gutsy player is one who shows immense desire to succeed, overcoming the temptation to back off for lack of patience or fear of failure. Some people might think it takes guts to cheat—but is that the same kind of guts?

Aristotle defined courage as a midpoint between the extremes of recklessness and cowardice. Reckless athletes heed no fear, whether it's reasonable or not. They stay on the summit of Everest too late to get back down. They run risky plays on fourth and long near their own goal-line. Cowards, on the other extreme, heed all fears—especially the

---

13. Bradley (1998, 67). "Resilience is what allows us to struggle hard and long with tragedy or loss or misfortune or change and still manage to dig deep and find our second wind. It's a kind of toughness."

14. See Kretchmar (1994, 238–40).

unreasonable ones. They worry about reliable equipment failing. They worry that teammates have conspired with the other team. Courage, the mid-point, means fearing only reasonable things. Athletes *should* avoid some risks, like playing football after a head injury or wrestling while severely dehydrated. Other risks, however, are accepted.

Having 'guts' means having appetites that follow the commands of the head. Having the guts to stick to a goal that is no longer reasonable, such as trying to ski a black-diamond slope as a beginner, is not courage but recklessness. Having the "guts" to do what the coach says, even when you think its wrong, is not courage but moral weakness. Having the guts to follow your head, to both enthusiastically pursue and revise goals where appropriate, is what courage in sport — and life — is all about.

When we say that athletes have guts, we mean that they have harmony of the soul; that their hearts are willing to follow their head's rational commands, and their guts contribute desire to the effort. The word 'courage' comes from the root meaning 'heart' — it's gut-level desire tempered by reason. The voice of conscience is sometimes hard to hear through the "noise" of emotion, but listening and heeding it is the central skill of courage.

Carrying It Over to Other Pursuits

As we learned early on, sport is a human construction and we can make of it what we want. We can use it to build character or to nourish moral callousness; the choice and responsibility belong to the individual athlete. Since virtue ethics teaches that happiness and the good life are the goals of moral excellence, it makes sense that a philosophical athlete would use sport to build virtues that could be applied throughout life. Philosophical athletes should put sport in the service of improving themselves rather than putting themselves in the service of sport. This means finding a place for sport in a life-long pursuit of happiness and exploiting the virtuous skills gained there in other life-pursuits.

The proper ordering of the soul, the orientation toward meaningful goals, the heartfelt motivation to pursue those goals, and the discipline to stay on a straight and narrow path are all elements of virtue-ethics that apply to sport. But they're only really worthwhile if they reach beyond sport to other areas of life. It's hard to imagine a happy life in which the *only* goals and achievements are athletic. Indeed it's hard to maintain exclusive enthusiasm for sport as our conception of the world and of ourselves grows and matures. Even the money and glory of sport lose their value in a life without meaning.

Thinking Activity: Drugs, Deception and Virtue

Question: Should athletes use performance enhancing substances?

Observe: The effects of self-deception about our plans for happiness range from a simple lack of motivation to a desperate search for short-cuts — easier ways to get to our goals. This is when the heart turns away from the head and starts following the gut. Remember that the gut seeks pleasure, readily sacrificing long-term goods in favor of immediate gratification. When the desire for pleasure replaces the desire for virtue, athletes focus on victory's side dishes rather than the main course. They think about the money, glory, or attention and justify their pursuit of the goal in those terms. But when a goal desired for the virtues behind it is achieved by other means, it is literally hollow. Like a victory gained in forfeiture or passing an exam by cheating, what you cared about in the test was not achieved

Analyze: Athletes can deceive themselves about their vision of happiness long enough to receive a medal and hear a national anthem. But once you realize that you have not become the person you wanted to be, once you understand that the relevant virtues still elude you, the false sense of happiness will escape.

Question Again: Here is a list of important questions for a philosophical athlete considering the use of performance enhancement:

1. Does using X and all its consequences fit into my big picture of happiness?
2. Would X be employed by the person I want to be?
3. Can I justify using X openly and rationally?
4. Is my heart following my head or my gut on this one?
5. Does using X develop a life-skill that can be applied to other endeavors?

Chapter Review

Summary: Virtue, Happiness, and Self-Respect

In virtue ethics, the same big picture of flourishing happiness motivates all action in sport and out. The clearer and more well thought out that picture, the easier it is to pursue it wholeheartedly. The challenges faced in any long journey are more easily overcome when we believe in our goal. For the philosophical athlete, virtue ethics comes down to self-respect. Sport offers us so many chances to discover our selves, our freedom, and our potential. If who we are is what we do, if life is a work of art we paint with our actions, why deface our work of art by throwing ethics aside?

Further Reading

Philosophy

Annas, Julia. 1993. *The Morality of Happiness*. New York: Oxford University Press. In this book, one of the great scholars of ancient philosophy in our time gives a contemporary analysis of ancient virtue ethics that focuses on pre-Socratic philosophers and modern moral problems. The first chapter is especially useful as an overview of virtue ethics.

Aristotle. 1953. *Nicomachean Ethics*. Translated by J.A.K. Thomson. Middlesex, England: Penguin. In Book II of this seminal work, Aristotle expounds his famed doctrine of the mean and his theory that the soul can be conditioned to right action.

Plato. 1992. *Republic*. Translated by G.M.A. Grube. Indianapolis, IA: Hackett. As the title advertises, Plato describes the structure of an ideal city in this dialogue. What many don't realize is that the ideal city is analogous to a properly-structured human soul, i.e. a virtuous person. The passage on the tripartite theory of the soul can be found in book IV.

Philosophy of Sport

On the issue of drugs in sport:

Simon, Robert L. 1984. "Good Competition and Drug-Enhanced Performance." *Journal of the Philosophy of Sport* XI: 6–13. This is an excellent overview of the philosophical issue of banning drugs in sport. It considers such issues as defining performance-enhancing drugs, risk, coercion, and informed consent, and how drug use affects competition.

Journalism and Literature

On the issue of drugs in sport:

Hoberman, John. 1992. *Mortal Engines: The Science of Performance and the Dehumanization of Sport*. New York: The Free Press. Hoberman offers a thoroughly researched history of the underlying drive for performance that inspires the use of performance enhancing drugs.

Prouty, David F. 1988. *In Spite of Us: My education in the big and little games of amateur and Olympic sports in the U.S.* Brattleboro, VT: VeloNews. This autobiographical account, by an official in the U.S. Cycling federation, explores the causes of and fallout from blood-doping at the 1984 Olympic games.

Solotaroff, Paul. 1992. "The Power and the Gory." In McGuane, ed., 176–196. This is a graphic account of the pharmaceutical "arms race" in professional body-building and the effects that it has had on competitors and their families.

Voy, Robert. 1991. *Drugs, Sport, and Politics.* Champaign, IL: Human Kinetics. This memoir from the former U.S. Olympic Committee head physician explores the causes and recommends potential solutions to the drug problem in Olympic sport. This book is noteworthy for the scope of if its view, which goes much farther than indicting individual athletes to suggest an overhaul of sports governance, at the local, national, and international levels.

Chapter 8

Showing Respect for Others

Chapter Preview

Introduction:
Sport, Violence, and Respect for Others

> *The way you demonstrate respect for an opponent is by playing your best against them.*
>
> —John Wooden

Jonathan E, the lead character in William Harrison's short story *Roller Ball Murder*, seems as much machine as man. A star in perhaps the most violent sport ever imagined, he stoically endures rule changes designed to increase the blood and death toll. He takes his coaches' orders, senses the bone and teeth of a competitor give way to his fist, and watches impassively as a teammate is killed during a game.

> Today I turn my best side to the cameras. I'm Jonathan E, none other, and nobody passes me on the track. I'm the core of the Houston team and for the two hours of play—no rules, no penalties once the cannon fires—I'll level any bastard runner who raises a paddle at me. [...] We move: immediately there are pileups of bikes, skaters, referees, and runners, all tangled and punching and scrambling when one of the balls zooms around the corner and belts us. I pick up momentum and heave an opposing skater into the infield at center ring; I'm brute speed today, driving, pushing up on the track, dodging a ball, hurtling downward beyond those bastard runners. Two runners do hand-to-hand combat and one gets his helmet knocked off in a blow which tears away half his face; the victor stands there too long admiring his work and gets wiped out by a biker who swoops down and flattens him.

The crowd screams and I know the cameramen have it on an isolated shot and that viewers in Melbourne, Berlin, Rio, and L.A. are
heaving with excitement in their easy chairs.[1]

Roller Ball Murder is an apocalyptic view of the future of sport,
but many would say that its feverish bloodlust and disregard for human
life differs from our modern sports only in degree. Aren't sports now
engineered to accommodate the fans' lust for violence? Won't coaches
sacrifice players' health to further their own careers? Don't athletes de-
spise their competitors? Aren't teammates viewed as disposable means
to personal ends? What role could respect for others have in such an
ugly environment?

Believe it or not, aggressive sports behavior may be permissible,
even expected, in certain situations. It's hard to imagine a non-violent
boxing match, for example. Boxers expect that their opponents will hit
and even try to knock them down. Since it's an accepted part of their
role as boxers and relationship as competitors, hitting hard can be regarded as a sign of *respect*—it might even be considered a duty.

How can we tell when apparently violent actions in sport represent
disrespect to a competitor? The trick is to understand the concept of
duty, the nature of the relationship, and the objectives of the activity.
The first step is to be precise about what we mean by "violence." In
general parlance, the term 'violent' may simply mean 'with extreme effort' as when we say of a lumberjack, "He swung the axe violently."
Baseball players certainly swing their bats with just as much effort, but
we'd hardly call that violence in sport. What we're concerned about is
violence directed at another person.

Still, we need to distinguish between actions that are accepted in a
given sport and actions that are not. One useful criterion, proposed by
sport-philosopher Robert Simon, is to distinguish between acceptable
"aggression" and unacceptable violence in terms of the *intent to harm*.
Players can be physically aggressive in their pursuit of a sporting
goal—causing a fumble, perhaps—without intending to harm their
competitor. But intentional harm is not part of the task at hand—it is
violence.

Of course the term 'harm' is open to interpretation. Even though
players expect a certain amount of potentially harmful activity when
they agree to participate in a given sport, they also expect that their

---

1. Harrison (1973, 31).

competitors will be pursuing sport-specific goals such as putting the hockey puck into the net.

Violence in sport, then, may be understood as harmful action extrinsic to the central objectives of the contest. Using this criterion we might even understand a sport such as boxing in which "harming" the opponent is one of the objectives. The parameters of such harm are defined by the rules and such actions as hitting below the waist, poking at the eyes, or gnawing on the ears (!) are violent in the sense that they are extrinsic to the test at hand.

To sum up, then, athletes have a duty to respect others' humanity, but also to understand and respect the particular relationships involved and the purpose of the activity.

Chapter Preview List

- Should athletes view their competitors as obstacles, facilitators, or friends?
- What does it really mean to be a good "team player"?
- Should an athlete ever refuse to obey a coach?

8.1 Competitors

Philosophical Background:
Respect, Duty, and Relationships

To understand what it means to respect others in sport, we must first explore the nature of duty and relationships. From a moral point of view, duty is understood as what is *owed* to others. The most widespread and profound expression of our duty to each other is the Golden Rule: "Do unto others as you would have them do unto you." It is an idea found throughout the world and its history from Buddhism to Zoroastrianism. Followed appropriately, the rule promotes social harmony while respecting individual values.[2] This simple command to give others the same consideration we expect for ourselves weeds out such corrupting ideas as "might makes right" without prescribing a particular set of moral values.

In the 19th century, Immanuel Kant developed his *categorical imperative*,[3] a version of the Golden Rule that derives its power from sheer reason, rather than divine command. Its most common formulation states:

> I ought never to act except in such a way that I can also will that my maxim should become a universal law.[4]

This means that to be a good person, I must to act out of duty to or respect for what is right (*not* personal interest). The way I test myself on this is to imagine what the world would be like if everyone did what I'm about to do—if it was a natural law as universal as gravity. A golfer tempted to shave a few strokes off his score, for example, could never will that all golfers did this.[5]

Kant's insight, much like the insight of the Golden Rule, is that most of the bad things we do could be avoided by looking at the big picture and seeing the similarity between others and ourselves. It seems that any moral system must have a basic level of not only self-respect, but respect for others as human beings.

---

2. MacIver (1952) calls this the "deep beauty" of the golden rule.

3. Kant called it 'categorical' because it applies to everyone at all times, and 'imperative' because it is an obligation.

4. Kant (1948, 70).

5. Cf. R.M. Hare (1970, 160–161) who objects that the Golden Rule and Kant's Categorical imperative might not deter a Nazi who honestly believed that he should be murdered if he were a Jew.

A second formulation of Kant's Imperative demands that we always treat others as ends in themselves.[6] This formulation prohibits you from using people—at least without their consent. Slavery is out, but caddies are in as long as they carry your clubs willingly and are respected as ends in themselves. That is, we must acknowledge others as being self-conscious, rational, and free—the same consideration that we are obligated to give to ourselves. The ethics of duty are built upon a foundation of respect.

Relationships are also important to the ethics of respect. Moral psychologist Carol Gilligan proposed an "ethic of care" to complement the traditional focus on universal rules.[7] For example, giving your best effort may be an expression of honesty within sport, but in situations where a parent is playing with a child, the particular concerns of that relationship may take precedence over the "universal" duty to play hard.

Kids remember fondly the first time they beat Mom or Dad in the driveway basketball court. There was a warm sense of triumph, of being better than you thought you were. And when we realize later that our opponent let us win that day, there's none of the anger or resentment there would be if the opponent had been a true rival. The special relationship of parent and child, as well as the objectives and expectations of the particular activity, condition our understanding of ethical respect.

In sum, respect for others demands (1) basic consideration for the other person as promoted by the Golden Rule; (2) an appreciation of the particular relationship involved; and (3) an understanding of the purpose of the activity and what is expected within it. The way we treat others reveals not only the kind of athlete we are, but also the kind of person.

For the philosophical athlete, an understanding of the nature of athletic relationships serves as the starting point for ethical behavior towards others in sport. From this understanding we can navigate our way though such issues as trash-talking, violence, running up the score, ball-hogging, and playing hurt for the team.

---

6. Kant (1948, 96): "Act in such a way that you always treat humanity, whether in your own person or in the person of any other, never simply as a means, but always at the same time as an end."

7. According to Gilligan (1982), such relationship-consideration is typical of the way women tend to think about morality. Gilligan isn't proposing that men and women follow different ethical theories, rather she believes that the universal and abstract concepts of western tradition should exist in tension with the particular and contextual concerns of relationships.

The Nature of the Competitive Relationship

The way you view the competitive relationship speaks volumes about your attitude toward sport. Many athletes view the *competitor as obstacle*—a barrier standing between me and what I want (usually, victory).[8] Indeed there's some truth to that view, especially when you're running second in a race or facing the last defender in a drive for the goal. Often competition is a "zero-sum" game that yields only one winner and one loser. It's either you or me, sink or swim, live or die. On this view, victory is understood as defeat of the other, the bet is all or nothing and the chances for hostility high.

The problem with the competitor-as-obstacle view, aside from the negative atmosphere it generates, is that it reveals a short-sighted and inaccurate conception of sport itself. Opponents provide all or part of the challenges faced in sport, but they are no more obstacles to our goals than Everest is an obstacle to the mountaineer. The challenge they provide is part of the sport; in some cases it *makes* the sport possible. Wrestling, for example, is inconceivable without an opponent. You can shoot baskets on your own, but you can't play basketball. You can run, but you can't race.

In every case competitors are only mistakenly conceived as opposites; in fact they are trying to achieve the same thing. The basic test of a sport—moving a ball down the field, sailing a boat around the buoy, roping a charging calf—is undertaken by all participants. What competitors do is increase the challenge by transforming the basic test into a *con*test—a testing together.[9]

On this view we see the *competitor as facilitator,* someone who makes the challenge, and in some cases the sport itself, possible. Especially in cases where the test is fairly simple, say running 100 meters, the contest provides most of the challenge. Running 100 meters is easy but running it faster than my contestants is anything but easy. In sports where the test is difficult enough, say climbing Mount Everest, contests are de-emphasized.

An even deeper understanding of sport may inspire us to view the *competitor as friend.*[10] To achieve this we must take another step back,

---

8. The terms "competitor as obstacle" and "competitor as facilitator" are used in a similar way by Fraleigh (1984, 83–84).

9. For more on tests vs. contests, see Kretchmar (1975).

10. This term and thesis are from Hyland (1978).

beyond the dimensions of competitor as obstacle and facilitator, to bring in the big picture of what we are seeking in sport in the first place. Philosophical athletes, at least, are seeking to understand and improve upon ourselves. We use sport as an arena in which we can recognize our imperfections and seek to attain excellence or virtue.

Now if our general drive as human beings is also toward excellence and perfection, then a friend would be someone who helped us to achieve that. Since excellence requires admission of imperfection and striving to do better, friends are people who point out our imperfections and challenge us to do better. A true friend will tell you if your prom outfit looks ridiculous. In short, a true friend challenges us to do our best, but then that's the mark of a good competitor also. On this view, the best competitors are ideally our friends.

So what does all this say about the competitive relationship? Should you be sending your opponents birthday cards and hanging out with them on weekends? Not necessarily, but it does show that competitors are there to help each other achieve excellence by providing a good challenge. In fact, sport philosopher Robert Simon *defines* competition as "a mutual quest for excellence."[11] The origin of the word *com-petito* means "to question or strive together."

This conception of the ideal competitive relationship creates an obligation to provide the best test possible for your competitor. As sport philosopher R. Scott Kretchmar puts it, to enter into a contest is to make a commitment to improve not only yourself but your competitors.[12] Playing hard isn't mean, it shows respect for the competitive relationship. By the same token, actions or attitudes that detract from the ideal competitive relationship—such as whacking your competitor on the knee so she won't be able to perform—are indefensible.

Using this understanding of competition and the philosophical conception of duty, let's look at some problem cases.

Trash Talking

Hey batta, batta, batta…SWING! Hey batta, batta, batta…YOUR MOMMA WEARS ARMY BOOTS! Trash talking is part of the fabric of

---

11. Simon (1991, 23).
12. See Kretchmar (1975, 39).

many sports, and in many peoples' eyes, a prime example of disrespect for opponents. What can we say about trash talking given our philosophical understanding of duty to others and the ideal conception of the competitive relationship?

First of all, from the perspective of the Golden Rule, competitors shouldn't say anything to their opponents that they wouldn't want said to themselves. Of course, even if this rule makes you keep your mouth closed, it may do nothing to quiet the blabbering of others. Should it? The fact is that trash talking is part of the history and tradition of many sports. That in itself doesn't justify the practice, but it may call for a *prima facie* tolerance of it until some other arguments against it are found. The old "Hey batta-batta" for instance, might be tolerated in softball while a "Hey shoota-shoota" would be totally inappropriate at a rifle contest.

Using the nature of the competitive relationship as our standard, we may conclude that trash-talking is wrong when it somehow interferes with the test. Being able to "psych-out" opponents may be a legitimate part of many athletic contests, as long as it respects more fundamental parameters such as the Golden Rule and respect for human dignity. Consider Larry Bird's penchant for trash-talking his defenders with comments like, "Who's guarding me?" or "Pass it to me, I'll just shoot right over this guy." Because they pertain to the test at hand, they don't seem foreign to the competitive relationship.

Racial slurs or comments about an opponent's mother are another matter, however. They may be *effective* in putting opponents off their game, but what do such distractions have to do with the contest? How do they enhance the test at hand? Bird's comments exacerbate the frustration of dealing with skilled opponents—an integral part of the game. An opponent's ability to ignore racist or personal slurs, however, is not integral to the game.

In general, comments designed to distract an opponent or provoke a brawl do nothing to improve the quality of the test. When trash-talking wanders away from the game it shows disrespect for competitors. Since good competitors are essential to a good game, trash-talkers ultimately threaten to harm their own interests.

Running Up the Score

Blowouts in which winning teams continue to play hard and score points long after victory has been assured are another common example of disrespect for one's opponent.[13] This situation seems to create a conflict between our competitive duty to play hard and the Golden Rule-inspired injunction against doing things that we wouldn't want done to us.

From the point of view of the categorical imperative, no serious competitor would wish for a world where blowouts were the rule rather than the exception. Vanquisher or vanquished, a lopsided test is a bad test and it does little to help either side improve themselves as athletes — or people.

On the other hand, such phenomena as tournament seedings, which purposely pit the lowest against the highest ranked competitor, are seen as a fair means of determining a winner. The objective of this, it should be noted, is to ensure that the strongest competitors arrive at the final. So the unbalanced contests *aim* toward a good competition.

At any rate individual competitors rarely have control over the selection of their opponents. They *do* have control over how they play the game, however. Should you pad your personal statistics by running up the score against much less skilled opponents?

Certainly there are questions about the validity of such numbers. Does a batting average earned, in part, against substandard pitching accurately reflect a ballplayer's skill? Does the college team who schedules a season of "creampuff" opponents deserve its "ten-and-oh" record? Aren't these numbers compiled with the hope that they will be interpreted as representing a higher level of skill than they actually do? No doubt this is part of sports reality. But the question is, should it be?

Serious competitors who reflect on the nature of the competitive relationship could never wish that sports were a blowout wonderland — even if they themselves were always the winner — because it would eliminate the conditions that make victory valuable in the first place. There would be no challenge, no tension, no question, and hence, no chance for improvement. What's satisfying and constructive is earning hard-fought victories: the "good game" we thank our competitors for in that ritual handshake.

Respect among competitors derives from their mutual interest in a quality test. Once the contest is over, there still may be an interesting test worth pursuing. But once the test is over, there can be little rationale for continuing to play hard other than humiliation of the opponent, which is disrespectful to both the opponent and the aims of the contest itself.

---

13. In fact, this has been the source of a continuing debate in the philosophy of sport. See, for example: Dixon (1992); Hardman et. al. (1996); and Feezell, (1999).

For example, a marathon runner may continue to press hard after victory is assured since the *test*, i.e. running 26.2 miles in two hours ten minutes (or whatever time challenges that individual) still remains. But a baseball game where the skill differential generates a hopelessly lop-sided score can hardly be considered a true *test* for either team. Neither team is being challenged, so neither competitor is fulfilling the role of testing and improving the other.

Thinking Activity: Respecting Competitors
Question: What constitutes ethical treatment of competitors?
Observe: Select an incident of competitor-conflict either from your personal athletic experience or from a newspaper or magazine article. Try to identify the motives of the player(s) in question and the effects of the incident.
Analyze: Using the criterion of competitors as friends who challenge each other to improve, evaluate the incident. Did it hinder one or both players from playing at a higher level? Was the effect of the incident to increase or decrease the skill-level required for victory? Did any advantage or disad-vantage that resulted reflect the actual skills being tested or not?
Question Again: Is there any way to defend the interpretation of sports competitors as enemies, rather than friends?

8.2 Teammates

The Nature of Team Relationships

"There's no I in TEAM." This slogan can be used as an encouraging reminder or harsh admonition. One of the great benefits of sport is the real opportunity to work with others as a team—to achieve together, to fail together, and to experience the human tension between individual and community. But what does it mean for athletes to show *respect* to their teammates? What are the boundaries of our moral obligations to these people who, in many cases, can be allies one day and enemies the next?

Teammates often adopt the role of competitor, when vying for a starting position or during a practice scrimmage, not to mention transfers to rival teams. Heck, I even played in a soccer game where we lent a player to the opposing team when one of their midfielders had to pick up her daughter from piano practice. All this shows is that teammates and competitors aren't really so different—often the same individual assumes both roles. But what *is* distinctive about the teammate relationship?

When teammates don a common uniform it represents a shared des-tiny. They are dependent upon one another, in some sense, for their success or failure. In traditional team sports such as rugby or water polo, there is only one win or loss to be shared. In other sports, such as cycling and wrestling, individual victories are combined with team prizes. Still other groups, such as commercial track and field teams or national Olympic teams, share uniforms and camaraderie without even competing in the same events. So what's the point of having a team from the athlete's point of view? It's similar to the competitor relationship, but with a twist: to become a better individual through association with the group.

It has been said so many times that we forget what it means: good teams don't suppress individuals, they make them better. In many cases this truism is built into the structure of the sport. Games such as football and soccer simply can't be played solo, and excellence in them depends specifically on individuals making particular contributions to a combined effort. Even if the best 11 soccer players in the world were all strikers, putting them all on one field wouldn't necessarily make the best soccer team.

Great team players perform their particular functions well and in harmony with their teammates. But beyond that, they have the ability to make others perform better. The crowning glory of any team player is to inspire teammates to improve their game. In cycling, a team-time-trial quartet will easily outpace four competitors racing only for themselves. Good team players work harder for the team than they would in an individual effort.

By the same token, an athlete who *doesn't* or *can't* perform can cause teammates to play worse. Journalist George Plimpton discovered this during a stint playing quarterback with the Detroit Lions. In the movie about his experience, *Paper Lion,* a teammate explains that the linemen just can't give their all to protect an incompetent quarterback who isn't going to help the team.

So your obligation as a team player is to bring out your teammates' best, both through the challenging example of your own excellent play and the support and understanding of a co-destined friend. Players who detract from the team effort by slacking off personally or dragging their teammates down abuse the teammate relationship.

Hogging the Ball

The most common example of disrespect for teammates in particular and the team in general might be loosely termed "hogging the ball." Most of us discover this concept as children, either by being the hog or by being a hog's bored teammate, forced to make a private game of collecting fallen leaves in the cleats of our shoes.

Apply the Golden Rule to the case of ball-hogging and results vary. We'd all like the opportunity to handle the ball for our team, but seeing that my destiny is tied to the team's success, I might rationally want for a skilled teammate to drive to the basket rather than passing it off to me for a chancier shot.

Maybe rather than thinking about what I'd like "done unto me," I could phrase the rule in terms of what I'd like done unto the team. This reflects the shared interests of teammates and coaches alike. Under this modified Golden Rule, I would pass off to others when it is best for the team, and want the ball passed to me when it is best for the team. Inflated egos are notorious for skewing individual judgment in these matters. Since teams share success and failure equally, however, individual agendas can't be justified when they threaten the interests of the team.

The same spirit derives from Kant's categorical imperative. How could an individual athlete wish that every player on the team, not to mention every player in the sport, played for their own glory rather than that of the team? Since you, as a team player, are obligated to make your teammates play better, keeping the ball away from them just denies them the opportunity to improve.

Throwing up your hands and trying to do it all yourself is bound to fail sooner or later. What's worse, the individual skills you develop as a *prima donna* are useless once you reach a higher level where the team element must be exploited for victory. This syndrome is a common problem for star high-school athletes making the transition to college or professional play. In the movie *Hoop Dreams,* college coaches at a high-school basketball camp repeatedly lament the inability of players to understand "team basketball," while the players complain that their teammates won't pass the ball.

The secret of great team players is not individual skill, but the ability to perform better in harmony with and out of obligation to the team. Individuals have to care about giving their all for the team. Once this is achieved, teammates will be inspired to perform better as well.

Individuals who imply by actions, attitude, or words that they must do their teammates' jobs fail not only to exploit the strength of team play, they also fail to bring out the best in their teammates. Back to the Golden Rule. Give others the opportunity to succeed that you would like to have back from them. Individual strengths and weaknesses can combine into a greater team force than any individual. There *are* "I's" in TEAM, they just recognize their roles.

Loyalty and Playing Hurt

One thing that's often considered a virtue among teammates, but in fact can be a damaging vice, is loyalty. In the view of sport-philosopher Johan Huizinga,

> loyalty is the surrender of the self to a person, cause or idea without arguing the reasons for this surrender or doubting the lasting nature of it.[14]

A sense of obligation to one's teammates can bring out the best in an athlete, but it also has the power to bring out the worst. This is especially the case when group sentiment overrides an individual's personal moral judgment.

As we learned earlier, you are always responsible for what you do— even things done as a result of peer pressure or out of a sense of loyalty. Rob Huizenga experienced such ethical dilemmas as a team doctor for the Los Angeles Raiders. Not only would players keep quiet about such shenanigans as "staged injuries" designed to hide talented but inexperienced prospects on the injured reserve list, they routinely risked their own health by playing injured out of loyalty to their teammates. Team doctors only exacerbated the problem by failing to inform players of dangers to their health, even their lives, if they continued to play.[15]

All this was done at the behest of the coaches and justified in terms of the good of the team. Didn't we just get through saying that the virtue of a team player is willingness to act for the good of the team? Didn't Keri Strugg become America's sweetheart when she vaulted on an injured leg at the 1996 Olympics, experiencing unspeakable pain and risking permanent injury, to score points for the U.S. team?

Remember that conflicts of duty should be resolved by considering particular circumstances and relationships. If an ideal teammate relationship is one that challenges and inspires athletes to be their best, how can putting pressure on individuals to compromise their physical health or moral principles do that? Encouraging teammates to play harder is different from pressuring them to play injured.

---

14. Huizinga (1949, 104).
15. Huizenga (1994, 141).

By the same token, doing something you would otherwise consider immoral out of loyalty to a team represents a failure on your part to use the team for self-improvement. In effect, you use the team to make yourself a worse person. Furthermore, the teammate who capitulates to peer-pressure only perpetuates a destructive cycle. Team players should also be ready to say "no" to a team's demands. Loyalty is not an excuse for immorality.

8.3 Coaches

The Nature of the Athlete-Coach Relationship

Coaches, like teammates, share a common athletic destiny with their players. Team success can be especially important to them, since coaching careers are made according to win-loss records. Much has been said about how coaches should treat their athletes, but what about the relationship from the athlete's point of view? What is an athlete's obligation to the coach? When should the athlete obey and when (if ever) not? How can an athlete learn from the coach without sacrificing personal autonomy?

There is a crucial sense in which the athlete-coach relationship is a pupil-teacher relationship. Almost always, an athlete is interested in learning from the coach about the sport in question. Coaches, like teachers, bring to the relationship expertise and experience in a mutually valued subject. More often than teachers, however, the coach is expected to impart lessons and wisdom beyond the domain of sport. Coaches are expected to act as role models, surrogate parents, even priests.

With these increased expectations comes increased power. In a classroom, every student takes the test. In sports, coaches decide who plays and who doesn't. Since athletes, almost by definition, have an intense desire to play and compete, coaches wield an enormous power over them. The coach distributes the goods the athletes want most, and athletes will do almost anything to get their share of the goods.

Ideally a coach's interests are identical to the athlete's: the latter's improvement as an athlete and an individual. Since you enter into a coach-athlete relationship with your personal improvement as the mutual goal, the relationship carries with it a *prima facie* duty on your part to make an honest effort toward that improvement. In deference to the coach's reputed expertise, you should follow the program prescribed for your training and be open and honest about how you respond to it.

These duties can be inferred easily by application of the Golden Rule or Kant's categorical imperative. Imagine that you were the coach, and ask yourself what kind of cooperation you would expect from an athlete that you were trying to improve. If all athletes lied to their coaches about the amount of training they actually did, what would happen to the institution of coaching?

By the same token, the coach-athlete relationship's commitment to an athlete's improvement precludes blind adherence to a program that isn't working. A coach's authority can't erase the athlete's personal responsibility for choices and actions. Just as with team loyalty, selling yourself out to the authority of a misguided coach is still a free choice, and you are morally responsible for it.

Athletes' relationships with their coaches are based, fundamentally, on a shared desire for team success. Part of an athlete's duty to the coach requires individual sacrifice for the good of the team; just how far such sacrifice should go deserves a closer look.

Obedience to Authority, Trust, and Intimacy

Infamous track sprinter Ben Johnson had unwavering faith in his coach and doctor. And why not? By following their directions religiously he improved steadily, eventually breaking the world record for the 100 meters at the 1988 Olympics in Seoul. Of course their program included the use of anabolic-androgenic steroids, which eventually showed up in his urine sample and cost him the medal, record, and several previous awards. His career ended in public disgrace.

Says former USOC medical director Robert Voy,

> The real key to this issue [Ben Johnson's steroid use], in my mind, is the absolute blind trust that Johnson had in his coach and Dr. Jamie Astaphan.[16]

Voy points out that we may never know whether the sprinter was aware of the risks of his drug abuse, but we do know that he was willing to follow his coach's directions. At a later hearing, Johnson played the role of a victim corrupted by evil coaches, saying he didn't think to

---

16. Voy (1991, 122).

question their methods since he was doing so well. His rationale may be understandable, but it is clearly indefensible.

In his groundbreaking experiments on obedience to authority, psychologist Stanley Milgram showed the shocking lengths people will go to please an authority figure. Milgram found that ordinary people would torture and even kill complete strangers when asked to by a scientist in a white coat.[17]

Given this fact about human nature, it's clear that coaches' authority comes with a huge amount of moral responsibility. Athletes trust their coaches to be guardians of their welfare as well as helpers toward excellence. Unfortunately, however, coaches have professional interests beyond the welfare of their athletes—specifically, in the win/loss records that dictate their professional reputations and even the terms of their employment.

None of this is secret. Athletes and coaches both know, when entering into a relationship, that there's the potential for exploitation and violation of trust. Both parties are aware of the power of authority. To the extent that either coach or athlete manipulates the relationship to achieve something other than the improvement of the athlete as competitor and human being, that person abuses the relationship. And that person is responsible for those actions.

Ben Johnson was able to ease his conscience about taking dangerous and illegal drugs by "trusting" his coach and doctor. But he is responsible for freely entering and remaining in that relationship as it dragged him down morally. Was it really so unjust that the athlete ended up taking most of the blame for his actions?

Trust is only a virtue when given on a foundation of reason. When I enter a car you're driving, I must trust you to drive safely. If I discover that you're driving drunk, it's up to me to speak up or get out if necessary. If I keep riding and we end up crashed, my injuries are largely my own responsibility.

None of this is to blame athletes for the abuses of their coaches. Child-athletes in particular need to be protected from unscrupulous coaches, especially since the coaching ranks sadly include a disproportionate number of child-molesters. But even among adults, the power imbalance in coach-athlete relationships makes romantic intimacy a risky and problematic proposition. For every example of an apparently

17. Milgram (1974).

successful relationship, such as that of Jackie Joyner and John Kersee, there are many more stories of abuse and failure.

In dealing with athlete-coach relationships, competitors should be aware that they're entering an ethical minefield that's most safely traversed by staying true to the central objective of personal growth and improvement.

The Coach as Role Model

It's funny how many athletes view their coaches as role models while disdaining that responsibility for themselves. The fact of the matter is, role models are chosen by those who look up to them. You can't choose *not* to be a role model, only to act admirably after you've been chosen. To the extent that coaches serve as role models, their athletes choose them. Nevertheless, the athlete's choice is a free choice, so decide whether and to what extent your coach *should* be a role model for you.

Since the athlete-coach relationship is based on personal improvement, an athlete should choose a role model who is the kind of person the athlete would like to be. Notice that I didn't say someone who has achieved what the athlete wants to achieve; that's only part of the equation. As we saw in the last chapter, excellence is about being a certain kind of person, not about earning a certain kind of award.

Of course, it's almost impossible to know anyone well enough to know what kind of person he or she is, especially when you're talking about famous people known only through highlight reels and magazine interviews. By the time you get to know a person well enough anyway, some chinks in the armor are bound to show up. Apply the Golden Rule here. Would you want to be emulated in every detail of your life? Since role models are ideals, real people won't do—unless you isolate the particular qualities you admire.

Coaches are most often admired and respected for their particular exploits. Laker coach Phil Jackson earned the respect of player Shaquille O'Neal largely because of the championships he earned coaching the Chicago Bulls. But O'Neal doesn't need to buy into Jackson's Zen philosophy in order to benefit from their athlete-coach relationship. He can isolate one aspect of Jackson's expertise, perhaps the triangle offense, and learn from that without trying to be a different type of person.

Again, the objective of the athlete-coach relationship is the athlete's personal improvement. Different coaches offer different things and it is the athlete's responsibility to benefit from each coach. I once had a coach who described it this way: Everyone has their own bag of tricks. You take a lesson from me and put a few of my tricks into your bag. You take a lesson from someone else and learn a few of their tricks. Eventually you have your own bag of tricks that's unique to you, you share these with others and the exchange continues.

Athletes are in charge of becoming the people they want to be. Coaches and other role models should be selected based on what they can contribute to the athlete's project for excellence.

Thinking Activity: The Ultimate Team Player

Question: What criteria should be used to select players in team sports such as football or basketball?

Observe: Think of a team selection process such as the NFL draft. Make a list of criteria coaches use to select players for their team. You might include physical qualities such as height and weight, intellectual qualities as represented by test scores, specific abilities such as speed, vertical leap, or skill at a particular position, and less-tangible qualities such as leadership and the ability to handle pressure.

Analyze: Looking at your list of criteria, try to rank them in order of importance. Is there any one quality that all players should have or does it depend on the composition of the rest of the team? If a player scored high in all categories except his or her ability to work well with others, would you still select the player? Is there any quality more important than ability to work with a team?

Question Again: How can an athlete develop the ability to make his or her teammates play at a higher level?

Chapter Review

Summary: The Courage to Be Yourself

Our examination of showing respect for others and the philosophical issue of moral duty has returned repeatedly to the foundational issues of personal excellence, freedom, and responsibility. Our projects as athletes and human beings needn't be sacrificed to accommodate the interests of others. We can respect competitors, teammates, and coaches by understanding the nature of our relationships with them. You control how you treat others and whether you will obey their commands. Ultimately it is up to the athlete to preserve personal integrity in dealing with others. Self-respect should be enhanced by the respect we show for others.

Further Reading

Philosophy

Gilligan, Carol. 1982. *In a Different Voice: Psychological Theory and Women's Development.* Cambridge: Harvard University Press. In working to understand the distinctive features of women's approaches to ethics, Gilligan discovered a major flaw in traditional theories such as the Golden Rule or Kant's categorical imperative: they don't take into account the particulars of human relationships. Gilligan argues that the particular must be combined with the abstract in attempting to develop a realistic moral theory.

Kant, Immanuel. 1948. *Groundwork for the Metaphysic of Morals.* Translated by H. J. Paton. New York: Harper and Row. One of the great classics of western philosophy, this little book succinctly explains the categorical imperative and its rationale.

Philosophy of Sport

Fraleigh, Warren P. 1984. "Relationships of Opponents." In *Right Actions in Sport: Ethics for Contestants.* Champaign, IL: Human Kinetics, 83–92. This clear and convincing essay shows the wisdom in seeing competitors as facilitators of athletic excellence rather than obstacles to personal success.

Hyland, Drew A. 1978. "Competition and Friendship." *Journal of the Philosophy of Sport* V: 27–27. Hyland draws on his knowledge of Plato to build on Fraleigh's insight and argue that our competitors are ideally our friends. This is a classic of sport philosophy.

Simon, Robert L. 1991. "Violence in Sports." In *Fair Play: Sports, Values, and Soceity.* Boulder CO: Westview Press, 51–70. This is a clear-headed and comprehensive account of the many forms of violence surrounding sport. Simon uses his definition of sport as a mutual quest for excellence to judge apparently violent actions in sport. He also considers the effect of violent sport on the larger society.

Journalism and Literature

Harrison, William. 1973. "Roller Ball Murder." Originally appeared in *Esquire.* Reprinted in Vanderwerken and Wertz, ed., 31–42. A fascinating and prophetic short story that paints an apocalyptic future of sport. Harrison tells the story of Jonathan E, a fading star in an increasingly violent sport owned by huge corporations and dictated by entertainment interests.

Huizenga, M.D., Rob. 1994. *You're Okay, It's Just a Bruise: A Doctor's Sideline Secrets about Pro Football's Most Outrageous Team.* New York: St.

Martin's. This book, detailing the author's stint as a pro football team doctor, reveals the extent to which athletes and coaches will go for the sake of the team.

Chapter 9

Showing Respect for Your Sport

Chapter Preview

Introduction
Can High-Tech Equipment Harm a Sport?

> *Respect for the game requires a respect for and adherence to the established customs of the game; but that doesn't excuse us from the responsibility for the formation of new customs. In fact, in some situations the expression 'It's part of the game' can become an excuse for behavior that is totally contrary to the very concept of a game.*
> — Clifford and Feezell, *Coaching for Character*

Sometimes ethical decision-making involves more than respect for yourself and respect for others. Sometimes it requires respect for your culture or community. In athletics, that means respecting your sport. As athletes we are often told to do things "for the love of the game," or "out of respect for the sport." But what does it mean to respect a sport?

Imagine the following scenario: you are a softball player and the night before your big game you receive a new, super-secret high-tech bat that promises to increase the velocity and distance of your hits by 10–20%! The bat looks and feels ordinary, but it's made of a special new alloy developed for the space program. The inventor hopes to eventually sell the bats for $10,000 each. Should you use the bat? Would it be fair to the sport?

The first thing to notice is that this *is* a matter of choice and a real ethical issue. Too many of us view technology like we view the weather: as an uncontrollable, inevitable force to which we have no option but to adapt. We don't try to stop the rain or question the necessity of its existence; we buy a better umbrella or raincoat. Likewise, the typical softball player doesn't try to stop the coming of high-tech bats, she buys one and uses it because she believes that she must to keep up with the inevitable tide of advancing sports technology.

The philosophical athlete, however, *will* ask the question, "Should I use this bat?" She will also recognize that it's different from asking why God made rain because unlike the rain, she has a choice about the bat. She will ask, "How will this bat affect my sport?" Notice that I said "the sport" and not "my performance." While improvements in individual performance are certainly important to athletes (and the driving force behind sports equipment technology), advantages gained through high-tech equipment can be worthless or even destructive to sport in the long run.

If the bat, and not the player, were responsible for a winning advantage, could she still take pride in victory? Her advantage would be erased once everyone had the technology, and is ethically questionable as long as it is available to only a few. The crucial quality of a top softball player might become the ability to obtain equipment and keep it out of the hands of others, rather than the traditional virtues of skill, courage, discipline, etc. This is why the athlete must look beyond individual performance to what's good for the sport in making these sorts of ethical decisions.

The first question our player should ask is whether this bat is allowed by the rules of her sport. We like to say that rules were made to be broken and indeed it's hard to imagine sports without deception, fouls, and incessant attempts to get away with something. Still, sports are made up of rules, so there's a sense in which breaking a rule means you're not playing the game. How can we discern when rule-breaking is part of the game and when it actually threatens the game? Would using this bat be akin to riding a motorcycle in a bicycle race? Would breaking the rules about proper bats mean that in some sense our athlete is failing to play the game? Respecting the game, first of all, means respecting its constitutive rules.

Say the bat is so new that no official rule exists banning it from the sport. What about the *unwritten rules* of sport? This second question reaches beyond official decrees to the little things that are often left unsaid, but nevertheless expected of all a sport's participants. Sports, in some sense, are little societies with certain customs and norms—like cultures. Might using this bat affect the culture of softball? Could it harm the playful atmosphere by threatening the safety of infield players? Would the bat's expense limit the class of participants to the wealthy? Respecting the game means, partly, considering the collective good of all who play it.

Ultimately, our player might ask her question from the perspective of sports viewed as "social practices"—entities with their own intrinsic values and objectives. By thinking about what makes her sport *worthwhile*, our athlete could produce a list of goods integral to the practice. In softball, the balance between offense and defense is critical. If the bat turned every hit into a homer, we might never get past the top of the first inning. Everything our player knows and loves about her game could be eroded and eventually destroyed by this change. Respecting a sport, finally, means preserving the goods that make it worthwhile.

So our ballplayer stands there eyeing her super-secret bat—and if she's a philosophical athlete she asks questions that reach beyond personal concerns. Introducing this bat may ruin her sport—or may make it better. The introduction of fiberglass poles to pole-vaulting helped to open that sport to such stars as Sergei Bubka, and an entirely new class of athletes: women. Our softball player's questions show her ethical responsibility: her respect for self, for others, and for the sport itself.

Chapter Preview List

- Does respecting the game mean always following the rules?
- Do sports have individual "cultures" that transcend written rules?
- What makes sport worthwhile and how do we preserve it?

9.1 The Rules

Sports Are Sets of Rules

What would sports be without rules? The soccer player eyes the goalie as he sets himself for the penalty kick. The official blows his whistle and the player slowly approaches the ball. Then, suddenly, he reaches down, picks up the ball, tucks it between both hands, and runs into the goal, bunting the goalie out of the way with a shoulder-block.

What game is he playing?! The objective of getting the ball into the goal has been met, but a host of other rules have been broken—rules that somehow define the game, that make it possible in the first place. Despite all our emphasis on competition, sports are in the first place cooperative human activities made possible by everyone's willingness to abide by certain public rules. We follow these rules, which restrict our personal freedom, for the greater good of all—much like society itself.

Given the importance of rules to sport and our rational self-interest in respecting them, it makes sense to view respect for sport as respect for the rules. Bernard Suits, whom we met in chapter 4, points out that sports, like all games, are essentially sets of rules. Without the rules, there would be no game.[1]

This view of sport, known as *formalism*, is based on a fundamental observation about the nature of sport itself. Each sport features a set of *constitutive rules* that specify the physical and temporal boundaries of competition, the objective to be attained, the acceptable means for achieving that objective, the equipment to be used, and criteria for evaluation (i.e. scoring and/or determining the winner).[2] For example, the rules of soccer include:

- The *dimension* of the field, height and width of the goal, time to be played, etc.
- The *objective* of putting the ball into the opposing team's goal.
- The *acceptable means* of using your feet, head, and so on but not your hands.

---

1. Suits (1973, 8).
2. List adapted from Fraleigh (1984, 68).

- The type of *equipment allowed*, including the size and weight of the ball.
- The *criteria for evaluation* as in one point per goal, the team scoring the most goals wins.

Games also have *regulations* that prescribe penalties for particular actions such as handling the ball or tripping another player.[3] Unlike constitutive rules, regulations can be changed or ignored and we would still have a game. Imagine a game of soccer with no rules about how goals are scored or what part of body may be used to handle the ball—could it be called "soccer" at all?

For constitutive rules to effectively define a sport or game, they should have the following qualities:[4]

- give meaning to actions within the game.
- be publicly known and understood.
- apply to all participants equally.

When you think about it, the acts of breaking a goal-line plane, putting a ball into a basket, or hitting a ball over a fence can have no meaning at all outside the rules of the relevant sport. Athletes can devote their entire lives to achieving something with absolutely no practical value or intrinsic meaning.

In fact, it is characteristic of sport to specify means or objectives that are purposely inefficient and meaningless in a practical sense.[5] A paramount example is the rodeo event of bull riding. Most rodeo events test skills that are useful in ranching, such as saddle-breaking a horse. But there's no practical reason to ride a bull—except that bulls provide a challenge to the athletes' skills that just can't be had with horses. So bull riding makes sense as a rule-defined sport, but is meaningless—even stupid—from any other point of view.

The second criterion, that rules be publicly known and understood, makes sense as well. If there were secret rules not known to all participants, legitimate games such as rugby would degenerate into something more like "calvinball"—the "game" played by the cartoon characters

---

3. Fraleigh (1984, 68–79) considers regulations to be among the constitutive rules. To clarify the "logical incompatibility thesis," however, I keep them separate.

4. Adapted from Rawls (1955, 294–295).

5. A point made repeatedly by Suits, see especially (1978, 22–41).

Calvin and Hobbes. Calvinball looks something like one-on-one foot-ball except that the rules are made up and changed as they go along.

As a result of calvinball's lack of fixed rules, Calvin and Hobbes spend most of their time arguing about who scored, what's out of bounds, and when the game will end. A predictable problem in calvin-ball is Calvin's frequent attempts to change the rules for his own advan-tage. This violates the third principle of rules: that they apply equally to all participants. Whereas the flowerbed was out of bounds for Hobbes last week, it's suddenly the end zone for Calvin today. The chaos of "calvinball" illustrates the need to have public rules that apply equally to all.

Philosophical Background:
The Greater Good

In connecting the notions of ethics and happiness, most of us think not only of personal virtue and particular relationships, but also of our duty to a more generalized idea often described as "the greater good." It seems as though ethical persons should be concerned with goods be-yond their immediate personal interests, but is such concern defensible? Even rational?

According to many conceptions of human nature, the answer is no. Humans are naturally self-interested and *altruism* (doing things com-pletely for the benefit of others) is impossible. Ethical theorists who want to work against the self-interested pursuit of pleasure and happi-ness have to deal with the apparent fact of *psychological egoism*—the belief that human beings are motivated to act only out of self-interest.

As it turns out, however, our desire for "the greater good" can be understood in terms of rational self-interest. In his famous work *Leviathan,* the 18th century British philosopher Thomas Hobbes ob-serves that human beings, like all living organisms, are interested in per-sonal survival. Our natural state is that of warring enemies in a world dominated by "scarcity and fear." But since we recognize that life in that state would be "solitary, poor, nasty, brutish, and short," we ra-tionally go against our natural inclinations and agree to live in peace, sharing our resources rather than fighting over them.[6]

The way we drive our cars is a good example of sacrificing personal freedom for the greater good. Rather than just charge ahead wherever

---

6. Hobbes ([1651] 1958, 107).

and however we want, we put money into a pot for road construction and maintenance, agree to limit our speed, and to drive on a particular side of the road. We consciously limit our own freedom as drivers to reap the benefits of safe streets and highways. Respecting the rules of the road, like respecting the rules of the sport, makes a worthwhile activity possible for everyone.

Can Cheaters Play the Game?

Fortunately for us, the rules of most sports contests successfully provide meaningful activities in which we can engage. To play a sport is to accept and abide by a specific set of rules. It involves the kind of agreement Hobbes (the philosopher, not the cartoon tiger) envisioned: we willingly accept restrictions on our freedom for the greater good of cooperatively playing a game.

The rules of sport are freely and openly accepted by participants, who can always opt not to play. In a sense, sports' rules are self-imposed by athletes—unlike the laws of the state. The formalist view that sports are sets of rules, combined with the resulting observation that participants agree to those rules just by playing a sport, leads to a very strict view about cheating: *if you break a rule, you aren't playing the game.*

This view, known as the *logical incompatibility thesis,* derives directly from the logic of the formalist view: if games are sets of rules, and cheating is breaking a rule, you can't cheat and play the game at the same time. The actual way that cheating is handled in sport seems to bear the thesis out. What happens in a basketball game when a foul is committed? The whistle blows and the clock stops, symbolically stopping the game itself. The violation has tilted the symbolic level playing field of sport, so penalty shots (free-throws) are assessed to regain the level playing field. Once the adjustment is made, the whistle blows again, the clock starts, and the game resumes.

The fact that penalties for broken rules are usually assessed outside the symbolic parameters of the game itself is testament to the view that cheating is antithetical to sport. So is the fact that habitual rule-breakers are ejected (banished) from the game. Cheating and cheaters are cancer to sport; they're not a natural part of it and must be controlled and removed to maintain the sport's health.

Of course the upshot of all this is that if you don't *play* the game, then you can't *win* the game. Since rules define how the contest is won, you can't be a winner unless you've played by the rules. Technically, a rule-violation such as traveling in basketball turns the game into something else. Rule-violators fail to play basketball as specified by the rules, so there's no way they can win.

But what if a rule violation is unintentional? Sport-philosopher Robert Simon recounts a 1990 football game in which the University of Colorado scored the winning touchdown on a "fifth" down awarded inadvertently due to a mix-up among the officials.[7] It's not hard to see that in a technical sense, Colorado didn't win the game because football rules limit you to four downs. However, the fact that Colorado didn't intentionally seek to gain a fifth down seems to absolve them from being morally reproached as cheaters. Perhaps they should have forfeited the victory after learning of the mistake, as Simon suggests, but they never deliberately ceased to obey the rules of football.

Sports rules are frequently violated out of ignorance or accident. If I tuck a basketball under my arm and start running down the court with it, it's safe to say that I'm not playing the game—even if I do this out of ignorance. On the other hand, an accidental fourth step violates the same traveling rule, but would we want to say that I've ceased to play basketball and no longer deserve to win?

Most formalists agree that intention matters. Sport philosopher Kathleen Pearson sees cheating in terms of the intentional deceit or dishonesty about what you are in fact doing. She says a cheater is someone who "has contracted to participate in one sort of activity, and then deliberately engages in another sort of activity."[8]

Of course, there may be some scenarios in which rules are intentionally broken for laudable reasons, as when a soccer player kicks the ball out of play to stop the game for the benefit of an injured competitor. Most often, however, rules are violated in an effort to gain personal advantage. Simon defines cheating in terms of intentional violations of public rules in order to gain advantage.[9] But even this can seem too narrow. Isn't the overarching goal of competitive sport to gain advantages over your opponent?

---

7. Simon (1991, 37).
8. Pearson (1973, 184).
9. Simon. (1991, 40).

The Good Foul

It seems plausible that playing a game honestly might include the intentional breaking of certain rules as part of the strategic pursuit of a game's objective. This is certainly the way real sports are played today. Not to confuse "is" with "ought," it nevertheless seems incumbent on the formalists to explain how certain intentional rule violations, such as offensive holding in football or fouling to stop the clock in basketball, are anything less than part of the game.

Pearson objects that rules violations are unethical because they interfere with the test of skills for which the sport itself is designed.[10] But the ability to find loopholes in the standing rules and use them to your advantage is arguably among the skills to be tested. Is there such a thing as a "good foul"?

Most so-called strategic violations of the rules are performed openly with a full intention to accept the penalty.[11] In these cases, a cost-benefit analysis of the rules determines that the advantage gained by breaking the rule outweighs the disadvantage of paying the penalty. The most common variety of this type of violation are fouls to stop the clock in close games with little time remaining. Such fouls are commonly accepted as part of the game in basketball and football, particularly since issues of skill enter into the decision. In basketball, you try to foul the worst free-throw shooter while the opposing team (expecting that you will foul) tries to keep the ball in the hands of its best free-throw shooters.

Sport philosopher Warren Fraleigh objects that such strategic rule violations cannot be considered part of the game and directly addresses the basketball case.[12] Although he thinks it acceptable to pursue the opponent aggressively in this situation, intentionally fouling violates not just the letter of the rules, but the spirit behind them. Since the rule against fouling wasn't intended to provide a way for opposing teams to stop the clock and gain a practical advantage, it shouldn't be used as such. Fraleigh notes that the clock-stopping foul in basketball is partly a flaw in the game's rules:

---

10. Pearson (1973, 183).
11. This description is similar to that of civil disobedience given by Martin Luther King, Jr. (1992, 90).
12. Fraleigh (1984, 79 f.).

If the rules make it possible and practical to violate them intentionally, then they reduce the possibility of keeping the contest one of positively prescribed skills and tactics.[13]

Rule-makers must do their best to eliminate such loopholes. In soccer, for example, an illegal hand-ball in the goal-mouth used to be punished by a penalty-kick. When defenders weighed the probability of a successful penalty-kick against the near certainty of a goal if they didn't use their hands, the only rational response seemed to be to grab the ball. But handling the ball (unless you're a goalie) goes against the most fundamental idea of what soccer is. So the penalty was changed to include a red-card (ejection from the game), and the problem was solved.

Even while advantages can be gained by manipulating rules, it's easy to see how intentional violations are a form of disrespect for the game.

Thinking Activity: What is Cheating?
Question: Can cheaters win a game? Have you ever lost to a cheater? Have you won because you or a member of your team cheated? Did knowledge of the cheating change your attitude toward victory?
Observe: Describe a contest in which rules were broken, but you thought the victory (or defeat) was deserved. Describe a contest where rules were broken in a way that made victory (or defeat) undeserved. Describe a contest where no rules were broken but victory (or defeat) was undeserved.
Analyze: Examine the differences among these scenarios and ask yourself what sorts of rules have to be followed in order to merit victory. How are they different from the rules that can be broken without affecting victory?
Question Again: Can you think of a rule change that would help the game to select a deserving winner more often?

9.2 The Culture

Sports Are Cultures

What about the "unwritten rules" of sport? The concept of unwritten rules and unspoken agreements among players suggests a theory of respect for sport as respect for a particular culture. This view understands sports not as sets of rules, but rather as groups of people with common values who share a history and tradition — like a family.

---

13. Fraleigh (1984, 80).

Some sports, such as Greco-Roman wrestling, have traditions that stretch back to ancient times. But even recently invented sports have their own discernable histories and traditions. Mountain biking, for example, grew out of an unofficial (and illegal) race down a Northern California trail. Early mountain bike races were lengthy, backwoods affairs in which riders were responsible for their own nutrition, navigation, and mechanical know-how. Today mountain biking is a "mainstream" Olympic sport, but it hasn't lost its rebel image and still requires riders to repair their own bikes—including flat tires—during the race.

Becoming part of any sport involves more than learning its rules, it involves initiation into a culture with its own history, lore, and *ethos*. Generally, an 'ethos' is the moral nature or guiding beliefs of a particular group. Critics of the formalist position say that individual sports have an ethos, too, which explains how rules are applied in concrete situations.[14] According to those who view sport as a culture, the formalist claim that cheaters can't play the game is out of touch with sport as it's practiced—not to mention lacking common sense.

Within the cultures and ethos of various sports, certain fouls are accepted while others are not. Sport-philosopher Craig Lehman points out that spitballs and corked bats are part of the lore of baseball. If it were true that throwing a spitball keeps the game from being baseball, we'd have to say that nearly every game pitcher Gaylord Perry played in was not a game of baseball.[15] What was it then? Admittedly if Perry repeatedly tossed the ball in the air and refused to throw to his catcher, we could say that he wasn't playing baseball. But some kinds of cheating are simply part of a sport's distinctive culture and generally accepted by its practitioners as such. Respect for the game is respect for the shared culture of the group—what makes everyone happiest.

Philosophical Background:
Utilitarianism

Ethical systems based on maximizing happiness for everyone affected are called *utilitarian*. In his *Principles of Morals and Legislation*, British philosopher Jeremy Bentham defined the rightness or wrongness of actions in terms of utility, and so became regarded as the father of

14. See D'Agostino (1981).
15. Lehman (1988, 285).

utilitarianism. Bentham understood utility generally as usefulness, and specifically as the ability to produce happiness in the community. What makes the community happy? Whatever is in its best interest. What is a community's interest? It's just the sum total of all the various interests of its members.

As appealing as utilitarianism is in theory, it presents problems in practice. Actions are judged in terms of real consequences for everyone affected. That means that as a utilitarian, I have to figure out not only whom my action will affect, but how it will affect each person in terms of their individual interests. It is notoriously hard to keep track of the chains of events set off by each of our actions; time machine movies like *Back to the Future* or *It's a Wonderful Life* provide ample illustration of this. But even if I could understand the scope of my actions, calculating their effects in terms of each individual's interests seems impossible.

To be fair, problems of accuracy exist in every ethical theory and subsequent refinements have addressed many of the key objections to utilitarianism. There still seems to be a problem, however, with the notion of sacrificing an individual for the benefit of the group. A utilitarian should jump on the hand-grenade if it's the only way to save three bystanders. Perhaps healthy individuals may be sacrificed for their organs if it would save several lives.

Nevertheless, the general idea of subordinating individual interests for the greater good seems plausible—even if our personal conceptions of community benefit are mistaken. Bentham himself had his body preserved so that he could be present forever at meetings of the board of trustees of University College in London. We can be sure he did it for the greater good—even if we can't be sure just what that good could be...

Respecting the Unwritten Rules

In fact, one may argue from a utilitarian point of view that maximizing the happiness within a sporting culture means abiding by its unwritten rules and unspoken agreements. Being a sanctimonious stickler for the rules may show respect for a kind of sporting law, but it is disrespectful to the people who make up the living culture of the game. There may even be cases where competitors agree to tolerate a limited amount of rule-breaking in order to *improve* the contest and make a better sport for everyone.

According to my husband Larry, who competed professionally, this is the case in some classes of motorcycle racing. Since "privateer" racers could not obtain the cutting-edge technology that factory-sponsored bikes had, there was an unwritten agreement that they would cheat on their engine parameters just enough to be competitive.

According to the rules of the sport, if riders suspect that a certain bike is illegal, they can have it broken down and inspected by officials. Since everyone was cheating to a certain degree, this option was only exercised when one bike seemed to dominate the others—apparently cheating "too much" and thereby making the race less competitive. This was all part of the culture of the sport, an accepted level of cheating agreed upon to make races more competitive and thus better for everyone.

If sports are viewed as cultures, and the happiness and well-being of a culture depends, to use Bentham's words, on the sum-total interests of all its members, it seems plausible that decisions about right and wrong in those sports should be left up to the agreement of participants.

In fact, participants often modify the rules according to their interests at a particular time—especially in "friendly" games such as playground basketball or Wednesday afternoon racquetball. Sometimes the workout or the sheer pleasure of playing outweighs concerns about accuracy of the tests. For example, in a friendly game of tennis, competitors play borderline balls since the shared interest in keeping the game going outweighs interest in an accurate score. In a famous article, James Keating actually distinguished "sport" from "competitive athletics" as an activity aimed at pleasure rather than victory.[16]

It's worth noting that the cultural "gentlemen's agreements" that shape the ethos of sport may also *prescribe* certain actions in the interest of sport that go beyond the written rules. In road cycling, for example, there are feed zones in which team officials hand out bags of food and water to the racers. The zones can be chaotic as riders try to find their trainers and feed-bags get dropped or caught in wheels, causing crashes and confusion in the race. For safety reasons, there is an unwritten rule that prohibits attacking in the feed zone. There is also an unwritten rule that prohibits attacking when a rival must stop for a crash, mechanical failure, or "nature call."

Now all these unwritten rules make sense in terms of race objectives—to test the rider's strength and endurance on the bike. Such un-

---

16. Keating (1964, 146).

written rules are especially respected among professional racers who share the need to keep safe so they can race (and earn) another day. When such rules are broken at the junior level, the penalty is usually a lecture from the coach, plus taunts from fellow racers, all threatening rejection from the community.

Problems with Social Context

Although the cultural aspect of sport cannot be denied, neither can it be depended upon to reliably promote behavior friendly to the sport, its participants, or even the general demands of morality. For one thing, our positive examples of unspoken agreements among competitors assume a kind of homogeneity that isn't always present in modern sport. Without explicit agreement about shared objectives, competitors always run the risk of disagreement and alienation.

Say, for example, that you and I go on a run together. You have the objective of beating me around the course, but I have the objective of a light workout and friendly conversation. Neither of us will be satisfied as long as we disagree about objectives, you'll be frustrated that I'm not helping to test your skills and I'll be frustrated that you won't slow down and talk.

Entering an official contest with written rules only improves the situation to a certain degree. The Harlem Globetrotters' objective in a given game is entertaining spectators. Imagine what would happen if the Washington Generals (or whatever the Globetrotters' opponent *du jour*) were to decide they wanted to win the game and expected the referees to start calling fouls.

You don't think this applies to real-life sports? You think part of sports' beauty is that sometimes a challenger can give the champion a real challenge right when it's least expected—as when fictional Rocky Balboa defeated a flabbergasted Apollo Creed, who complained, "He doesn't realize it's a show, he thinks this is a *fight!*" The point is that formal rules and explicit contest objectives make such upsets possible. If the rules and objectives were subservient to ethos of a particular sporting culture, they could change like back-to-school fashions.

Consider how the emphasis on profit already threatens the integrity of certain pro sports. Many basketball purists have chafed at what they saw as an unwritten agreement among the coaches, players, and referees of the NBA to ignore certain formal rules of basketball such as traveling or palming the ball. The NBA tolerated such play, not in the interests of the game itself, but in the interests of producing a more marketable product for spectators. In a similar vein, some argue that fighting has been allowed and even condoned in the National Hockey League for its entertainment value. This is particularly true in warm weather expansion markets such as Arizona and Texas where spectators have not been brought up with the game and so are unable to appreciate its intricacies.[17]

One way to interpret these phenomena is to say that the culture of the sport is changing—just like the hemlines of basketball players' shorts—and eventually the rules will follow suit. But as sport adapts to the interests of entertainment, is there any cause to argue that the sport itself has been damaged? Will the ESPN-invented and controlled Winter X-games replace traditional winter sports? Will NBC's huge financial stake in the Olympics eventually influence how the games are staged and which sports are included?

In many ways the whole idea of morality in sport and society itself can be called into question.[18] No doubt sports are, in many ways, cultures. But unless we retain some deeper sense of their unique nature, the whole idea of respecting sport collapses into relativism.

Thinking Activity: Sport and Culture
Question: What should be included in a sport's culture?
Observe: Think for a minute about some aspects of your sport's culture distinguishing which traditions derive from a social culture and which derive from the sport itself. For example, the sumo wrestling ritual of casting salt into the ring derives from cultural and religious beliefs. The cycling ritual of shaving legs derives from practical sporting concerns of massage and healing abrasions.
Analyze: Do any of the social traditions harm the sport? Do amateur requirements discourage athletes from a lower socioeconomic class, thus lowering the level of competition? Do any of the sports traditions run counter to certain cultures? For instance, do dress traditions discourage participation by groups such as Muslim women who may have religious dress restrictions?
Question Again: Is there something your sport could change to make it truer to its objective goals?

---

17. See, for example, Lasch (1979, 192).
18. An observation astutely argued by Eassom (1998, 57–78).

9.3 The Internal Goods

Sports as Social Practices

If the formalist idea of sport is too tight and the cultural idea of sport is too loose, perhaps there is a middle ground that keeps the best of both worlds while avoiding some of the problems. Some have suggested that the solution is to view sports as *social practices* of the kind described by contemporary philosopher Alasdair MacIntyre: cooperative human projects interested in specific internal goods.[19]

Social practices are conceived of as cultural entities whose histories and traditions have, among other things, the important function of establishing standards of excellence. But unlike Bentham's idea of a community, social practices have their own particular objectives, which are independent from the personal interests of the group's members. In this way, sports as social practices can accommodate the formalists' concern with the purpose of the contest[20] and the spirit of the rules,[21] without discounting the force and presence of a sport's particular culture. At the same time social practices avoid the charge of relativism, since they have interests of their own that cut across social context and are distinct from the individual interests of practitioners.

Respect for sport viewed as a social practice, then, would be respect for and preservation of the special interests of that sport.[22] Simply put, the interest of a social practice is to preserve its internal goods. Since the constitutive rules of a sport aim to produce those internal goods, athletes who respect their sport will honor and obey its rules.

However, the rules and regulations of a sport are *themselves* merely means toward the attainment and preservation of a sport's intrinsic goods. Therefore, practitioners may choose to break selected rules when it's in the interest of the sport's internal goods, such as the case with our motorcycle racers agreeing to break some rules in the interest of a more competitive race.

Furthermore the social practice theory can account for those unwritten rules of sport—such as cyclists not attacking in a feed zone—

---

19. Specifically, Morgan (1987) and Butcher and Schneider (1998).
20. Pearson (1973, 184).
21. Fraleigh (1984, 70–71).
22. A similar definition is given by Butcher and Schneider (1998, 9).

and evaluate them using a coherent set of criteria: the interests of the sport itself. What's distinctive about viewing sport as a social practice is that its internal goods provide a standard for moral criticism independent of constitutive rules, social context, and individual interests.

Philosophical Background: Social Practices

In his 1981 book, *After Virtue,* Alasdair MacIntyre put a novel spin on the ideas of community and the greater good. He introduced the concept of *social practices* as the areas in which human virtues are exhibited and cultivated. MacIntyre describes a social practice as

> any coherent and complex form of socially established cooperative human activity through which goods internal to that form of activity are realised in the course of trying to achieve those standards of excellence which are appropriate to, and partially definitive of, that form of activity, with the result that human powers to achieve excellence and human conceptions of the ends and goods involved, are systematically extended.[23]

Some examples may help with this. Endeavors such as farming, music, and architecture would be considered practices while specific skills such as killing weeds, beating on a drum, or doodling are not. Sports such as speedskating and field hockey most definitely *are* social practices.

In connection to the issue of the greater good, practices might be viewed as sub-communities that carry with them specific standards of excellence as well as collectively valued *internal goods*. So, for example, the practice of cross-country skiing demands particular skills such as balance, rhythm, and aerobic endurance while valuing a set of internal goods derived from silently gliding through winter wonderlands.

Individual practitioners must submit to a practice's standards for excellence and they must manifest to some degree its required virtues in order to secure the internal goods of the practice. If I have a team of huskies pull me along on my cross-country skis, I fail not only to manifest the virtues appropriate to the practice, but also to forfeit my chance at its internal goods. I still have a shot at the *external* good of getting from A

---

23. MacIntyre (1981, 175).

to B across a snowy expanse, but that good could be achieved by a snow-mobile or other means and is therefore not *internal* to the practice.

Now practice-communities are important because they act as a kind of garden for cultivating individual virtue. The virtues I cultivate in pursuit of being an excellent skier, surgeon, or musician are central to my being able to lead a good life (remember Aristotle's goal of *eudaimonia*). Furthermore, a good life will contain participation in a certain number of worthwhile practices. On MacIntyre's view, then, practices are important both for individual morality and the ethical health of the larger community.

So nurturing and preserving these practice-communities becomes a new way to generate the greater good. The cultivation of personal excellence requires submission of self to something larger. It entails a respect for and understanding of each practice-community's history. And it requires an engagement with other practitioners, past and present.[24]

MacIntyre's conception of social practices ties together the ethical concepts of virtue, duty, relationships, and utilitarianism in a way that seems tailor-made for the philosophical athlete. Respect for oneself, for one's fellow practitioners, and even for the history and customs of the practice itself combine into a tried and true formula for achieving a good life.

Preserving Internal Goods

If sport is best understood as a social practice, then respect for sport boils down to preserving its "internal goods." But to understand what that means, we must first distinguish these internal goods from other goods in which we might be interested. External goods such as money, fame, or physical fitness can be acquired in a variety of ways. Internal goods, by contrast, can only be achieved or obtained by engaging in the practice itself. As such, they are hard to describe to those not familiar with the practice.

One good apparently internal to sports is the experience known as "flow," sometimes called "being in the zone." Many athletes identify these experiences as the main reason they participate in sport, but the experience is notoriously hard to explain to non-athletes.[25] One thing

---

24. MacIntyre (1981, 181).
25. See, for example, Jackson and Csikszentmihalyi (1999), or Murphy and White (1995).

we can say is that the internal benefits of sport, such as flow, often re-sult from closely-fought battles and appropriate challenges—things the practice itself is designed to preserve. One useful guide for thinking about a sport's internal goods is to imagine an ideal contest and ponder the nature of its benefits.[26]

To be sure many athletes partake in sport more for its external goods than for its internal ones. In fact, many of the ethical problems we worry about in sport derive from athletes' pursuit of external rather than internal goods. Perhaps we can invoke a formulation of Kant's cat-egorical imperative and admonish ourselves to treat sport as an end in itself, and never *just* as a means to some external good.

But a more practical formulation of the same idea might be never to harm the interests of the sport itself just to gain some external goods. This rules out most cases of cheating, drug use, and athlete exploitation without invoking ethical criteria from an external source. For example, almost all sports aim for the ideal of equality, so behavior that chal-lenges that ideal—say spending several million dollars to develop a technological super-bike that will only be available to one team's ath-letes—goes against the interest of sport and should be avoided.

Toward this end, MacIntyre makes a useful distinction between *practices* (i.e. stock-car racing) and the *institutions* that support them (i.e. NASCAR). Institutions are concerned with the acquisition and dis-tribution of external goods—usually money, prizes, and other material things. Furthermore they tend to be structured in terms of power and status. Since sports depend on institutions to support them, it's no won-der that institutions' concern with external goods can corrupt them.[27]

The sad part is that we often depend on these institutions to pre-serve the interests of our sport, when in fact their natural tendency is to corrupt it. No wonder the entertainment industry seems to corrupt our cherished games. No wonder sports governing bodies have largely failed in the battle against dope.[28] No wonder universities, colleges, and now high schools engage in the ritual exploitation of athletes. None of these

---

26. This tactic is used by Fraleigh (1984) who employs the example of a rewarding badminton match.

27. McIntyre (1981, 181–182).

28. Robert Voy (1991, 101) argues that leaving governing bodies in charge of anti-doping programs is akin to having the fox guard the henhouse: "There is simply too much money involved in international sports today. One needs to understand that the officials in charge of operating sport at the amateur level need world-class performances to keep their

204 THE PHILOSOPHICAL ATHLETE

institutions is ultimately interested in the internal goods of sport—only the practitioners themselves even understand what the internal goods are. It's up to athletes—active and retired—to police a sport's institutions and to preserve the sport's interests.

Being a Caretaker

So ultimately respect for the game means acknowledging one's role as a caretaker of one's sport. Athletes who choose to exploit their sports in order to gain external goods will eventually bleed the sport dry, leaving nothing behind for others. This is not to say that preservation of sport means spurning those external goods; many athletes who earn a fortune from their sport also play the role of conscientious caretaker. Their sense of responsibility for preserving the sport they love takes them beyond obeying the rules and honoring a sport's culture. It leads them to adopt the interests of sport as their own and to perform acts or even make innovations to sport in accordance with those interests. Says sports ethicist Russell Gough, "playing by the rules and keeping winning in perspective go hand in hand."[29]

Being a sport's caretaker means recognizing and affirming the internal goods of one's sport, then using those goods as a basis for criticism of one's own behavior as well as that of other athletes, coaches, officials, and institutions. Being a caretaker of sport means honoring the customs and traditions of your sport, but it also means taking responsibility for changes in that culture—both as instigator and as critic.[30]

Finally, being a caretaker means going beyond the rules and customs of sport to act in new ways that cultivate a sport's internal goods. In the 1999 Giro d'Italia, pro cyclist Paolo Savoldelli compromised his own chance at victory by telling the teammates of his rival, Marco Pantani, that their leader had dropped his chain and was in need of their help. That is, he compromised his chance of a victory based on luck and thereby preserved his chance at a genuine victory based on strength and skill. He showed respect for his sport by constructively acting to preserve the internal good of a battle well fought. As a matter of fact,

---

businesses rolling forward...And sometimes that means turning their backs on the drug problem."

29. Gough (1997, 85).

30. A similar point is made by Clifford and Feezell, (1997, 69).

he lost the race to Pantani but the sport itself was made better by Savoldelli's gesture of fair play.

Thinking Activity: Your Sport as a Social Practice
Question: What are the internal goods of your sport?
Observe: Make a list of all the good things you get from participation in your sport. Distinguish internal from external goods, first by singling out goods that can only be obtained in sport, next by identifying goods that can only be obtained in your particular sport.
Analyze: Can you identify threats to internal goods of your sport? For example, does the pressure to perform at the college level detract from your pure enjoyment in sport? Do friends, coaches, parents, or institutions try to motivate you using external goods?
Question Again: Is there a better way to get the external goods you seek?

Chapter Review

Summary

Ethics is the means we use to guide our actions toward a satisfying and meaningful life-story. The main criterion we use is respect: reflective care and concern for things that are important in that life-story. For the philosophical athlete, respect has three general dimensions: respect for self, respect for others, and respect for sport itself.

Self-respect derives from a clear understanding of personal goals and objectives which drives the heart and gut to pursue those goals with passion. Knowing the kind of person you want to be is the giant first step toward behaving like a champion.

Respect for others requires a basic understanding of the respect due to all human beings combined with a specialized analysis of particular relationships. Once we understand the role that others play in our meaningful lives, we can develop appropriate interactions with them.

Finally, respect for the game demands its own understanding—this time of the internal goods inherent in a sport's rules and culture. Getting clear about those and acting accordingly will help our pursuit of meaningful lives and preserve what's good in the sports we love.

Further Reading

Philosophy

Bentham, Jeremy. 1789. *An Introduction to the Principles of Morals and Legislation*. London: T. Payne. It was in chapter one of this book that Bentham first introduced the principles of utilitarianism. Although Bentham invented the concept, his colleague John Stuart Mill refined and wrote about it more. Mill's essay "Utilitarianism" is more commonly read.

Hobbes, Thomas. [1651] 1958. *Leviathan*. Indianapolis, IA: Bobbs-Merrill Co. Hobbes' stark realism about the nature of man is both compelling and sobering. The reasons man suppresses his natural instincts to obey society's rules is detailed in chapter 17, "Of the Causes, Generation, and Definition of a Commonwealth."

MacIntyre, Adasdair. 1981. *After Virtue*. Notre Dame, IN: University of Notre Dame Press. MacIntyre's account of social practices has been profitably applied to sport by a variety of sports ethicists. The book begins with a critical history of ethics. In chapter 14, "The Nature of the Virtues," MacIntyre explains his theory of social practices and their connection to virtue.

Philosophy of Sport

Butcher, Robert and Angela Schneider. 1998. "Fair Play as Respect for the Game" in *Journal of the Philosophy of Sport* XXV, 1–22. This excellent essay uses MacIntyre's principles to define fair play in sport as an effort to preserve a sport's internal goods.

Fraleigh, Warren P. 1984. *Right Actions in Sports: Ethics for Contestants*. Champaign, IL: Human Kinetics. Chapter 5 of this seminal work in sports ethics deals with the issue of rules. Fraleigh is a formalist and disparages "the good foul."

Lehman, Craig. "Can Cheaters Play the Game?" in Morgan and Meier, ed..1988. 283–288. Lehman argues against the formalists that sports should be seen as cultures and not just sets of rules.

Pearson, Kathleen M. 1973. "Deception, Sportsmanship, and Ethics" in Morgan and Meier, ed..1995. 183–184. Another formalist account of why cheaters can't play the game in sports.

Suits, Bernard. 1973. "The Elements of Sport" in Osterhoudt, ed. *The Philosophy of Sport: A Collection of essays*, 48–64. Reprinted in Morgan and Meier, ed..1995. 8–15). Suits offers an analytical approach to the connection between sport and its rules.

Journalism and Literature

On Technology in Sport:

Bjerklie, David. 1993. "High Tech Olympians" in *Technology Review*. January, 23–30. This is an interesting review of the effect of high-tech equipment in various Olympic sports.

Jerome, John. 1980. *The Sweet Spot in Time*. New York: Summit Books. His examples may be a bit dated, but chapter 14, "Tools" is an excellent discussion of the role equipment technology plays in sport.

Part Four

Working with Others

Section Preview

Introduction:
Drugs, Sport and the Just Society

> *The variety of circumstances in which elite athletes find themselves can be described as a continuous spectrum involving various degrees of pressure from trainers, sports federations, and even governments. At one end is the consenting adult who lives free of official pressures to overtrain or take drugs, while at the other end of the spectrum is the child-athlete who is pressured into a punishing training regimen and perhaps fed anabolic steroids without his own or his parents' knowledge.*
> — John Hoberman, *Mortal Engines*

What is Justice?

Advocates of children's sports are fond of claiming that sport teaches social values. By participating in the micro-community of sport, we learn to work with others, to follow rules and laws, to strive for the greater good. There is a sense in which sports are communities, but are they *just* communities? Do they reflect the best sort of society? Does sport really value such social ideals as liberty, equality, and fairness?

Sports have rules, but are rules more or less respected than society's laws? Do the rules protect the safety and liberty of participants, or do they protect the interests of those in power? Athletes share a common starting line in a race, but do they really have equal opportunities? Does the elaborate structure of local, national, and international governing bodies guarantee fairness in sport?

209

Perhaps sports do not resemble just communities at all. Consider the attitude of most athletes, coaches, and governing bodies toward performance-enhancing drugs: they all seek to prohibit their use. Is that the stance of a truly benevolent and just community?

Banning Drugs is Paternalistic

Imagine that your school or workplace decided to ban the performance-enhancing drug: caffeine. Would that seem just to you? Wouldn't you defend your liberty to drink whatever you want with your morning bagel? Wouldn't you argue that your consumption of double-espressos gives you no special advantage over your colleagues, and defend your right to risk any ill-effects to your health? Wouldn't you consider the mandatory urine tests an unfair search of your personal space? Wouldn't you plead that your caffeine consumption poses no harm to anyone but yourself? In fact, if you're like me, you pose *less* of a threat to others with your morning caffeine fix than without it.[1]

In fact, your complaints would be taken seriously by most just societies. Personal liberty is among the rights most prized by communities, who tend to limit it only to prevent harm to others. In fact, liberty is so important that many civic-minded philosophers of sport might find themselves in the unexpected position of advocating the legalization of performance-enhancing drugs such as steroids, growth hormone, and EPO.

Why? Because banning such drugs, so long as they harm no one but the athlete who takes them, is *paternalistic*. Paternalistic laws may be justified for children or the mentally impaired, but adult athletes of sound mind know better than the government what to put in their bodies. So why not let athletes take anything they want in pursuit of victory? It might promote such important social values as liberty, equality, and fairness.

Liberty, Naturalness, and Risk

We have already discussed the importance of freedom in sport. If sport values athletes' liberty, then why does it try to control what we put into our bodies at home? Athletes would never stand for a sport in which a particular diet was required for competition. So what's the difference between my freedom to choose a pre-game meal and my freedom to use performance-enhancing drugs?

---

1. Caffeine example adapted from Simon (1984, 211–212).

You might argue that unlike spaghetti and peanut butter, drugs are not *natural*. There are two problems with this argument. First, many natural substances are banned for their performance-enhancing qualities. *Ma huang*, a natural form of ephedrine found in various herbal supplements, is on the IOC's banned substance list. Testosterone and human growth hormone, among the most reviled of performance enhancing substances, occur naturally in the body. Furthermore many accepted performance-enhancing substances, such as Gatorade, are not natural.

Perhaps the spirit behind the naturalness argument is concern about the *risks* of ingesting chemicals foreign to the body. But sports are themselves risky. Injuries and even death are a real danger that athletes face constantly. Most governments allow citizens the liberty to take risks as long as they understand the danger. Isn't it hypocritical to assume that athletes can give informed consent to participate in a risky sport like hockey, but are incapable of informed consent with respect to the drugs that they take? Legalizing drugs would eliminate the hypocrisy of allowing only natural or risk-free substances in an activity that is by its very nature artificial and risk-producing.

Equality and Fairness

Another argument for banning performance-enhancing drugs is that they violate the principle of *equality*, giving some athletes an *unfair* advantage. This brings up the question of just what equality and fairness are in sport. If an athlete has severe asthma, as does Jackie Joyner-Kersee, is it unfair for her to treat this condition with medicine prescribed by a doctor? "No," some might say, "as long as the medicine only restores her to a normal condition and doesn't provide an advantage."

But this reply assumes that there is some definable baseline understood to be "normal." Elite athletes are anything but normal in their capacities. Should an athlete with naturally high lung capacity be compelled to reduce it chemically so that he doesn't have an unfair advantage? Attempting to quantify a normal capacity, as many sports do by setting parameters for blood hematocrit or testosterone levels, seems to unfairly exclude those who naturally exceed such levels. It also entices those who naturally fall below the level to take enough drugs to get them up to that level.

"But those who chose not to use drugs," one might object, "could never be *equal* to the dopers." This is another compelling point until you consider that sports aren't really equal to begin with. Athletes are born unequal in terms of genetics. Then they have unequal access to coaching, facilities, nutrition, medical assistance, sponsorship, etc. The third-world athlete forced to train with rocks does not have opportunity equal to the United States team member who has access to the latest equipment and coaching. The runner who can fund a high-altitude training-camp is not on equal footing with her competitor who must train at sea level.

Making drugs legal might actually encourage fairness and equality by giving every athlete access to the same chemical advantages. It might also provide chemical compensation to athletes who are genetically, financially, or geographically deprived.

Do Drugs Threaten a Sport's Internal Goods?

Given the weakness of these traditional arguments, can an athletic community that values liberty, equality, and fairness, justifiably ban drugs from its sport? Perhaps the relevant question to ask is whether the use of performance-enhancing drugs actually does harm other athletes by harming the sport itself.[2] More specifically, does the use of drugs threaten a sport's internal goods?

This is more or less the tactic taken by sport-philosopher Robert Simon, who argues that drugs stop sport from being a contest between persons. If drugs were allowed, Simon contends, the winners could be those who respond best to chemicals rather than those who respond best to the challenge of the test.[3] This would transform the nature and spirit of most sports.

Remember MacIntyre's claim that social practices exist to define and preserve certain mutually valued virtues. Is the virtue valued in your sport the ability to respond to chemicals? Remember also that sports practitioners, rather than institutions, need to police the rules in such a way that the internal goods of sport are preserved. This means that decisions about banning drugs must be left up to the *athletes,* who have a vested interest in the internal goods of the sport. Governing bodies, sponsors, event promoters, even coaches cannot be relied upon to make and enforce these rules since their interests may conflict with those of the sport itself.

---

2. This is the general line taken by Holowchak (2000).
3. See Simon (1984, 71–92).

The legalization of performance-enhancing drugs might address concerns about liberty, equality, and fairness. It might also show respect for individual athletes' right to harm themselves freely. But if the use of such drugs would in fact harm the sport, it threatens the entire sport-community, which is made up of practitioners who deserve certain protections.

The Values of Sports Communities

A sports community, like any community, is only as good as the values of its members. The values of a particular sport, like the values of any well-planned community, can serve as a guideline to making and implementing rules and regulations that preserve rather than destroy a sport community. To this end, sports might develop their own sorts of constitution; perhaps we can imagine an athlete's bill of rights. Ultimately our participation in sports as philosophical athletes can teach us to be better citizens of all the communities we value.

Section Preview List

- What are an athlete's rights and obligations in a sport-community? (Chapter 10)
- Can sport value *equality* when its objective is to point up differences? (Chapter 11)
- What is the scope of *fairness* in sport? (Chapter 12)

Chapter 10

Liberty and Authority

Chapter Preview

Introduction
Freedom of Expression or Excessive Celebration?

> *Here, then, we have the first main characteristic of play: that it is free, is in fact freedom.*
>
> —Johan Huizinga, *Homo Ludens*.

The wide-receiver from State U. leaps into the air and plucks the football from the sky, landing in the end zone for a touchdown and setting off screams of hysteria in the crowd. He then takes off his helmet and performs an exuberant victory dance for the camera. His teammates rush to congratulate him and share in the euphoria.

The referee throws a flag. The team is penalized for "excessive celebration."

Is this an act of oppression, an unjustified truncation of the player's freedom of athletic expression? Or is it an attempt to preserve order in the sport-community—to *promote* freedom by enforcing the athlete's obligation to his sport?

Rules in sport, like laws in society, are intended to preserve individual liberty. But one athlete's liberty depends on another athlete's obligation not to interfere, and on all athletes' responsibility to preserve the ideals of their sport.

The question of whether celebration is "excessive" and when (if ever) it should be penalized, is a question about the limits of individual freedom in a community. To answer this question properly, we must examine the relationship between an individual and her community. How important is athletic freedom to a sport-community?

The 19th century British philosopher John Stuart Mill believed that individual liberty was the foundation of any healthy and productive society. He thought that truth could best be found in an open "marketplace of ideas" where all opinions could freely be expressed and held up to scrutiny beneath the light of reason. Communities are deprived of truth not only by squelching unpopular opinions that may in fact be true, but also when majority opinion cannot be enlightened by dissenting voices. Says Mill:

> The peculiar evil of silencing the expression of an opinion, is that it is robbing the human race, posterity as well as the existing generation—those who dissent from the opinion, still more than those who hold it.[1]

Mill also thought that liberty is needed to promote individuality, which benefits communities as well as their citizens. Albert Einstein, for example, was certainly not a conformist and to some extent his genius depended on his freedom to be eccentric. Says Mill:

> Genius can only breathe freely in an *atmosphere* of freedom.[2]

Indeed Mill thought liberty was needed for improvement itself. Left to their own devices, the general tendency of the masses is to move toward mediocrity. To go with the flow is to go nowhere. Mill thinks that this human drive toward conformity caters to our lowest faculties:

> He who lets the world, or his own portion of it, choose his plan of life for him has no need of any other faculty than the ape-like one of imitation.[3]

Social restrictions on individual liberty, then, threaten nothing less than our mental energy and moral courage. By harming the quality of individual people, they harm the quality of society as a whole.

Is this true of sports and athletes as well? How is freedom engendered and preserved within a sport-community? How does freedom benefit that community? When should athletic freedom be limited? When should it be preserved? Philosophical athletes who understand the nature and scope of these questions can make responsible decisions, both for themselves and for the preservation of their sports.

---

1. Mill (1859, 16).
2. Mill (1859, 62).
3. Mill (1859, 56).

Chapter Preview List

- What does the individual athlete gain from a sport-community?
- What must the individual athlete *give up* for a sport-community?
- What does the individual athlete *owe* to a sport-community?

10.1 Sport as a Social Contract

Liberty in Sport Compared to Society

You could argue that individuals are less free in sport than in almost any other area of life. Unlike the carefree ideal of child's play and frolic, the "playing" of organized sport is bound by interminable sets of rules. The space and time within which we play are strictly limited and those limits are painstakingly enforced. Not only are our actions regulated, we are restricted in how we may dress, what we may say, where we may stand.

Even our lives off the field may be regulated by sport. There are requirements pertaining to age, place of residence, and grade point average. We have to be careful about the medicines we take and the foods we eat—not just in terms of a sensible diet—but because there are rules regulating the ingestion of such apparently innocuous substances as caffeine, Visine, birth-control pills and most cough syrups. We might be required to provide urine or even blood-samples so that they may be searched for signs of subversive activity. All this seems a far cry from the inherent liberty of play.

On the other hand, you could argue that individuals experience more liberty in sport than in society itself. In previous chapters we marveled at an athlete's sense of freedom and the foundation it provided for self-understanding, personal responsibility, and ethical conduct.

But even beyond such philosophical considerations, any cop or lawyer can tell you that actions permitted on the football field, rugby pitch, or wrestling mat would be illegal assault if performed on the street. Most of what car, motorcycle, and bicycle racers do would quickly earn a traffic ticket. In some ways, the rules of sport can be more permissive than civilian law.

Athletes in competition often feel a kind of release from social rules and norms. Sociologists are fascinated by the way football players can hug, cry, and pat one another's behinds without incurring the usual social derision for being sissies. Women participating in "Ladies' rugby tournaments" or carrying the nickname "Lady Tigers" exhibit behavior considered anything but lady-like by society.

So liberty in sports seems at first to be a paradox. Sports' elaborate web of rules and regulations have the ironic effect of producing a sense of freedom. When we look at the theory of the *social contract*, however, we can see that liberty must be given up in order to be gained.

Perhaps sport itself can be viewed as a social contract in which athletes agree to abide by certain rules in order to achieve certain benefits, chief among them a heightened sense of freedom.

Philosophical Background:
Liberty and the Social Contract

Liberty is perhaps the most treasured of all social values in the western tradition. It has been described as the natural state of man, a God-given entitlement, and foremost among the list of "unalienable rights" guaranteed by the United States Constitution. You may never have thought about it this way, but the preservation of individual liberty is one of the key reasons we humans leave our natural state and form civil communities.

The idea, as expressed by the 17th century philosopher Thomas Hobbes, is that humans sacrifice some of the freedom inherent in their "natural state" of war and agree, for their mutual benefit, to concentrate on more productive things than fighting one another. We give up freedom to get freedom because it's in our rational self-interest. This seems backwards, until you realize how busy you would be protecting your self and your stuff if there was no civil agreement (and no means of enforcement) to obey certain laws. More to the point, imagine what chaos there would be on the roads if we didn't all agree to drive on one side, stop at the signals, or yield to oncoming trucks.

This agreement among the members of a community to abide by certain laws came to be known as the *social contract*. Its modern champions, John Locke and Jean-Jacques Rousseau, put a more positive spin on the agreement. Locke believed that liberty was a natural human right, given by God and guaranteed by reason. In Locke's view, citizens construct the state to preserve the freedom that they all recognize each other as having.[4]

According to Locke, individuals retain their liberty within the state because the power of the state depends entirely on the citizens' continuing consent. The social contract is therefore contingent upon the state's ability to preserve and protect individual liberty. If it fails, the citizens are likely to withdraw their support—as illustrated by the phenomenon of a revolution.

As we observed earlier, freedom of any kind comes coupled with responsibility. Likewise, in civil society, rights come coupled with obliga-

---

4. Locke (1689b, 218).

tions. Rousseau's interpretation of the social contract emphasizes the obligation of citizens to put aside their personal and partisan concerns in favor of the collective good or general will of the group.[5] In this way, group membership actually limits one's ability to act strictly according to personal interest, but only because it is already in one's personal interest to maintain harmony in and receive the benefits of the group.

Is it likewise plausible that we agree to the rules governing sport in the effort to achieve a greater good? We enter into sport freely, making a conscious choice to accept its rules. This is a situation much closer to the ideal of a social contract than nations, for example, into which we are unwillingly born. But if sport *is* a social contract aimed at achieving some good, just what sort of good is it trying to achieve? [6]

The Benefits of Athletic Freedom

Social contracts aim to preserve, first and foremost, a kind of individual liberty that is often described in terms of human and civil rights. Since (as we have observed) freedom always comes at a price, the price is usually justified in terms of benefits to the community. Freedom of speech, freedom of religion, and freedom of association are protected because of their benefits to the United States.

Is there such a thing as athletic freedom that can be justified in terms of benefit to a sport-community? A limited amount of individual autonomy certainly seems central to the health of sport. Individual liberty in sport is a necessary prerequisite for the benefit of learning about personal responsibility and ethics, as we saw earlier in the book. Indeed athletic freedom seems crucial to sport as an area where virtues are creatively expressed.

Compare freedom of expression in sport to issues of freedom in art, academics, and religion. Artists should be allowed to express their creativity without fear of censorship from a disapproving cultural elite. Professors should be free to follow the path toward truth, whether administrators approve of their findings or not. Religious people should be allowed to worship as they please, regardless of the popularity of their beliefs.

---

5. Rousseau (1761, 425).

6. Eassom (1998) has argued very persuasively that sports are in fact much more complicated than social contract analogies would have us believe. I am willing to concede that point. I use the social contract analogy here as a tool for clarifying our ideas about the scope of individual rights and obligations in sport.

These "freedoms" are granted in the form of protection from individuals and organizations in the community who might otherwise use their power to squelch opposing views. This restriction on the free exercise of power is justified in terms of benefit to the community. As John Stuart Mill observed, a society needs a diversity of products in the free marketplace of ideas, if it hopes to pursue truth.

How does athletic freedom benefit sport-communities? Chiefly, it helps athletes in the myriad of ways previously discussed. First, freedom is necessary to preserve the spirit of *play*. The more sport comes to resemble work, the less it can be differentiated from conventional society as a sanctuary for self-discovery and understanding. Ancient Roman gladiators, who competed on pain of death for the entertainment of the masses, could hardly experience sport as an opportunity to contemplate their existence. Professional athletes who compete to pay their bills may differ from the gladiators only by degree.

Second, freedom is a prerequisite for any understanding of personal responsibility to be gained in sport. Calling football plays from a skybox, telling cyclists to attack through earphones, or guiding racecar drivers from the infield may increase the chances of victory. But the more coaches prescribe and preordain athletes' moves, the less an athlete learns about personal responsibility.

Third, a certain amount of freedom in *how* one tackles specific sporting challenges is needed for athletes to test themselves intellectually and physically in sport. If the task of moving a soccer ball downfield were reduced to dribbling it as fast as possible in a straight line, the opportunities to acquire such skills as creative and strategic thinking or physical agility and toughness would be lost.

Finally, freedom of athletic expression is needed for sport's great innovations. The high jump's Fosbury flop, basketball's slam-dunk, or cross-country skiing's skating technique all started as the creative expression of some individual athlete. Each technique was resisted initially but eventually added to the beauty and texture of sport.

Rights and Obligations of Athletes

The fact that individual autonomy has its benefits in sport does not imply that absolutely anything goes, however. The sports innovations listed above suffered attempts by rules committees to ban them. The reason is that liberty always comes at a price, and decisions to pay that price are guided by values. Generally, the liberties granted in a particular community reflect the values of its culture and heritage. For example, the pilgrims came to America to escape religious persecution, so it makes sense that America values and protects religious freedom.

Likewise, the benefits of liberty in sport must reflect some particular set of values. But if these values merely reflect some particular *social* culture, how can sport adapt to a variety of world cultures? How can the rules and regulations of soccer, for example, accommodate the values of every culture represented in the World Cup? Is it possible that sports themselves, and therefore sport-communities, have their own sets of accepted values? If so, such values would provide a useful guideline for determining rights and obligations of athletes that would resonate across cultural boundaries.

Put more forcefully, sport may need to be protected from the interests of such powerful ideologies as capitalism and patriotism. Just as the freedom of artists and academics is protected from disapproving cultural ideals, so too athletic freedom must be protected in order to preserve the internal goods of a particular sport.

The history of basketball's slam-dunk provides an instructive example. Once the move was introduced it was quickly banned in several leagues. The battle over the dunk quickly took on racial overtones and became at some level a clash of values between white and black American cultures. The traditional "white" style of play seemed threatened by the upstart "black" style. Many of those in the white power structure expressed a fear that African-American players might "take over" the game—a fear that assumes whites somehow "owned" the game in the first place.

But battles such as these should be about what's good for the sport, not which social group has "possession" of it. Sports have intrinsic goods that benefit all practitioners. Protecting the rights of individual athletes should go hand in hand with protecting the goods of the sport itself.

Agreement about a sport's internal goods may come about as a kind of social contract among athletes. The athletes may explicitly consent to the contract by means of a ceremony—as in the athletes' oath taken at the Olympic Games. Or, they may consent implicitly simply by partaking of the benefits of sport. In any case it should be left up to athletes and ex-athletes—people who understand and are motivated to protect the internal goods of sport—to initiate and perpetuate this athletic social contract.[7]

---

7. In fact this is the model for determinations of free speech, academic freedom, and freedom of worship. History offers many reasons to prefer self-government to external

> **Thinking Activity: Making a Sports Social Contract**
> **Question:** What would a social contract be in your sport?
> **Observe:** Choose a particular sport that you're familiar with and write down all the "internal goods" of that sport. Remember that MacIntyre defined internal goods as benefits (a) available only to practitioners and (b) achieved while trying to achieve standards of excellence appropriate to the activity.
> **Analyze:** Determine what sort of activities must be permitted in order for practitioners to achieve these internal goods—call these an athlete's "rights." Determine what sorts of activities threaten the achievement of these internal goods—call these "prohibitions."
> **Question Again:** How do the terms of your contract compare to the reality of how your sport is practiced? Can anything be done to improve the situation?

10.2 Negative Freedoms in Sport

Prevention of Harm to Others

In imagining sport in terms of a social contract, we must first ask what sort of actions will be prohibited. Certainly, constitutive rules provide an immediate framework for the limitation of athletes' liberties. If we let volleyball players kick the ball, we wouldn't have a volleyball game at all. Beyond the rules that actually *define* a practice, however, how much freedom is needed to preserve the goods of a given sport? Or, to put it another way, to what extent must athletes be free from interference?

For many of us, the very concept of "interference" is first learned in sport. I remember that in front yard football, I had to count a certain number of "elephants" before interfering with the opposing quarterback; and still I wasn't allowed to just maul the quarterback. Even among kids using flowerbeds as end-zones there's an implicit agreement to avoid harming one another. After all, if someone gets hurt and has to go home or to the doctor, the game would be over.

Harm is typically a central issue in any social contract and sports are no exception. Even what some may call violent sports have safety regulations and rules generally prohibiting "dangerous play."[8] Using the

---

control, ranging from book-burnings and witch-trials to modern debates about religious cults and pornography.

8. On the other hand, harming others seems to be the *object* of some sports. Boxing is an obvious example, but even non-combat sports that emphasize endurance—ultra-

view of sport as a social practice, we can say that harm to others should be prohibited, except where it is essential to a sport's central challenge and therefore the production of its internal goods.

This might lead to a distinction between necessary and unnecessary harm within sport, as reflected in American football's "unnecessary roughness" penalty. For example, you wouldn't have boxing if you banned punching altogether, but you can—and they do—ban such unnecessary violence as hitting below the belt. Even the ancient Olympic sport of *pankration,* which allowed all sorts of boxing and wrestling moves, prohibited such actions as biting, gouging of the eyes, and breaking of opponents' fingers because those actions seemed to threaten the spirit of the contest.[9]

Philosophical Background:
Negative Liberty and Paternalism

Since gaining liberty through a social contract requires us to give up some liberty, it's worth asking what we mean by the right to individual liberty and why it should be preserved. The most basic understanding of liberty is the absence of physical impediment—if I'm locked behind bars or bound by shackle and chain, I'm anything but free.[10] In a social sense, liberty is generally understood as lack of interference from government or fellow citizens. This is often called *negative liberty* since it's characterized by the absence of interference rather than the presence of assistance.

As we saw in the chapter introduction, negative liberty's most eloquent defender was John Stuart Mill, whose classic essay *On Liberty* has had a huge impact on law and government in the western world. Given the importance of liberty to the health of the community, the question is how to maximize its benefits without society exploding into a state of chaos. Mill's answer is the *harm principle*:

---

endurance running and extreme-races such as the *Raid Gauloises*—seem to include physical harm as a part of the essence of their challenge. It may not be harm to *others* in the sense that I'm not punching you with my fist, but it's arguable that by trying to make an opposing runner "crack" on a long climb in an ultra-marathon race, I am indeed attempting to harm that person.

   9. Swaddling (1980, 60–62).

   10. Of course shackles and chains can also be metaphorical—what if someone holds a proverbial gun to my head, manipulates my decisions, or molds my attitudes through propaganda and indoctrination?

The only purpose for which power can be rightfully exercised over any member of a civilized community, against his will, is to prevent harm to others.[11]

This means that we can't interfere with another person's action (no matter how imprudent, stupid, or even self-destructive that action may be) unless it's to prevent harm to other people.

If Evel Knevil wants to jump across a canyon on some rocket-cycle, he should be allowed to do it. I can tell him I think he's nuts, that he's immorally negligent of his own life and his family's feelings — but I can't stop him. That's my duty, my obligation to others, *as demanded by my own right to liberty.*

The spirit of the harm principle is reflected in our laws, especially in the opposition to such things as motorcycle helmet laws and mandatory fastening of seatbelts. Even if there's wide agreement that they're a good idea, it's hard to justify forcing those attitudes on others. Of course helmet and seatbelt laws are common these days, but often they are restricted to persons under 18. Mill made exceptions to the harm principle for minors, the mentally ill, and those who cannot take care of themselves. But only in these cases is *paternalism* — the restriction of an individual's liberty for his or her own good — justified. The word 'paternalism' derives from the Latin word for 'father' and it is rightfully associated with such ideas as parental controls over what kids view on television or the Internet.[12]

Safety and Paternalism

While regulations prohibiting harm to others are relatively uncontroversial, at least where harm is unnecessary for securing the internal goods of a particular sport, attempts to prevent individuals from harming themselves are much more problematic. It's one thing to make sure that an athlete can give *informed consent* — that is, that the athlete understands the risks of undertaking a given activity — and another to actually stop the athlete from taking such a risk.

---

11. Mill (1859, 9).
12. The connection between paternalism and issues of free-speech is very real. Although pornography, for example, is considered by many to be offensive and even socially destructive, the benefits of free speech demand that only children can be legally "protected" from it. Likewise, flag-burning is hurtful to many, but it is protected as a mechanism for criticism of the government. If the government or majority can squash all dissenting views, what's to keep it from descending into tyranny?

There are many athletic regulations that seem paternalistic. These range from required safety equipment to rules banning particular moves, to regulations banning the use of certain substances, to all-out prohibitions of risky activities such as B.A.S.E. jumping. Can such regulations be justified by the internal logic of sport?

The move to require helmets and to make them conform to standard safety criteria seems to have grown in tandem with the rise in civil litigation to recover massive medical costs. The United States Cycling Federation finally required hard-shell helmets after lawsuits from riders who had been seriously injured while wearing traditional leather strap helmets threatened to end bike-racing altogether in the U.S. The Federation needed the hard-shell rule in order to obtain insurance.

Meanwhile its members charged that the rule violated their civil liberties and suggested that the USCF was receiving kickbacks from helmet manufacturers.[13] When the international governing body tried to require pro cyclists to wear helmets in the early 1990's, the riders staged strikes and defied the rules by refusing to pay fines. Eventually the rule was rescinded.

It does seem condescending to protect professional athletes from themselves, even when there's no good reason not to reduce the risk. Remember that helmets in professional hockey had to be grandfathered in, by limiting the requirement to new players. In most cases where paternalistic safety rules are discussed, the arguments emerge that pros serve as role models for youth or that athletes are forced by peer-pressure to forgo reasonable caution. These attempts to justify paternalism by appealing to the protection of youth or claiming that athletes really don't have a choice can be interpreted as failure to respect the athletes' intelligence.

The issue gets stickier, however, when taking unadvisable risks might result in a competitive advantage. The paradigm case here would be doping. Should athletes be free to ingest dangerous substances for the purpose of performance enhancement? If so, would the legalization of such substances effectively coerce other athletes into taking them just to compete? This issue is discussed in the section introduction.

In some cases, required safety equipment can actually encourage athletes to take more risks than they otherwise might. This seems to be the case with American football, where the transition from soft to hard-shell helmets has tempted players to use those helmets as weapons. Spearing,

---

13. These events are recounted in Prouty (1988, 192–199).

ramming, or butting an opponent with the crown of the helmet is banned at all levels of football—as much for the protection of the hitter as the hittee.

In 1993, Arizona Cardinal safety Chuck Cecil was fined $30,000 by the NFL for two such hits, even though his opponents were uninjured and no penalty was called on the field at the time. The league fined Cecil under a rule banning unnecessary roughness, but admitted that their actions were at least partly intended to protect Cecil from himself.[14]

Individual Liberty vs. the Interests of the Sport

Perhaps paternalistic intervention, like the prevention of harm to others, can be regulated in terms of the preservation of a given sport's internal goods. Let's revisit the issue of sports innovation. Initial objections to the Fosbury flop were based on safety, since not all high jump pits could safely accommodate jumpers landing on their backs or heads. But that consideration, while valid, was not a threat to the basic test of getting over the bar.

Compare the case of an ingenious swimmer who discovered that an underwater dolphin-kick propelled him much faster than the breaststroke. The swimmer would dive into the pool, dolphin kick three-quarters of its length, then surface for only a few breaststrokes. Unlike the Fosbury flop, this "innovation" seemed to threaten the very ideal of excellence at the breaststroke by *avoiding* the stroke as much as possible. Swimming has since changed the rules to require that swimmers begin the prescribed stroke a short distance from the edge of the pool. In this case the internal logic of the sport was used to prevent abuse of its values.

Can the internal logic of sports also be used to justify safety requirements? The case of the U.S. Cycling Federation teaches an important lesson: organized sporting events almost universally involve some entity that needs financial protection from liability claims. Whether a sporting arena is on a college campus, private estate, or public park, insurance is needed and insurance companies want to hedge their bets by requiring various safety-measures.

Even if we can agree that an athlete's liberty ought not to be interfered with, we can also agree that entire sports ought not to be sacrificed just to protect an individual's rights to risk his or her own safety. After all, the internal goods of a sport are available only to participants. What

---

14. See Telander (1993, 44).

good is a situation in which athletes have freedom, but nowhere to exercise it?

Adults can ride their bikes bareheaded on the street all they want, but if you want to enter a race you have to wear a helmet. One way to look at the difference is to remember that when you enter the race, the risks you take are no longer simply your own. A serious injury to you is apt to result in huge medical bills, which will be paid indirectly by all competitors through higher insurance fees. So in a sense you *are* risking "harm" to others, by potentially forcing them to pay for your mistake.

If sport can be understood as a social contract among athletes, a central goal of that contract should be to preserve the opportunity to compete. If that goal requires certain appropriate safety-measures, then they reasonably can become part of that agreement. Individual athletes don't lose the liberty to eschew measures, they simply forgo that liberty temporarily as part of a freely-accepted agreement among competitors.

Thinking Activity: Athletes' Bill of Rights
Question: What would an athletes' bill of rights look like?
Observe: Working from a general idea of your sport's internal goods, list 3–5 athletic freedoms that you think are essential to your sport. Phrase each item on your list as an athlete's "right."
Analyze: Go over your list and explain how denial of that "right" would change the sport—what specific benefit of the sport would be lost if the freedom were denied? Is that benefit essential to the values of the sport community itself, or does it reflect the values of some particular person, culture, or society?
Question Again: Might any of your rights be applicable to all sports? Are there universal sports values from which we can derive such an Athlete's Bill of Rights?

10.3 An Athlete's Obligation to Sport

You Are Your Sport

While viewing sport in terms of social contract there comes a time to reflect on a version of John F. Kennedy's famous statement: Ask not what your sport can do for you, ask what *you* can do for your sport. Remember Rousseau's point that individuals who enter into a social contract must change their mode of thinking from personal interest to the interests of the group.

The first thing to acknowledge is that athletes are not related to their sports as subject to object. You may say, "I play water-polo," but what that statement implies is that you (in some sense) *are* water polo, where water polo is a practice and you are among its practitioners. Take all the athletes from a sport and what do you have left? The coaches? The officials? The equipment? The arena? The rulebook? None of these things would exist if there weren't first a group of people who wanted to play. The health and preservation of your sport depends on you and your fellow athletes.

A corollary to this observation that athletes *are* their sports is that sports are nothing more than what the athletes (and other concerned participants such as coaches and officials) make of them. If track sprinters decided to run their race in a pool they'd end up with a sport closer to swimming. But beyond changes in the constitutive rules, decisions made by the citizens of a given sport can profoundly change it. Remember that MacIntyre's definition of a practice held that practitioners determine the standards of excellence. The *virtue* and skill demanded by a practice depends largely on those standards of excellence, which are set and changed by the top practitioners.[15]

Generally, these virtues and skills change quite slowly. Even revolutionary changes in a sport's standards of excellence—for example, the four-minute mile—do not greatly change the kind and amount of virtue demanded by the practice. Still, they make us aware of an evolution. For a long time in running history, the idea of sprinting for an entire mile was anathema, but at some point speed became a virtue of the miler. In this way, the practice was changed by its practitioners, but its internal goods were preserved.

An ethical question arises, however: given that athletes have this power to transform the nature of their sport, do they also have some *obligation* to preserve and protect it?

Philosophical Background:
Positive Freedom Requires Obligation

Having observed that a right to liberty always carries with it the obligation to respect the liberty of others, one gets the sense that as free-

---

15. MacIntyre (1981, 177).

dom expands so does obligation.[16] For example, your right to free speech not only restricts my freedom to interfere with what you say, it may even create an obligation for the community to provide a forum in which you can be heard. The obligation to facilitate the exercise of freedoms—to provide not a freedom from, but a freedom to—is generally known as *positive freedom*.

In his important essay "Two Concepts of Liberty," the 20th century philosopher Isaiah Berlin notes that freedom involves more than having a choice. I may have the choice of giving my wallet to the mugger or being shot, for example, but you'd hardly call my action free. Freedom depends, among other things, on the number of possibilities open to me and how easy or difficult it is for me to actualize these possibilities.[17]

Granted government action can do nothing about the *natural* impediments to my playing in the NBA, but it can do something about the *social* impediments to my becoming a medical doctor: it can provide appropriate opportunities for education and tuition assistance. Arguably, it is obligated to provide these insofar as it is interested in my liberty. But enhancing my liberty in that way means infringing on the liberty of at least some of my fellow citizens, perhaps in the form of taxation or by denying that same medical education to someone else.

Berlin argues that whereas negative freedom is a question about *what* I am free to do, positive freedom is question about *who* decides what I can and cannot do. This is not obvious at first. Consider again that my freedom, for example, to play high-school football requires that others act to provide me with the opportunity. The people who provide the equipment, facilities, and opportunity to me actually control my liberty to play.

Sometimes they must be forced by law or some other authority to give me the chance, and in that case it's the government who controls my freedom. Granted, governments provide many such opportunities. The many girls who now play high-school football have that chance specifically because the government requires it. The caveat is that such freedoms are gained only at the expense of other freedoms. The same government that allows my participation now prohibited it in the past.

---

16. At least insofar as we are equal, hence the justification for less liberty being granted to minors. Equality is the topic of the next chapter.

17. Paraphrased from Berlin (1969, note 10).

Positive liberty, therefore, is nothing more than what those in power believe it should be at a particular point in time. There's always the risk that whoever controls my freedom will have values or attitudes different from mine. As Berlin notes, even the most oppressive tyrannies and totalitarian regimes claim to be promoting freedom—they just have narrow visions of what a human being should be: "Enough manipulation with the definition of man, and freedom can be made to mean whatever the manipulator wishes."[18]

Once we see that liberty comes always with an obligation not to interfere with others, and then that it's regulated by different conceptions of truth, the near-chaos that results from maximum social liberty seems to show order after all.

Obligation to Prevent Exploitation?

Most of us participate in sports to gain certain benefits. As we noticed before, the most important of these benefits are internal—that is, they're derived directly from the practice of the sport itself. An internal good of sailing, for example, might be the magic feeling of being pushed along by the silent power of wind.

Internal goods are available to every practitioner of the sport, without coming at the expense of anyone else. Unlike such external goods as victory, which must come at the expense of the vanquished, or monetary rewards, which must be taken from someone else, the internal goods of sport are available to everyone who pursues the sports' ideals and standards.

Now the exclusion of such things as winning and prizes from the internal goods of sport does not imply they must be eliminated. What's important to see is that the internal goods are the heart of a sport and our social contract must be designed to preserve them. Practicing sport solely for its associated external goods amounts to its exploitation. As basketball coach John Wooden says, "the journey is better than the end"[19]

The term 'exploit' means to make use of something. In its most pejorative sense it means to unjustly use something or someone solely for one's own advantage. This brings to mind Kant's injunction against treating others *merely* as means to an end. Granted athletes "use" their

---

18. Berlin (1969, 95).
19. Wooden quoted in Packer and Lazenby (1998, 29).

sport as a means to its internal goods. For example, you may strive for excellence in softball as a means toward the end of the feelings it provides and the personal virtue that striving engenders. But in doing that you can also respect your role within the sport by preserving its history, standards, and internal goods.

On the other hand, athletes *exploit* sport when they use it *merely* as a means to some external good (say, money) that can be theirs only at someone else's expense. Athletes who exploit their sport solely for personal advantage are no better than universities that exploit their athletes for profit.

Notice that accepting external goods is not necessarily exploitation. What's characteristic about exploitation is that it bleeds a thing dry for one's own advantage. The difference is similar to a gardener who lovingly tends her tomato plants, then takes their fruit judiciously without harming the vines. The exploiter tramps into the garden of sport and plucks as many tomatoes as he can, never caring for the health of the plants that produce them.

Usually there are enough "gardeners" in sport that the damage done by exploiters fails to destroy the practice. Social contract theorists call those who reap the benefits of the community without contributing "free riders." It is widely agreed that free riders act unethically, although most communities have them. The problem we face in sport is that free-riding rhetoric about the central role of winning or making money off sport is spreading quickly. What's to keep all the gardeners from going home and leaving the free-riders with nothing but a bare patch of dirt?

For the Love of the Game

Athletes are, in principle, free to make of sport what they want. But there's always the danger that we will eventually destroy its internal goods. In the United States, the most pressing threat seems to be the push to make sports a business. And why not? Sports are great entertainment, capable of generating billions of dollars in revenue. But unless we find a way to preserve the garden that produces that fruit, we risk losing everything.

Consider the example of "professional wrestling." Few consider it a true sport, not even the wrestlers themselves. They freely admit that they're in the business of entertainment. Matches are rigged—without apology—for maximum spectator appeal. Pro wrestling has more in common with the circus than it does with the Olympic sport practiced in high schools and colleges around the world. But what keeps other entertainment-oriented sports such as professional hockey from becoming mere entertainment? In a word, it is the *intentions* of (most of) the athletes.

The preservation of sport depends on its practitioners, not only because they effectively *are* the sport but also because they are in a position to know and appreciate the internal goods of the game. Notice that since we base their qualification on the knowledge of internal rather than external goods, victories and paychecks are not relevant. In fact, the external temptations that professional and elite athletes face make them *less* trustworthy as caretakers of sport than those who play "for the love of the game."

Sports institutions, as we saw in the last chapter, are the least qualified to preserve a sport's "garden" since they, almost by definition, are concerned with external goods. When average athletes look into the mirror, what they should see staring back at them is the best hope their sports have for preservation and survival—but this is only true as long as the average athlete understands the goods of the game.

The trick to telling "gardeners" from exploiters in the world of sport is to look at their intentions. Anyone who has lived through a sport's popularity growth spurt should recognize the "jerk factor"—namely that the number of obnoxious jerks involved in a given sport seems to be related exponentially to the growth in the number of overall participants. Typically, small sport communities are often populated exclusively by those with true passion and dedication for the sport. As a sport grows and the possibility for external goods such as money and popularity increase, the percentage of truly caring participants seems to shrink.

The community becomes populated by what sport-philosopher Bernard Suits calls triflers, cheats, and spoilsports.[20] Triflers follow the rules of a game without seriously pursuing its objective. Cheats pursue the game's objective—or, more commonly, the spoils associated with that objective—without following rules or (therefore) truly playing the game at all. Spoilsports care neither for the rules nor the objectives; that's why they "spoil" the sport.

---

20. Suits (1978, 44–48).

Those who demand athletic freedom, then, must do it within the confines of a social contract that preserves the interests of the sport. Ask not only what sport can do for you, but also what you can do for sport.

Thinking Activity: Gardeners vs. Exploiters
Question: Are you a caretaker or exploiter in your sport?
Observe: Take a clean sheet of paper and make a list on the left side of things you personally "get out of" your sport. Then, on the right, list things you do that "give back" to others in the sport.
Analyze: Does your "get out" list contain more internal or external goods? Do the items on your "give back" list focus more on internal or external goods? Would you call yourself more an exploiter or a care-taker?
Question Again: What can you do to be a better care-taker of your sport?

Chapter Review

Summary: Justice in the Sport-Community

Athletes' relationships to their sports are analogous to citizens' relationships to their communities. In fact sport is a kind of community, a group made up of individuals from a wide-variety of social and cultural backgrounds who are brought together by the shared values of their sport. Just as citizens benefit from their membership in a community, so athletes benefit from their participation in sport. But these benefits come with obligations, obligations not to interfere with others and to nurture and preserve the community. Some view sport as a place to learn about citizenship. Philosophical athletes know it's more than an analogy. Citizenship within ones sport-community is as important a responsibility as citizenship in one's state.

Further Reading

Philosophy

Berlin, Isaiah. 1969. "Two Concepts of Liberty." In *Readings in Social and Political Philosophy*, Robert M. Stewart, ed. Oxford: Oxford University Press, 90–97. A contemporary insight into the role of power in our interpretation of liberty, this essay shows how different sets of values will define liberty different ways and justify oppression according to such concepts.

Locke, John. 1689. "Second Treatise on Civil Government." In Cahn, ed., 217–292. This classic, conservative approach to social contract theory justifies the social contract in terms of individual rights.

Mill, John Stuart. 1859. *On Liberty*, edited by Elizabeth Rapaport (1978). Indianapolis, IA: Hackett. This is a true classic of social and political philosophy that has had enormous impact on modern law. Mill explains the benefits to the community of individual liberty and institutes the harm principle as a prerequisite for government interference.

Rousseau, Jean-Jacques. [1761] 1967. *The Social Contract and Discourse on the Origin of Inequality,* edited by Lester G. Crocker. New York: Simon and Schuster/Pocket Books. Rousseau offers more liberal interpretation of the social contract that emphasizes the need to recognize one's stake in community welfare and think for the group.

Philosophy of Sport

Eassom, Simon. 1998. "Games, Rules, and Contracts." In McNamee and Parry, ed., 57–78. Eassom argues very persuasively that sports are in fact much more complicated than social contract analogies would have us believe.

Morgan, William J. 1994. *Leftist Theories of Sport: A Critique and Reconstruction.* Urbana and Chicago, IL: University of Illinois Press. This is a definitive contemporary look at the social and political theory of sports by one of the foremost scholars in the field.

Suits, Bernard. 1978. "Triflers, Cheats, and Spoilsports." In *The Grasshopper: Games, Life, and Utopia,* Toronto: University of Toronto Press, 44–48. Suits explains various forms of bad sports citizenship in terms of failure to respect a game's rules and/or objectives.

Journalism and Literature

Prouty, David F. 1988. *In Spite of Us: My education in the big and little games of amateur and Olympic sports in the U.S.* Brattleboro, VT: VeloNews. This is an inside-view of sports government from the former head of the United States Cycling Federation. It includes his struggle with liability issues, the helmet rule, and blood-doping.

Telander, Rick. 1993. "Headlong and Headstrong." *Sports Illustrated,* October 11, 42–45. This article tells the story of American football player Chuck Cecil's battles with the NFL over his helmet-first hits. Since the rule Cecil breaks is intended to protect him, his case is relevant to the discussion of paternalism.

Chapter 11

Equality and Difference

Chapter Preview

Introduction:
White Men Can't Jump?

> *As a rookie, in 1957, I was the only black player on the Boston Celtics, and I was excluded from almost everything except practice and the games. Exactly twenty years later I was coach and general manager of the of the Seattle Supersonics, which only had two white players on the team—and they were excluded from almost everything but practice and the games. The black players left them out of meals, conversations, parties and anything else that makes a lonely road trip bearable. I told the blacks how unfair this was, and they made a token effort to change, but they said the white players were just too different. In basketball, it took only twenty years to go from the outhouse to the in-crowd.*
>
> —Bill Russell, *Second Wind*

In December of 1997, *Sports Illustrated* published an article entitled "Whatever Happened to the White Athlete?" The article was the result of extensive interviews and a nationwide poll of middle-school and high school kids. What it found is that "*White Men Can't Jump*" is more than a movie title. White athletic inferiority is the belief of a plurality of schoolboys, white and black.

What's more, recent psychological research indicates that beliefs about superiority and inferiority based on racial stereotypes actually affect performance. Says University of Arizona Psychologist Jeff Stone,

237

"When people are reminded of a negative stereotype about themselves—'white men can't jump' or 'black men can't think'—it can adversely affect performance."[1]

Statistics show that white participation in the major team sports is down and getting smaller with each passing year. White parents steer their kids away from sports, coaches steer white players away from the speed positions, Nintendo gets richer as the nation's young become obese. *S.I.*'s study also showed that nearly half of the black kids believe they can play professional basketball, while only 20% of whites thought they could. Of course the real odds are much worse for both groups. But the really troubling statistic is the paucity of blacks who think they can have careers requiring post-graduate study.

Many view the myth of white athletic inferiority as a welcome turning of the tables in the otherwise white-dominated social game. But it may be that the myth of black athletic superiority is tied to our inability to accept equality. Once upon a time, the athletic *superiority* of whites was taken as justification for their social, economic, and colonial authority. But the inherent equality of sport eventually allowed blacks success where none was expected. This situation begged for an explanation that could uphold the status quo of white social superiority. Enter the myth of the dumb jock, accompanied by the idea that black athletes don't work but have natural talent. There is even a troubling belief in the equation of black male athleticism and criminality—an association apparently validated by such characters as Mike Tyson.[2]

The trade-off between athletic and mental superiority hasn't helped anyone. It can make black athletes overconfident athletically and cause them to downplay academic achievement. It discourages white athletes from participation in sport, and all the goods that come with that. Furthermore, it promotes the pernicious fallacy that anyone who wants to appear intelligent and successful had best steer clear of sport.

The psychological effects of stereotypes remain a problem off the field as well. Reminders about race and gender actually affect students' scores on tests. Asian women, for example, scored lower on math tests preceded by questions that reminded them of their gender and scored higher when a similar test was preceded by questions about their eth-

1. Begley (2000, 66).
2. For more on this connection, see Hoberman (1997, 209–220).

nicity (a reinforcement of the stereotype that Asians are better at math).[3] Discoveries about the power of stereotypes may also help to explain the racial divide in standardized tests.[4]

One provocative and encouraging fact *S.I.*'s survey did uncover was that athletes at integrated schools, black and white, were least likely to buy into the myths.[5] That is, kids who actually competed with kids of other races were less likely to believe in one group's superiority to the other. The solution to the problem, then, seems clear—forget the stereotypes, shut-up, and go play.

The issues of race and gender stereotyping point to an important paradox in modern sports: they try to promote *equality* while seeking *inequality*. On the one hand, it seems obvious that sport values equality. As in any worthwhile human community, players are given equal opportunity to compete on a level playing field and to be judged by unbiased standards. On the other hand, it seems just as obvious that sport is about *inequality*—the whole purpose of a contest is to point out differences in ability, performance, even virtues. Athletes strive to rise above their foes, to distinguish themselves from others, to stand alone on the winner's podium.

So which is it?

Both. The internal logic of sport attempts to provide equal opportunity and reward sport-relevant differences without regard to such issues as race, gender, or ethnicity. On the other hand sport is hardly immune from the stereotypes and prejudices that infect society at large. As philosophical athletes we can be aware of this situation and embrace the egalitarianism of sport in order to rise above the petty prejudices and damaging stereotypes that plague our society.

Chapter Preview List

- Is sport the promised land of equality or a wasteland of discrimination?
- Do social and cultural ideas of inequality affect sport?
- How can equality be promoted within sport?

---

3. Begley (2000, 66).
4. Begley (2000, 68).
5. Price (1997, 45).

11.1 Equality in Sports: Ideal and Real

Competition and Inequality

Every year in Scotland a soccer game is played between mortal enemies — or so it seems. The match, called "The Old Firm," pits a Catholic against a Protestant team in a rivalry that mirrors an old and bitter war. Spectators need to be corralled into sections separated by high barbwire fences and an empty neutral zone. Fights and riots in town are expected. A supporter of one team says of the opposing team: "They're animals, I hate everything they stand for, everything they believe in. As soon as I see them, my blood starts boiling." When asked why, he shrugs, then confesses, "It's just the way I was brought up."[6]

In stark contrast to the riotous fans are the players themselves, who exhibit none of the spectators' hatred toward their opponents on the field. Play is, if anything, less "dirty" than usual and the religious rivalry — which is no longer reflected in the actual religions of the players — is practically a non-issue compared with the sporting rivalry that often decides the Scottish title.

The phenomenon of the "Old Firm" illustrates the central paradox of equality in sport. From the pure perspective of sport, players are equal — race, religion, even gender and age make no difference to the soccer ball being kicked. And the players themselves had better concentrate on the game and *treat* their opponents as equals if they're to have a chance at securing victory.

But this pure game of sport is played in a sea of partisan spectators for whom the whole contest is an issue of proving one group of people superior to another. And who's to say that the spectators are wrong? After all, sports are defined in terms of winners and losers; they are built on a foundational belief that humans are unequal and their purpose is to publicly expose those inequalities.

On the other hand, human equality is a different concept than the kind of equality associated with numbers. Social equality is often described in terms of runners sharing a single starting line. Equal *opportunity* is not to be confused with equality of ability, motivation, or outcome.[7]

---

6. *Sports Illustrated*, May 17, 1999, 57.
7. This distinction is profitably made by Simon (1991, 27–32).

In fact sports' apparently inherent egalitarianism can make them seem like a haven from the universal plague of social prejudice. In the "Old Firm," the players are separated from the spectators by psychological as well as chain-link fences. For those who don't fit the profile of the power-elite in their society, sports seem to provide a golden opportunity to transcend social prejudice and be judged on merit alone.

It might surprise you to learn that in colonial times, whites looked to the unquestioned egalitarianism of sport to validate beliefs in their natural racial superiority and thereby ease their consciences about their oppression and brutality.[8] Some whites even rationalized slavery as part of an ethical duty to protect the inherently weak Negro race from extinction![9] Ultimately, however, egalitarian sport has proved athletes of African descent to be anything but inferior and weak.

It's no coincidence that sport has been able to provide such opportunities. Like all well-founded communities, sport considers equality of opportunity to be a foundational value. For all its ability to transcend social prejudice, however, sport has at the same time reinforced and perpetuated social inequities and the biases that inspire them. So the question remains open—is sport the promised land or a wasteland for equality?

Philosophical Background:
Social Equality as an Ideal

When Thomas Jefferson declared it a "self-evident truth" that "all men are created equal," he was echoing a social ideal that has existed nearly as long as civilization itself. Equality is a central value in almost every society. Plato believed in the political equality of the sexes and envisioned women in military and governmental positions in his *Republic*.[10] Aristotle also defines justice largely in terms of equality,[11] but he notes that human beings could never be equal in the sense that 2 + 1 is equal to 3, or the way four quarters equal one dollar; we're too different from one another for that.

Human beings *can* be equal in particular respects, however. For example, two people may be of equal height, equal weight, or equal age.

---

8. A detailed historical study of this phenomenon can be found in Hoberman (1997, 99–114).

9. Hoberman (1997, 153).

10. See especially *Republic* IV, 454de.

11. See especially *Nicomachean Ethics* III.

Equality in the social-political sense asserts that people are equal in certain relevant respects, while remaining different in other respects. This equality entitles us to equal treatment in our societies. But the big question is: just what are these "relevant respects" of equality?

Unfortunately for the ideal of equality, the answers to that question are almost always conditioned by irrelevant social and cultural beliefs. Hence the reality of equality changes from epoch to epoch and community to community. Slavery, lack of voting rights, and countless forms of racial, ethnic, and religious discrimination have taken place—and continue to thrive—in countries who proclaim undying esteem for liberty and equality. Even Thomas Jefferson was a slave owner. But that disturbing fact needn't tarnish the wisdom of his words.

Equality resonates as a social ideal because it puts the burden of proof and justification on those who would deny equal rights to others. The Roman stoics split from the Greeks and declared that even slaves possessed a natural equality to their masters, based on human rationality.[12] Christianity proclaims that all souls are equal in God's eyes.[13] And the early social contract theorists such as Hobbes, Locke, and Rousseau tried to reflect the natural equality of mankind within their ideal states.

Although women, foreigners, and people of color were excluded from many of these idealists' conceptions of equality, the downtrodden have asserted their rights by reaffirming the principle of equality and dispelling only the arguments about relevance. Jefferson saw the folly of slavery end within his own lifetime. But this did not represent a change in his ideas about equality, just a broadening of the mind about who was in fact equal.

Sport as the Promised Land of Human Equality

From the perspective of many a racial or religious minority, sport has proved to be a promised land full of opportunities denied in society at large.[14] As Clifford and Feezell point out, "sport sets up an arena in

---

12. A noteworthy example is Seneca.

13. Galatians 3:26–29.

14. I'm using the term 'minority' to identify any group having less power in a society—not necessarily fewer numbers. In South Africa, for example, Blacks have been a majority numerically, but a minority in terms of power.

which an ideal equality reigns: everyone is equal in relation to the opportunities or possibilities provided by the rules."[15]

An optimist might read Dr. Martin Luther King Jr.'s famous *I Have a Dream* speech and believe that modern sport has achieved that dream. King echoed the American ideal that all men are created equal, just as sport assumes that they are. He hoped that the "sons of former slaves and sons of former slave owners [would] be able to sit down together at the table of brotherhood...."[16] This became a reality at the integrated training-tables of Southern sports teams. And he dreamed that people would be judged by the "content of their character" rather than the color of their skin. Stopwatches and goal-lines are inherently colorblind in the "judgments" they make of our athletic character.

Sport has overcome many racially defined barriers, giving many of us our earliest and most intimate contact with people of other races and ethnicities. I still recall quite vividly how as an Anglo child growing up in Southern California, an elementary school softball game dispelled some powerful myths about race in my own mind.

I had heard grave warnings from my classmates about a mythical monster named Virginia—the 12-year-old Latina pitcher on the opposing team. She was said to have three-inch fingernails painted blood red so they would blend with your blood when she tried to scratch your eyes out! At the game, I spotted her immediately—seven feet tall with eye shadow and claws, ready to kill us all.

After I received the first pitch, however, I realized she was closer to five feet tall and her pitches weren't even that hard, much less aimed at my head. I remember so clearly standing there on a rubber first base, looking at Virginia and just wondering where all the fear and lurid stories had come from. Virginia was just a girl, like me, who liked to play softball and was pretty good at it.

Sport has helped so many of us in our personal battles against social and cultural bias. It forces us to treat others as equals—at least for as long as the game is on. It makes it hard to retain stereotypes by exposing us to individuals. Looked at another way, however, you might say that it's as much a part of the problem as the solution.

·

15. Clifford and Feezell, (1997, 64).
16. King Jr. (1992, 104).

Sport as the Wasteland of Discrimination

Sport does seem to be ahead of society in terms of discrimination — but only slightly. The Jim Crow mentality of "separate but equal" ended in sports long before it ended in schools. But then sports integration was based on exploitation. Jackie Robinson was hired by the Dodgers to improve the team, it wasn't (consciously) an act of affirmative action — an attempt to redress historical wrongs. And Robinson, like so many who followed in his footsteps, still faced rampant racism within the sport and without.

The sad thing is that rising minority participation in modern sports has not done much to alter the dynamics of exploitation. Minority athletes have done much for their universities to improve the quality and profitability of sports. But universities don't always make good on the promise of a solid education that is offered in exchange.[17]

Despite the highly publicized (and often inflated) salaries, professional sports have not done much better in terms of athlete exploitation. Phillip Hoose observes a kind of slave-plantation economics in several professional sports. Where else in the modern world do you have a business where the majority of the workers are black while the foremen (coaches), managers, owners and customers are almost exclusively white? Just the term 'owners' is disturbing when used in an industry where players are bought, sold, and traded.[18]

Pro sports continue to provide excuses and make efforts to resolve the racial disparity between the front-office and the defensive backfield, but meanwhile the plantation analogy seems hauntingly apt. It's funny how people complain about the inflated salaries of (often minority) players, but seldom criticize the wealth of team owners and managers. Why does it seem more appropriate for management to prosper from labor, than for labor to exploit the demand for its services? Does race have anything to do with this?

Some scholars believe that sports actually exacerbate the phenomena of racism by pointing out differences. After studying the phenomenon of race and sport in Germany, researchers Thomas Alkemeyer and Bernd Bröskamp concluded that sports promotes "strangerhood" — or

---

17. To be sure, the responsibility for getting that education lies primarily with the student, but some schools do little to ensure that student-athletes have the preparation, time, and resources to convert scholarships into valuable educations.

18. Hoose (1989, xxiv).

seeing others as essentially different and foreign.[19] It does this in a particularly visceral way by focusing on the body and therefore reducing cultural or personality differences to physical differences, at least in our popular imagination.

We're all familiar with sports-inspired stories of human difference: blacks have an extra muscle in their legs, Latinos have a chemical imbalance that makes them prone to anger, women's adaptation for childbirth makes them more tolerant of pain. The problem with attributing social and cultural differences to physical phenomena is that it makes strangerhood seem insurmountable; we will never see each other as equals because our differences are physical, unchangeable, and therefore irreconcilable.

The reality is that historically, even "scientific" studies about race and gender differences have been tainted by social prejudice.[20] And for all its internal emphasis on equality, sport is not immune to such diseases as racism and sexism. The first line of defense, as always, is awareness.

Thinking Activity: Sport, Society, and Equality
Question: Is Sport More or Less Biased than Society?
Observe: Selection for sports teams is usually based on try-outs. Selection for social positions such as jobs is usually made on the basis of interviews. Reverse these two systems for a second and imagine that candidates were interviewed for sports teams and given try-outs for jobs. Maybe you could imagine yourself interviewing candidates for a basketball team and having try-outs for a position as a stock broker.
Analyze: Is the race, sex, or ethnicity of the candidate more a factor in one system than in another, why? Would you be more likely to select a black person over a white person for your basketball team? How would the change in selection-system affect the quality of candidates?
Question Again: Should the race, sex, or ethnicity of the person who makes the selection make a difference?

11.2 The Hidden Power of Social Inequality

Are Minorities Taking Over Sports?

Most of us would like to believe that we have escaped from the petty social prejudices of our ancestors and our less-enlightened peers.

---

19. Alkemeyer and Broskamp (1996).
20. See Hoberman (1997, 143–186).

But sometimes we fail to notice things that are in plain-sight. Those who have been harmed by social prejudice often—but not always—are better at seeing bias in sport. For all of us, however, an awareness of the assumptions hidden behind our thoughts is needed. It's the only way to liberate ourselves from them.

Start by considering the apparently straightforward comment, "Blacks are taking over the NBA." On the face of it, this comment seems honest and uncontroversial. The number of black players has risen steadily to the point where they make up around 80% of the league's athletes today. The observation that relatively few coaches, managers, and owners are black does, in some sense, take away from the force of this statement. But people who say that blacks are 'taking over' are intentionally referring to the player population and the apparent "natural superiority" of black athletes.

To see the hidden assumptions behind the statement we need to take a closer look at just what it says. First, the verb 'to take over' is used when one group owns or controls something and another group seizes that control—as when one business takes over another (sometimes called a hostile take-over) or a dissident group takes over a government.

The point is that saying "Blacks are taking over the NBA" implies that someone (presumably not black) owns or controls that league, or basketball in general. Or, more precisely, it implies that some racial group owns or controls the sport. It may even suggest, indirectly, that one racial group is the *rightful* owner or controller of that sport and therefore this take-over is a cause for concern (or celebration, depending on which race you think is the sport's rightful owner).

To see this point more clearly, contrast the statement "Tall people are taking over the NBA." Why is this different? It seems just as obvious; even if you defined 'tall' as something like 'over 6 foot-5 inches,' you could probably show that more than 80 percent of players are tall. Tallness is something you're born with; it's genetic. Whether or not there are race-linked physiological factors that constitute an athletic advantage,[21] no one would dispute that tallness is a natural advantage in the sport of basketball. But neither does anyone suggest that this advantage is unfair.

---

21. Although there is widespread popular belief in the athletic superiority of the black race, science has had a hard time proving it, partly because it's hard to isolate the physical factors in athletic performance form others such as training, psychology, and environment, partly because it's difficult to find any single characteristic specifically linked to race—including skin color. See Hoberman (1997, 223).

So what's at the heart of the difference between the statements, "Blacks are taking over the NBA" and "Tall people are taking over the NBA"? The answer to this question seems to involve a lingering assumption of privilege and entitlement based on race. White males, at one time, could rely upon status and privilege to secure certain goods, including athletic goods. When such race-based entitlements are reduced or lost, it makes sense to say that things are being "taken over."

Less subtle in the racialized statement "Blacks are taking over the NBA" is the wistful belief that blacks are athletically superior to whites. Whether true or not, such a belief wields more damaging psychological power to blacks *and* whites alike than scientific evidence could ever justify.[22]

But the real difference between tallness and race as selecting factors in a sport like basketball is that tallness is a *sports-relevant* inequality, while race carries tons of *sports-irrelevant* social and historical baggage. As philosophical athletes, part of our task—and a central opportunity provided to us by sport—is to see beyond such social and historical bias and to view individuals as players from a sports point of view which doesn't itself make distinctions for race.

Philosophical Background:
The Struggle for Equality in America

The struggle for equality among women and racial minorities in sport simply reflects their social experience in America and beyond. African-Americans at one time legally counted for only 3/5 of a man—and that only if they were in fact male. Just as the equality of sport cannot erase racism, the achievement of equal political status—i.e. the right to vote and to be represented in government—has not meant true equality for many citizens.

In 1903, the African-American thinker W.E.B. Du Bois described poignantly the experience of achieving political equality only to face much more serious social barriers. He explains the ironic tension between American ideals and black social reality. On the one hand he was an American citizen, equal to others. But always this fact was second to the color of his skin:

---

22. As Begley (2000) shows, stereotypes can affect both academic and athletic performance.

It is a peculiar sensation, this double-consciousness, this sense of always looking at one's self through the eyes of others, of measuring one's soul by the tape of a world that looks on in amused contempt and pity. One ever feels his twoness, — an American, a Negro; two souls, two thoughts, two unreconciled strivings; two warring ideals in one dark body, whose dogged strength alone keeps it from being torn asunder.[23]

The idea that social minorities are equal but not equal is a troubling reality that flies in the face of the ideals of our social contract. Minorities' struggles for equal rights in countries supposedly founded on that ideal back up the observation made earlier that the parameters of equality — the decision about what the relevant qualities are — is a largely social decision made by those in charge. Contemporary African-American thinkers have argued, plausibly, that their groups were excluded from the free world's social contract. They have postulated a hidden racial contract in society — an agreement among the powerful to exclude those unlike them.[24]

What's important to remember, whether you agree with such theories or not, is that society looks different depending on who you are and where you stand. Those of us who are white can never imagine exactly how the world looks to our fellow citizens of color. Those of us who are female can never understand exactly what it's like to be male.

Equality doesn't mean being the same as your neighbor — it means being entitled to equal treatment where differences are irrelevant. And in this sense, equality is compatible with difference — with the diversity of styles, attitudes, and perspectives that various community members bring to the table.

Du Bois was concerned about how to preserve the cultural distinctiveness of his group while striving for equality. Malcom X advocated a kind of domestic cultural separatism that might preserve black identity while mitigating the effects of racism. And contemporary thinkers such as Cornel West have suggested that the perspectives particular to minority groups be assimilated into an improved popular consciousness that would at last reflect the richness of our social diversity. The challenge for the philosophical athlete is to preserve the benefits of diversity in sport while striving to break through the damaging effects of racism.

---

23. Du Bois (1995, 45).
24. See Mills (1997).

The Sad Truth About Stereotypes

Every once in a while a scientific study will come out that apparently validates the myth of black athletic superiority. It might be proved, for example, that African-Americans have a higher percentage of fast-twitch muscle fibers—a characteristic associated with speed. Regardless of whether such studies are valid or not, it seems that little good can come out of them.

It's important for athletes of all races to believe their athletic potential is roughly equal to their peers. Needless to say, it's important that their competitors believe the same thing. The reason is that even if the study *is* right, and *in general* African-Americans are to some degree superior in sprinting potential, nothing can be justly concluded from that about a particular athlete.

Short of testing the muscle fibers of each athlete individually, no one could conclude this black athlete is any faster than this white athlete. That's what the athletic *contest* is for. Whites are generally taller than Asians, too, but if you know nothing about me other than my race you can't conclude from that that I'm taller than your Asian friend.

The problem is, people *do* draw such individual conclusions—not so much about tallness, but about intelligence or athletic ability or other things that are socially weighted and potentially dangerous.

Stereotypes aren't identical to scientific studies, but they have the same prejudicial effect. And stereotypes are as present in sport as they are anywhere. Blacks are portrayed as undisciplined brutes who don't like to work but are blessed with natural talent. Said pro basketball player Isiah Thomas of the stereotype, "It's like I came dribbling out of my mother's womb."[25] Latinos are considered to be emotional and hot-tempered, naturally blessed with explosive speed. White athletes are characterized as physically inferior but able to succeed through brains and hard work.

Claims that such stereotypes derive from honest observation make no difference. Even if the stereotypes could be proved through objective scientific inquiry, they would never justify judgment of a particular individual. That's why it's called *pre-judice*—judging an individual before you've had the chance to collect the relevant data. What it amounts to is intellectual laziness—so it will probably never go out of style. What

---

25. Thomas is quoted in Hoose (1980, xviii).

250 THE PHILOSOPHICAL ATHLETE

philosophical athletes can do is be aware of the power of stereotypes and do our best to battle against them.

The psychological power of social stereotyping may not seem like a big deal—especially when the stereotype is positive as with Asian superiority in mathematical ability or black superiority in running and leaping. Even if stereotypes can risk becoming self-fulfilling prophesies, what's the danger of every African-American boy believing that he's destined for athletic greatness?

The danger is that self-prejudgment closes doors. Putting all one's eggs in a professional athletic basket is dangerous, not only because the risk of failure is astronomical but also because the commitment makes development in other areas all but impossible. Many thinkers worry that the exaltation of professional athletes in the African-American community exacerbates the lack of achievement in more conventional pursuits.[26] To be sure, black youth are inspired by Michael Jordan, but they are inspired to practice their jump-shots, not to open their books.

The myth of athletic superiority comes with the stigma of intellectual inferiority.[27] Ah yes, the "dumb jock" stereotype. By retaining a sense of intellectual superiority, whites are able to reconcile their social authority and privilege in the face of black athletic success. In this sense, even "positive" stereotypes can be destructive and must be resisted.

Thinking Activity: Sportscasters and Stereotypes
Question: Do television sportscasters perpetuate athletic stereotypes?
Observe: Watch one or more televised athletic contests in which athletes of various races participate. Keep a tally of the types of adjectives used by sportscasters to describe athletes of different races. Classify adjectives that suggest (1) natural talents (i.e. gifted, natural, blessed, size, speed, etc.) (2) hard work (i.e. persistent, tough, determined); (3) intelligence (i.e. smart, tactical, clever) and (4) emotions (hot-headed, passionate, a tinderbox).
Analyze: Do you find any correlation between race and the types of descriptions used? Does the correlation reflect the social stereotypes regarding that race?
Question Again: Assume that the sportscaster's descriptions just happen to be accurate, reflecting no racial bias. Should we worry that they reinforce stereotypes anyway?

---

26. Among these is Hoberman (1997, 3–27).

27. Hoberman (1997, 225) calls this the "Law of Compensation: which postulates an inverse relationship between mind and muscle, between athletic and intellectual development."

11.3 Equality in the Sports Contract

Philosophical Background:
Equality and the Veil of Ignorance

How can athletes get past the damaging and distorting affects of racism and sexism in sport? We might begin by adopting a "veil of ignorance." In his groundbreaking work, *A Theory of Justice,* John Rawls argues that equality would come naturally to any group of people seeking to establish a just community. Rawls builds upon the theory of a social contract by imagining what kinds of principles a group of free, rational and self-interested persons would adopt in forming a community. To eliminate all the circumstances irrelevant to the project of justice, Rawls stipulates that these principles be decided from behind a *veil of ignorance* that filters out all purely personal concerns.

The veil of ignorance is a hypothetical situation in which individuals are ignorant of their social situations—such factors as race, gender, class, career, or income. In addition, the individuals are ignorant of their "natural assets and abilities," such as intelligence, size, strength, and agility.

From this "original position," Rawls claims, rational free agents cannot help but make equality in the assignment of basic rights and duties a central principle of their just society:

> Since all are similarly situated and no one is able to design principles to fit his particular condition, the principles of justice are the result of a fair agreement or bargain.[28]

Like a group of children distributing cookies, we are naturally inclined to divide things evenly when no argument can be made for favoring one individual over another.

Rawls' intuition that equality is in some sense the elimination of concern about irrelevant human differences can be confirmed by performing our own thought experiment. Imagine that we are part of a small group of people locked inside a time machine. Say we know our races, genders, economic standing, SAT scores etc.—whatever differences determine advantages or disadvantages in our current society. The caveat is that we have no idea where in the world, or at what time in history, we will land. How would we treat each other then?

---

28. Rawls (1971, 12).

We can carry over the prejudices of the society we come from, but the situation might be reversed wherever we land. What if we find ourselves among an Amazon tribe of female warriors? What if we land in a place where blue-eyed people are enslaved? Will strength be valued over smarts in this new place? Wouldn't we be forced to see one another as equals once extracted from our particular societies?

Notice that Rawls' theory does not confuse equal opportunity with equal outcome—the idea is to begin as equals in the eyes of the community, just the way runners start their races from a common starting line. From there, relevant differences may manifest themselves in the form of social or economic advantages—just as differences in running ability manifest themselves within the race.[29]

Rawls shows that thinking people, deprived of any social or cultural basis by which to rationalize bias, would choose equality as in their own best interest. Philosophical athletes, as thinking people, should adopt their own veil of ignorance when considering questions of equality in sport.

Equal Opportunity in Sport

Imagine you're one of a group of athletes designing the rules for a contest in which you will all participate. For the sake of argument, let's say that it will be a running race. Given that everyone is free and rationally self-interested, each athlete will try to design the race to his or her own advantage. If you're a sprinter you'll propose a short race. If you're a poor runner you might want a handicapped (staggered) start. Maybe you have money and want to set things up so advantages can somehow be bought.

But wait. Behind the veil of ignorance, you're not allowed to know any personal information about your race, class, gender, skills or ability. You might even be paralyzed from the neck down and unable to run at all. Behind the veil of ignorance what kind of race would you agree to? You would agree to one that would give each competitor as equal a

---

29. But Rawls thinks that an agreement among equals will recognize that each person has certain "inviolable rights" that can't be overridden, even for general good. In this way he salvages individual rights from the ideals of traditional utilitarianism. The sacrifice or exploitation of an individual or group may promote the overall good—slavery, for example, can be a benefit to the economy—but a rational individual would never agree to it as long as there was the chance she might be the slave.

chance as possible. You'd design a race that looks very much like the races we have today.

This is because sports are already designed to provide equal opportunity to all competitors. In his seminal work on sports ethics, Warren Fraleigh gives equal opportunity for optimal performance the *highest* priority among guides for right action.[30] This means that insofar as you are a serious athlete, you treat others from the point of view of sport itself: as equals in all the relevant respects.

How do we know which respects are relevant to sport? Try looking at athletes from the point of view of the game itself: the constitutive rules. When the rules identify a player, what definition do they assume? Do they specify race, gender, or socioeconomic class? Better yet, imagine that you are a javelin being hurled into the air. When you land in the ground after so many meters, what matters to you about the person who threw you? Just that person's skill, strength, and timing. Sport gives us the chance to evaluate ourselves and others according to merit alone—but only if we first give sport the chance to do that by mentally transcending the social biases that pervade our world. It's as simple as taking the point of view of the ball.

Classes, Handicaps, and Economic Differences

Of course, sport as practiced in the real world is full of distinctions and differences. Athletes commonly compete in classes differentiated by gender, age, weight, or skill level. At one time they were also classified by race, but that distinction is no-longer (widely) accepted. When is such classing justified and when is it not?

Most classes are made in the effort to improve the quality (i.e. closeness) of competition. This is certainly the justification of handicapping in sports such as golf; it is a convention that accounts for different levels of skill in order to let players of varying ability enjoy a close game. It's important to notice, however, that handicaps are variable and based (ideally, at least) on sporting skill, not social categories.

Other distinctions, such as the one between amateurs and professionals, are based on factors extrinsic to sport and have frequently proved themselves worthless. Most Olympic sports have eliminated the distinction while those that retain it, such as the National Collegiate Athletic Association, struggle constantly to define it.

---

30. Fraleigh (1984, 114).

Age-group distinctions can function like handicaps, especially in events such as marathons, triathlons, and cross-country ski races where there may be thousands of competitors and only one absolute winner. It is important, however, that age not be used to *prohibit* an athlete from competing for the absolute prize.[31]

An "unofficial" distinction that often does exclude an athlete from competition is wealth. Costs for required equipment, entry fees, facility use, coaching, and transportation can be exorbitant. Furthermore, in much of the world, economic distinctions manifest themselves along racial lines. The result is a lack of diversity in expensive sports such as equestrian, sailing, and motor racing. To keep economic differences from being a threat to equality, many sports develop grassroots programs and adjust rules to defray costs.

Seeing Beyond Social Prejudice

Equality, then, is a central value of our sports contract. Philosophers have shown that equality is essential to the project of designing a just community. The intrinsic egalitarianism of sports' constitutive rules has borne out that ideal, even while sport serves to distinguish differences among people.

We have also seen that the reality of equality in sport, just like the reality of equality in politics, is threatened by social bias and stereotyping. Sport has been and continues to be infected by irrelevant social prejudices and concerns. On the other hand sport is often ahead of society in the task of rising above unfounded bias. The sense of equality embedded in sports' logic can help philosophical athletes to discern the social prejudices that obscure human judgment in so many ways.

It is naive to think that any of us is immune from the biases of our society; those who deny racism or sexism are among the most likely to be entangled in its web. In order to overcome prejudicial thinking, we must first admit to our tendency toward it. Fortunately for us, sports participation does much to dispel harmful stereotypes. It allows us—

---

31. In such sports as women's gymnastics and figure skating, minimum age requirements have prohibited the best athletes from competing for championships. While there certainly are valid (paternalistic) concerns about the exploitation of children athletes, it seems wrong from the point of view of sport to exclude a potential winner on the basis of age.

sometimes even forces us—to see through to the reality of individual merit.

Sport provides the opportunity to see what you can do, free from social perceptions. It even provides the opportunity to experience cultures different from our own. Sport itself is enriched by the variety of styles and interpretations brought to it. But all these opportunities exist only insofar as we are willing as athletes to liberate ourselves from prejudice about social and cultural differences irrelevant to sport.

Thinking Activity: Sport from Behind a Veil of Ignorance

Question: Do irrelevant interests affect your sport?

Observe: Form a group of 3–4 people who will invent a new sport. Base the sport on something like soccer in which a ball is put into a goal, then have each person suggest a rule about how the game will be scored, whether style will count or not, whether you can use your hands or not. First suggest the rules based on what would give you personally an advantage. Next, revise your rules from "behind a veil of ignorance"—a position in which you know nothing about anyone's strengths and weaknesses, including your own.

Analyze: How are the two games you invented different? Which one do you think is better as a sport? Which one is more like the sports we have today?

Question Again: Can you think of rules in sports today that reflect the personal biases of the rule-makers?

Chapter Review

Summary

Equality is an ideal treasured in almost every conception of a just community, including sports-communities. Of course human differences cannot be ignored, so equality for us must be limited to certain relevant respects. In sport the relevant respects are easy to decipher—teams have an equal number of players, competitors are given an equal amount of time, goals and running lanes are of equal dimension. In sport, we strive to give athletes equal opportunity to display relevant differences of ability.

Sport is not immune, however, to the stereotypes and prejudices that infect society. By trying to view each other with the unbiased eye of sport, we might learn to overcome such prejudices and to further the ideal of equality in our lives.

Further Reading

Philosophy

Aristotle. 1984. *Nicomachean Ethics*. In *Complete Works*, edited by Jonathan
    Barnes. Princeton, NJ: Princeton University Press, 1729–1867. See book
    III for Aristotle's distinction between numerical and human equality.
Du Bois, William Edward Burghardt. 1995. *The Souls of Black Folk*. New
    York: Penguin. Published in 1903, this is a touching and prophetic classic
    of African-American thought, as relevant today as the day it was written.
Plato. 1992. *Republic*. Translated by G.M.A. Grube. Indianapolis, IA: Hack-
    ett. *The* classic work in social-political philosophy. See book 5 for the dis-
    cussion of relevant differences and the inclusion of women in the military
    and other traditionally male aspects of society.
Rawls, John. 1971. *A Theory of Justice*. Cambridge, MA: Harvard University
    Press. This book is a contemporary classic. An overview of the theory, in-
    cluding the veil or ignorance, can be found in chapter III, section 24.

Philosophy of Sport

Alkemeyer, Thomas and Bernd Broskamp. 1996. "Strangerhood and Racism
    in Sports." *Sport Science Review*, v. 5, n. 2: 30–52. This scholarly article
    condemns sports' role in emphasizing racial and ethnic differences, thereby
    exacerbating stereotypes.
Hoberman, John. 1997. *Darwin's Athletes: How Sport has Damaged Black
    America and Preserved the Myth of Race*. Boston: Houghton Mifflin.
    This enlightening look at the history of sport and race really helps us to
    gain perspective on the situation in which we find ourselves today. Hober-
    man makes clear, for example, that doubts about athletes' intelligence are
    at least partially motivated by a need to justify white social privilege.
Hoose, Phillip M. 1989. *Necessities: Racial Barriers in American Sports*. New
    York: Random House. Hoose offers an accessible overview of the phe-
    nomenon of racial stereotyping in American sport. The book contains in-
    terviews with athletes and interpretations of events such as Al Campanis'
    claim that blacks don't have the "necessities" to manage pro sports.

Journalism and Literature

Begley, Sharon. 2000. "The Stereotype Trap." *Newsweek*, November 6,
    66–68. This is a short and accessible review of psychological studies that
    show how stereotypes affect academic and athletic performance.
Price, S.L. 1997. "What Ever Happened to the White Athlete?" *Sports Illus-
    trated*, December 8, 30–51. This is a clear article that uses statistical sur-
    veys and questionnaires to explore the demise of white participation in
    American sport.

Chapter 12

Fairness

Chapter Preview

Introduction:
Title IX

> *In this age of woman's movements, few people have realized yet that the movement which is doing most for womankind is centered in our High Schools. A new type of girl has sprung up in our country. A girl more perfect mentally, morally, and physically than the girl of twenty years ago. This is the basket ball girl. Many are her detractors; numerous are her critics, but her champions and supporters see in her the future greatness of American womanhood.*
>
> —A Kokomo High School Student, 1909

Among the hottest controversies in modern sport is Title IX—a law that has provided athletic resources to women, sometimes by taking them from men. In a college-sports world where men outperform women, generate more revenue, and have greater professional prospects, one may ask why female athletes should receive similar support. The short answer is because it's the law. But is such a mandate *fair?*

Title IX of the Educational Amendments Act of 1972 prohibits exclusion, denial of benefits, or discrimination on the basis of sex in any *educational program* that receives funding from the federal government. The crucial assumption made in applying Title IX to school athletic programs is that those programs are educational. Arguably, any program maintained by a school, whether it be theatre, music, computer science, or philosophy, should be justified in terms of its educational value.

It's non-controversial that educational resources such as library books and math classes should be evenly distributed between the sexes,

257

but sport seems to many to be a separate sort of case. For starters, the physical differences between males and females mandate separate classes of competition. Furthermore, interest and ability have traditionally been much greater on the men's side.

Not surprisingly the NCAA argued initially that Title IX should not apply to athletics.[1] But how can colleges and universities defend their sponsorship of athletics at all if they're not part of the institution's educational mission? Eventually the NCAA ended its resistance to Title IX and began to demand that its member-schools at least make progress toward compliance with the law. Unfortunately, this "progress" has sometimes eliminated opportunities in "minor" men's sports such as wrestling or swimming. These men often think they are losing scholarships to women, when it's just as true that they are losing them to "major" men's sports such as football and basketball. Remember the statute *prohibits* discrimination on the basis of sex.

The problem with Title IX is not so much sex discrimination as it is lack of funds. In a perfect world, women's sports would simply be added to existing men's programs. But resources are scarce—so the question goes back to fair distribution. In sport, rewards are distributed according to performance in open competition. In business, salaries are paid according to revenue generated. In college sports, men seem to possess the advantage in both such categories.

But colleges are neither sports leagues nor businesses—they are educational institutions. Therefore, in Title IX, considerations of ability and revenue are irrelevant (at least in principle). Since the goods in question are opportunities for participation rather than prizes awarded for success in competition, the fact that men generally outperform women athletically or the fact that men's programs sometimes generate more revenue should not guide decisions; educational values should.

In terms of educational value, is a wrestling program really less worthwhile than a jayvee football team? The answers to such questions may not be clear. What is clear is that these are the sorts of questions that should be asked. Title IX, above all else, reminds us to view scholastic sports as educational programs and to make decisions about the distribution of sports resources according to educational concerns. It is a reminder we needed to have.

---

1. Polidoro (2000, 142).

We have already seen that sport can value equality even while it celebrates and rewards differences. But can it be *fair* while distributing resources according to performances that are influenced by such involuntary factors as gender, talent, and genetic inheritance? When divisions are made in sport—between male and female competition for example—does one division deserve more opportunities, accolades, or resources than the other? What happens when the internal logic of sport collides with our social sensibilities about justice and fairness?

Chapter Preview List

- What is meaning of equal opportunity in sport?
- Can sport reward for merit and still be fair?
- Should sport compensate for inequities or even handicaps among athletes?

12.1 Fair Play in the Sports Contract

Fair Play and Open Competition

Sport is famous for—and justly proud of—its improbable success stories: athletes who overcome social obscurity to achieve worldwide recognition and admiration. In ancient times, sport gave Roman gladiators the chance to transcend their status as slaves. And in 1973, when Billie Jean King defeated Bobby Riggs in tennis' battle of the sexes, she redefined the popular idea of what women could do. There is perhaps no other area of human endeavor in which success has been open to so many as in sport.

This fact is testament to the central value of *fair play* in the sporting contract, a value given force and incentive by constitutive rules and, in an important way, isolated from the corrupting influences of society. Race, class, and economic status are not officially factors in sport. Athletic success (at least in most sports) can be had by almost anyone, unlike success in such areas as business, academia, or politics.

Fair play in sport is based on two interdependent principles: equality of opportunity and reward according to merit. When claims of unfairness are made—it's almost always when someone was denied the opportunity to compete, or a reward was given to an "undeserving" individual. A close look at competitive rules also reinforces fair-play values: competitors start out on equal footing and expect to be rewarded according to demonstrated merit.

It's important to notice, when considering fair play, that the requirement of equal opportunity is primary. To find the best athlete in any sport, we first maximize the pool of participants, then distribute additional opportunities and material rewards according to performance in open competition. Envision the structure of a single-elimination tournament, any of the masses of first-round competitors can forge a path to the championship on the basis of demonstrated merit.

But merit-based selection is only justified as long as no one has been arbitrarily excluded from the lowest level of entry.[2] Forced exclusion from competitions such as the Olympic games has a direct impact on the perceived worth of the victories earned. Unfortunately, the theoreti-

---

2. Even Nozick (1974), who defends entitlement, recognizes that it is compromised when people are unfairly excluded from competition.

cal ideal of everyone having access to sports' greatest prizes is impracti-
cal. But sports communities must realize that when selections for opportunities are made outside of competition the ideals of fair play are
threatened by the possibility for "contamination" from external factors
such as race or social class. The effort to stick to the ideal of fair play in
sport requires us to minimize those barriers and thereby maximize the
chance of finding deserving victors.

Philosophical Background:
The Utility of Equal Opportunity

Title IX is a contentious issue less because it deals with gender and
sport than because it concerns the distribution of scarce resources. This
is always the biggest challenge to the ideal of equality in any just society. The intuitive mandate for numerical equality among citizens (one
person, one share) becomes a problem just as soon as there aren't
enough goods to go around.

When beliefs about equality meet the realities of scarcity, fairness
becomes less an issue of equal distribution than the best form of unequal distribution. How is that to be determined? French philosopher
Jean-Jacques Rousseau believed that the fairest distribution would be
closest to distribution in nature—an idea that suggests Darwinian competition.[3] Indeed, opportunities such as starting positions, college slots,
and jobs are awarded according to competition. It serves the egalitarian
ideal by providing equal opportunity while profitably utilizing inequalities in talent, training, skill, and motivation to select the best candidates
for given positions and improve society as a whole.

Plato saw the utility of equal opportunity and open competition and
used it in *Republic* to justify the inclusion of women in the guardian
class:

> If the male sex is seen to be different from the female with regard
> to a particular craft or way of life, we'll say that the relevant one
> must be assigned to it. But if it's apparent that they differ only in
> this respect, that females bear children while males beget them,
> we'll say that there has been no kind of proof that women are dif-

---

3. Rousseau (1967, 246).

ferent from men with respect to what we're talking about, and we'll continue to believe that our guardians and their wives must have the same way of life.[4]

Not everyone in history has been so open minded about women, of course. More often, Rousseau's principle of natural selection has combined with social assumptions about "natural superiority" to work *against* the ideal of equal opportunity.

The 18th century philosopher Mary Wollstonecraft argued that Rousseau himself made such an error when he claimed in *Emile or a Treatise on Education* that the purpose of a woman's education was to make her as pleasing as possible to men. Wollstonecraft agreed with the egalitarian philosophy of Locke and Rousseau, but insisted that it be accompanied by an assumption of gender equity. After all, Rousseau's assumptions about the "natural" inferiority of females could only be confirmed if both genders were offered equal socialization and equal education. Says Wollstonecraft,

> Girls and boys, would play harmlessly together if the distinction of sex was not inculcated long before nature makes any difference.[5]

Reflecting Plato's logic for opening the military to women, Wollstonecraft argues that the exclusion of girls from practical education deprives the community of potentially great leaders. Her ideas were echoed the following century by John Stuart Mill, the same man who wrote *On Liberty*. Mill's *On the Subjection of Women* makes a utilitarian argument on behalf of a woman's right to compete socially with men. Noting that queens rule with no less skill and effectiveness than kings, Mill claims that society only harms itself by excluding women from the most important social offices.

Rousseau, Plato, Wollstonecraft and Mill were all arguing for the values of fair play: equal opportunity and reward according to merit. What the latter two observed was that the scarce resource of opportunity is not always distributed according to these principles—even by those who espouse them. This is because social and cultural assumptions about the "nature" of certain groups of people are used to justify their exclusion from open competition. Can our sporting contract improve on the social contract in this category?

---

4. Plato, *Republic*, 454de.
5. Wollstonecraft (1790, 81).

Does Sport Provide Equal Opportunity?

At first glance, equal opportunity appears to be a given in sport. There's a fundamental assumption that everyone who has the desire to compete should and will be given the chance. In the eyes of the rules, everyone can play, at some level, and anyone capable of performing the activity can be a player.

Gender is rarely a barrier to participation in sport these days but sex-segregation persists. Males and females play in separate leagues, run different distances, use different-sized balls, and in some cases play different versions of the same game (i.e. baseball and softball). Does such segregation violate the principle of equal opportunity?

It seems consistent with the logic of sport to use age, size, and sex as *classifications* in the effort to enhance competition, as long as they don't become a barrier to participation at the highest level. Rather than reserving a sport such as field hockey for women, a team should be created for men. Or, if appropriate, mixed teams should be developed. Title IX has allowed girls to participate in high school football and boys to play field hockey with the girls.

But gender segregation is unfair if it excludes one sex from competing for the highest prizes against the other. According to the United States Cycling Federation rules, women may compete with men of the same category (skill class) or a category lower, if they so choose.[6] This rule allows an exceptional woman athlete to seek out the challenge (and greater prize money) of men's races without forcing her to race against men all the time.

In many sports, however, women and men aren't even allowed to test themselves against the same standards. Their races cover different distances, their game balls and throwing hammers are different sizes. Until recently, women weren't even allowed to throw the hammer, compete in the pole vault, or run the marathon. The problem with these restrictions is that they deny athletes the opportunity to compare their performances in truly open competition.

There may be reasons to keep things that way, given the social humiliation of being beaten by a woman. Such humiliation has been cited as an argument against high-school wrestling in some states, where athletes are divided only by weight-class. The boys say wrestling a girl is a

---

6. United States Cycling Federation 2000 Rulebook, p. 19. Rule 1H2. Men don't have the same luxury because, theoretically, they can seek better competition in a higher category.

no-win situation because if you lose you lost to a girl, and if you win you only beat a girl. As a result, many boys forfeit their matches rather than face the challenge. But how can this be good for sport? From the mat's point of view, if you win you beat a wrestler and if you lose you lost to a wrestler, period. The rest is social bias.

But if it seems wrong to restrict women to competing only against each other, it may also be wrong to deprive men of a gender-specific category. Perhaps women need the lighter equipment and shorter distances to encourage greater participation. Perhaps men need a place to play alone. In any case there should be some standard class with standard measurements of excellence that views men and women equally as athletes, because from the point of view of sport that's all they are.

Providing the opportunity to compete on equal terms is not to say that women's performances should be measured in terms of men's performances; men are not the yardstick, the yardstick is the yardstick. Objective measurements of individuals that can be compared to each other regardless of gender seem to be dictated by the internal logic of sport, and a provision that would be made in any sporting contract formed from behind a veil of ignorance. Women's and men's classes should remain to preserve the sporting value of close competition, just like age-classes and handicaps do, but they should not be used to exclude athletes from the opportunity of testing themselves against the best.

Are Female Athletes Attractive?

In some ways it seems that women athletes have transcended social prejudice. They compete for athletic scholarships and have opportunities to play in professional leagues.[7] Sports participation no longer leads to assumptions about sexual orientation. The 1999 Women's World Cup Soccer Tournament filled stadiums and captivated a television audience. Its champions, the American team, were honored both by *Sports Illustrated* and by *Glamour* magazine. The athlete is considered by many to be the new paradigm of feminine beauty

Audiences marvel when female jocks appear on evening award shows, decked out in sexy dresses, high heels, and make-up. Men fork over their hard-earned money to buy fund-raising calendars of partially-

---

7. Shulman and Bowen (2001, 155) observe, however, that these "advantages" have a downside. Many of the problems that plague big-time men's collegiate sports (i.e. academic underperformance) are now starting to surface with women's teams.

nude world class athletes. The Associated Press described one such calendar of American track and field athletes as making "Victoria's Secret models look matronly." A high jumper who appeared in the calendar said, "This is not a calendar of bimbos. These are world-class athletes with brains. Don't try to argue otherwise."[8] The fact that female athletes exploit their looks for money, the fact that they can play soccer but still feel feminine and attractive—these are welcome changes from the days when beauty and athleticism were considered mutually exclusive for women.

But what's disturbing about the question "Are female athletes attractive?" is the very assumption that it matters at all! The hockey puck doesn't care about the size of your breasts. The word "attractive" puts others into control because "being attractive" is a *passive* phrase. When female athletes worry about their attractiveness they stray from the ideals of sport and the opportunities it provides to transcend such social concerns. Even when women athletes use their attractiveness to get the camera's attention and the lucrative endorsement contract, they are wielding a kind of power that betrays the real power cultivated within sport.

Thinking Activity: The Limitations of Female Athletes
Question: Will a woman ever play in the Super Bowl?
Observe: We don't know just what women can do yet. Women's sport is in its infancy, its performances are derived from a relatively small gene-pool who suffer social disapproval for their participation, not to mention inferior funding, coaching, and facilities. Even the biological evidence for male athletic superiority is unconvincing when compared with "medical evidence," accepted in the late 19th and early 20th centuries, that blacks were physically inferior to whites and in danger of extinction.
Analyze: Is there a way to isolate athletic potential and performance from social consideration? Our mammalian kin, race horses, are presumably less affected by social pressures. Fillies usually race in their own class and marginally under-perform the colts, but some exceptional females have made it to racing's triple crown. Winning Colors was the first filly to win a triple-crown race, can women athletes be far behind?
Question Again: How can female athletes minimize the effect of social pressures on their self-perception and performance?

Although sport itself is intrinsically egalitarian, our worldwide sports culture reflects the gender bias of society. Think about the sports-

---

8. Quotes appeared in *The Women's Sports Experience,* vol. IX, no. 2, p. 4.

metaphor of "scoring" being used to describe sexual domination.[9] Think about the troubling phenomenon of male coaches sexually advancing on female athletes. Think about the widespread occurrence of body-image diseases such as anorexia nervosa that affect so many female athletes.

Fortunately, sport's intrinsic fairness gives philosophical athletes the chance to rise above society's sexism.

12.2 Rewards, Merit, and Entitlement

Competition and Reward According to Merit

In effect, the purpose of competition is to establish desert—as in who *deserves* to play and who *deserves* to win. As with opportunities, there are often more deserving individuals than there are rewards to go around. A large pool of dedicated and hardworking athletes compete for playing time, prize money, scholarships, and salaries. Even if we agree to distribute such rewards according to merit and desert, how can we do so fairly, especially when some athletes are male and some are female?

On the face of it, fair play would dictate that everyone have an equal opportunity to compete for such scarce resources as slots on the football team. But the obvious objection to that kind of sex "integration" in sport is that women, "the weaker sex," would lose out in open competition. Giving them the "equal opportunity" to make a single football or basketball team would only lead to a *de-facto* exclusion on the basis of physical weakness.

So, in the spirit of equal opportunity, schools provide separate teams that offer an equal number of slots for men and women. It's not enough to provide an equal number of teams, since teams for sports such as football, open only to men, are much larger than a corresponding team in, say, women's soccer. As a result, smaller men's sports such as wrestling have been cut as schools try to equalize the number of opportunities for men and women while preserving their football teams.

Suddenly it doesn't seem fair that a male wrestler of the highest athletic merit should be denied his opportunity to compete so that a slot can be created for a female swimmer, who may not be skilled or even interested in serious competition. Heck, the wrestler might even be able

---

9. An issue explored by Mariah Burton Nelson (1994, ch. 5).

to out swim this woman. But the key question here is whether *athletic* merit should be the deciding factor in how opportunities for participation are distributed. As we noted earlier, college sports are *educational* resources and should be distributed according to relevant educational criteria, rather than pure athletic merit.

But what about the distribution of other goods in sport? Do women athletes deserve "equal pay for equal work"? Do professional athletes deserve their astronomical salaries? Are resources justly distributed within the sports community?

Philosophical Background:
Desert and Entitlement

According to some philosophers, the first thing to consider in determining the fairness of merit-based distribution is the perspective of the least-advantaged member of the community. Since we all (theoretically) sacrifice some natural freedom to enter the social contract, doesn't each of us deserve at least some benefit?[10] Keeping this perspective in mind, John Rawls developed his second principle of justice, the difference principle, which holds that social and economic inequalities are only just when they benefit *everyone* in a community, particularly the least-advantaged members.[11] It's a species of the rising tide principle that says you should only pump more water into the bay if it helps to float all the boats higher, not just your own.

Rawls observes that even in the most just societies, natural differences of ability among individuals will yield certain social and economic inequalities which eventually result in unequal life-prospects. These inequalities can only be justified by greater benefit for all. Hence the social and economic advantages enjoyed by doctors are "fair" as long as they result in top-flight medicine, which benefits the entire society. Even the least advantaged members of society would suffer if medicine were not allowed to flourish.

The general idea is that you only ought to gain from your natural ability and talent as long as you compensate by also benefiting others in the community. But philosopher Robert Nozick questions whether the better endowed members of society would consider Rawls' principle to

---

10. Rousseau (1967, 230) says those with no property to protect must get something else out of social membership.

11. Rawls (1971, p. 14 and section 13).

be fair.[12] Instead of observing society from a bird's-eye view as Rawls does, Nozick focuses on individuals and what resources they are *entitled to*—that is, what they can justly call their own. Nozick's *theory of entitlement*, has three simple principles:

1. A person who acquires a holding in accordance with the principle of justice in acquisition is entitled to that holding.

2. A person who acquires a holding in accordance with the principle of justice in transfer from someone else entitled to that holding, is entitled to the holding.

3. No one is entitled to a holding except by (repeated) applications of 1 and 2.[13]

For Nozick, distributive justice amounts to everyone being entitled to what they have justly acquired. He feels that the system should allow individuals to profit freely from their skills and talents, without being compelled to benefit others as Rawls demands.

Nozick illustrates his idea with a hypothetical example of basketball fans paying 25 cents out of every basketball ticket directly to Wilt Chamberlin. The special consideration paid to Wilt is justly acquired and deserved. According to Nozick, society should not be allowed to *re*distribute resources except in cases of unjust acquisition or transfer. Resources won in fair and open competition (or by gifts of inheritance) are entitlements—not to be disturbed by government idealists.

Entitlement to just deserts versus obligation to the larger group—these two principles are in tension during any discussion of fairness.

Fair Distribution of Material Rewards

Once equal opportunity for participation is secured in a sports community, material rewards such as scholarships, prizes, and salaries can be distributed according to merit. Arguably, this system benefits the entire community by encouraging excellence. The criteria for merit will depend on whether the sports community is professional or educational. In either case, however, there are legitimate questions about entitlement and benefit to others that have to be addressed.

---

12. Nozick (1974, ch. 7) says the term 'distributive justice' is misleading because there's no central distribution. In reality, we're talking about *re*distribution of resources.

13. Nozick (1974, 151).

The simplest form of material reward in sport is of course the victory prize or purse and there is little dispute that this rightly goes to the victor. Questions may arise, however, about how such rewards are to be split among the team. Professional cycling teams are often run like the old whaling ships with each member receiving some fraction of the total haul. Team leaders often remit their own share of the winnings back into the general pot as a sign of gratitude to the team. Such gestures are hardly altruistic. Leaders expect to be repaid in terms of loyalty, and the costs are offset by higher salaries and endorsement contracts.

This brings up another hot issue: pro athletes' entitlement to their enormous salaries. In some sports, star athletes receive huge sums of money. Even after we consider that these individuals are among the very best in their chosen field, that they have only a few years to cash in on a lifetime of dedication to sport, and that the contract amounts are inflated by agents' and lawyers' fees, the amounts seem too large. Are athletes really *entitled* to such riches just for playing a game?

Another look at Nozick's Wilt Chamberlin example might put the question in perspective. Nozick imagined that if fans would pay an extra quarter just to see Wilt play, then he was entitled to those proceeds. The reality of pro sports salaries is not so different. The athletes aren't paid simply for playing the game; if they played the game behind closed doors, they wouldn't earn a cent. What they receive is a percentage of the revenue generated by the *business* of professional sports. Why shouldn't they be allowed to negotiate the worth of their labor in a free market, just as movie-stars and corporate CEOs do? If a ticket price goes up to pay an athlete's salary (and fans still buy the ticket) the athlete seems entitled to those funds.

Should Men and Women Athletes Be Paid Equally?

One fact rarely mentioned in the debate over sports salaries is the fact that these riches go almost exclusively to male athletes. Is this fair? Is it a violation of Title IX? Whatever happened to the principle of equal pay for equal work? Some people say that what's refreshing about women's sports is that the athletes aren't money-grubbers. They play for low salaries or the pure love of the game. Does this mean they wouldn't take the money if it was there?

First of all, Title IX *does* demand that sports resources such as scholarships, equipment, and publicity be divided proportionately among men's and women's teams. But Title IX applies *only* to educational institutions receiving federal funds and justifies those mandates in educational terms. Professional leagues such as the Women's National Basketball Association have certainly benefited from Title IX-inspired reforms, but they are not regulated by it—any more than General Motors is.

Professional sports leagues are for-profit enterprises and therefore justified in distributing their resources according to free-market principles. Should WNBA salaries be equal to those in the NBA? Only in the event that WNBA *revenues* are equal. By the same token, female athletes in such sports as professional ice-skating may be able to justify higher salaries than men based on their greater spectator appeal. It is not an issue of equal pay for equal work. Such demands would be akin to an apprentice actor demanding a fee equal to that of a box-office superstar like Brad Pitt for playing the same role.

A related, but not identical issue is disparities in prize money for competitions with men's and women's classes. This has been an issue in professional tennis as well as other, less visible, sports. Of all grand-slam tennis events, the U.S. Open was first to offer equal prize money to men and women. Wimbledon and others that continue to offer unequal prizes often cite the fact that men's matches are longer as reason for the superior pay. This seems unfair given that this difference is stipulated by the rules and out of the control of the players themselves. Again, there's no intrinsic reason why women should play a different game than men.

Thinking Activity: Entitled Advantages in Sport
Question: To what competitive advantages are athletes entitled in sport?
Observe: Make a list of sports advantages that can be gained with money or social connections (including performance-enhancing substances, services, equipment, etc.)
Analyze: Reexamine your list to determine which you think are entitlements, not to be tampered with e.g. Gains made by access to weight training vs. gains made through expensive dietary supplements.
Question Again: Does allowing those advantages help or harm the situation of the least advantaged athletes

---

The relevant criterion in professional sports should be revenue generated—not athletic merit. In sports where *no revenue* is generated, a local 10K race for example, there seems to be little justification for unequal prize-money. As long as some athletes are barred from open competition, disparities in prize money can't be justified according to performance. A plausible solution, sometimes employed in sports such as triathlon, is to make all competitors eligible for prizes in an open competition, while providing additional rewards for women and certain age-groups. The point is to make equal opportunity prior to selections based on merit, then to use classes to encourage participation and close-competition—all key values of any sports community.

12.3 What Are the Limits of Fairness?

Should Sport Compensate for Inequities?

Thousands of golfers use carts everyday to play the game they love. They are not incapable of walking the length of the course—in fact it would be better for most of them health-wise to leave the cart behind. Yet when fellow golfer Casey Martin asked to use a cart in tournament play, an unexpected cry arose from the cart-jockey masses: Casey's request was *unfair!*

Perhaps only those who use a cart can say how much of an advantage it provides, but Casey's case seemed special. Born with a degenerative disease that makes walking long distances impossible, Casey argued that he needed the cart to compensate for his involuntary defect. The cart, he argued, would put him on a level playing field with his competitors. It would actually give him a fair chance.

The Martin case raises several interesting questions, not least of which is whether fairness requires special compensation for the disadvantaged. We have seen that the intrinsic fairness of sport is constantly corrupted by social prejudice in the real world. In this sense sport seems to resemble other kinds of social practices, such as education and economics, in which the removal of legal barriers has been insufficient to provide truly equal opportunity. In society, calls to end segregation and discrimination are often accompanied by calls for "affirmative action," a general term referring to various programs that actively promote opportunities for disadvantaged groups. The idea is that positive action must be taken to compensate for the historical and continued disadvantage of the underprivileged.[14]

---

14. Such programs can be controversial because they seem to violate the ideal of equal protection under the law. According to Hall (1992, 357), proponents argue that affirmative action promotes equality by making "more equal in law the less equal in life."

Because they reward according to merit, sports have fared well in the battle against racial prejudice. But what are we to say of desert outside of athletic merit? Shouldn't everyone have the opportunity to participate, regardless of ability to perform? Can't compensations be made to render lesser athletes competitive? Social benefits, such as voting, cannot be denied to a citizen based on race, sex, color, creed or even literacy. What about the benefits of sport? Should measures to encourage women and the physically disabled—who may never be able to compete equally—be taken by sport?

Philosophical Background:
Affirmative Action

We have seen that the ideals of equal opportunity and reward according merit have been limited in reality by who is and who is not considered a full citizen. This fact raises a big question about just what "fair competition" is—and whether it's even possible in real-world societies.

Nozick admits that we're not entitled to the ill-gotten gains of such means as theft, fraud, slavery, and excluding others from competition. Keeping in mind that unjust acquisition at any point in the chain of transfer taints the entire chain, can you say that every coin in your pocket traveled a completely just route from the mint to you? What about property originally taken from Native Americans? What about wealth accumulated through slavery? What about educational opportunities once distributed according to race or class?[15] Can anything be fairly won in imperfect social competition?

Most of the historical barriers to fair competition in society—exclusions based on sex, race, ethnicity, even socioeconomic class—have been legally eliminated. But members of these groups continue to lag behind in competition for goods such as education, income, and political power. To what can we attribute these groups' apparent failure?

If the competition were fair, then it might reflect some kind of deficiency in preparation or natural ability. But just what would it take for social competition to truly be fair? Advocates of affirmative action believe that the removal of legal barriers cannot by itself level the social playing field. Fairness requires actively offering opportunities to the disadvantaged.

---

15. Nozick (1974, 153) says he knows of no sophisticated treatment of such issues.

The experience of women and racial minorities in America is testament to this claim. Three centuries of feminist thought has inspired many changes, but women still lag behind in "open competition" against men. Wollstonecraft's dream of equal education is as close to reality as possible and yet girls still trail boys in such subjects as math and science.

Could women's status as a "second sex" in fact be justified by biology? Scientific studies suggest important physiological and hormonal differences between the sexes. Perhaps there are still social factors holding women and minorities back. What should society's response be to all this? Is affirmative action required to "level the playing field" for disadvantaged groups?

As with liberty and equality, fairness is a simple ideal that becomes exceedingly complicated in real life. Where distributive justice relies upon fair competition in its effort to distribute goods according to merit, social prejudices and economic advantages threaten to fix the race before it is run. Even if inequities are based on accidents of birth or inheritance, it is an open question whether society should compensate for them. Affirmative action has made some progress toward the goal of fair play in society—can it do the same for sport?

Should Sport Adapt to Women, or Should Women Adapt to Sport?

In 1991, Mariah Burton Nelson wrote a book called *Are We Winning Yet? How Women Are Changing Sports and Sports Are Changing Women*. Her subtitle really hits the issue on the head. The massive increase in female sports participation has indeed changed women in many positive ways. It has given them, among other things, a place where they can transcend their *alerity*—French philosopher Simone De Beauvoir's word for the otherness that pervades women's experience of themselves in the world. The question is: Is this for the better?

Sport in many ways has allowed women to retain the active exuberance that they all had as young girls. In the *Second Sex* (written in 1949), De Beauvoir poignantly describes the way young girls' bodies are turned against them by society.[16] She notes that girls start out active but face a future of passivity beginning at adolescence when their activity is curtailed by social ideas about clothing and appropriate activities. Their body changes are seen as a handicap: breasts, menstruation, and

---

16. De Beauvoir (1949, 306–312).

increases in fat are thought to make girls unsuited for physical effort. This perceived physical weakness leads to real weakness, by keeping her inactive and sapping her self-confidence:

> This lack of physical power leads to a more general timidity: she has no faith in a force she has not experienced in her body; she does not dare to be enterprising, to revolt, to invent; doomed to docility, to resignation, she can take in society only a place already made for her. She regards the existing state of affairs as something fixed. [...] Not to have confidence in one's body is to lose confidence in oneself.[17]

At this point there is nothing for the young girl to do but wait, passively, to become the possession of a man. De Beauvoir points out that her future will not be actively conquered, but passively given over to a "new master."[18] De Beauvoir proposes sport as the antidote to this tragic female demise:

> Most professions call for no greater energy than woman can offer. And in sports the end in view is not success independent of physical equipment; it is rather the attainment of perfection within the limits of each physical type: the featherweight boxing champion is as much a champion as is the heavyweight; the woman skiing champion is not the inferior of the faster male champion: they belong to two different classes. It is precisely the female athletes who, being positively interested in their own game, feel themselves least handicapped in comparison with the male.[19]

The empirical evidence, not just from my personal case, but from observing my female student athletes, seems to bear out De Beauvoir's suggestion. Every year it seems that fewer of my students have even heard of the concept of a "MRS degree."[20] Female athletes worry less about how their bodies look to others than how they perform in competition. Their bodies are *their own*, subjects of personal ambition rather than mere objects of desire.[21]

---

17. De Beauvoir (1949, 310).
18. De Beauvoir (1949, 308).
19. De Beauvoir (1949, 311–312).
20. This expression refers to a woman attending college for the sole purpose of finding a husband.
21. For all this they are not immune to social pressures—eating disorders such as bulimia and anorexia nervosa remain a problem among female athletes.

So sports *have* changed women, but not everyone agrees it's for the better. The kinds of aggression and competitiveness required for success arguably run counter to civil society as well as feminine nature itself.[22] Philosopher Jane English (who died in 1978 while climbing the Matterhorn) suggests that sporting equality may best be reached if sport adapts itself to more feminine qualities.[23] Noting that feminine characteristics that are disadvantages in traditional sports—i.e. smaller size, wider hips, different hormones—are *advantages* in other sports (such as the balance beam), English calls for the introduction of a wider variety of sports to accommodate a wider variety of physical types.

This idea need not be implemented by declaring traditionally female activities such as cheerleading and aerobic dance to be competitive sports. Nor should it be an excuse for excluding women from traditionally male sports. Rather the idea is to affirmatively promote and design sports in which women (and appropriately-endowed men) have the opportunity to reach the highest levels of excellence—making sport itself more fair.

Compensation for Disability

Another group demanding affirmative action in sport is the physically disabled. In the mid-1970's the United States barred discrimination against the disabled in education. Then in 1978, the Amateur Sports Act affirmatively endorsed the promotion of athletic opportunities such as the Special Olympics and Paralympics, as well as special classes in traditional events such as the Boston Marathon. The Americans with Disabilities Act of 1990 further banned discrimination in employment, public transportation, services, and accommodations—including sports and recreational facilities.[24] Since that time, athletes and coaches have sued under the act to gain unprecedented access to sport. The question is, how much accommodation can be made for physical disability in a practice designed to reward extraordinary physical ability?

---

22. Of course this view makes rather bold assumptions about what society and femininity *should* be, assumptions that have the potential to limit women in just the way De Beauvoir laments. To say that a woman who is competitive and enjoys hockey is in some way *masculine* is to insinuate that she is in some way defective.

23. English (1978, 287).

24. Information on these laws can be found in Polidoro (2000, 84–85).

In 1998, golfer Casey Martin sued and won the right to compensate for a degenerative leg disease by using a cart in the Professional Golf Association's Nike Tour. Central to Martin's argument were the claims that shooting rather than walking is the skill being tested in golf, and that his rare genetic disorder should not bar him from employment as a professional golfer.

The PGA countered by making a clear distinction between providing *access* to play and watch the game and providing *accommodation* to compete in the sport at its highest levels. It argued that pro golfers are not employees and defended its right to make the rules governing competition. The PGA's main reason for resisting Martin's claim was that it would tilt the level playing field because being allowed to use motorized transportation gives an individual an advantage over the rest of the field.[25] What's interesting is that Martin views the cart as a way to compensate for an involuntary *disadvantage*. From his point of view, the playing field is already tilted against him. Both Martin and the PGA seek the same thing: a level playing field; but who determines what that is?

There's no question that social bias against the disabled exists, and such biases ought to be overcome. Barriers to the disabled are more than psychosocial, however. The inability to climb a set of stairs or to read a standard book are tangible. As a professor I have provided special accommodation to disabled students not available to the rest of my class. The rationale is that it compensates for an involuntary disadvantage, but what about other involuntary disadvantages? Students with poor analytical ability are also handicapped in the study of philosophy. Should I provide accommodations for them? It seems not, since one of the things philosophy exams do is to *test* analytical ability.

Likewise if sport were to accommodate for all disabilities, its purpose of selecting and rewarding according to *ability* would seem to be compromised. No one doubts the benefits of programs like the Special Olympics that provide sports opportunities to the disabled. But to what degree can or should disability be compensated for in tests of merit? Some athletes defend their use of drugs as compensation for genetic disadvantages. Would it be possible to determine some baseline level of ability, for which every athlete who falls below could artificially compensate? Is the opportunity to compete against the best in the business

---

25. www.sportsline.com/u/golf/martin/pgastatement.htm

an entitlement of every athlete? Just what are the limits of fair competition in sport?

> **Thinking Activity: Affirmative Action in Sport**
> **Question:** Should disabilities be compensated for in competitive sport?
> **Observe:** It is widely agreed that the opportunity to participate in sport should not be denied to anyone on the basis of disability. How might sport level the playing field for certain disabilities without harming competition?
> **Analyze:** What do your answers say about your idea of equal opportunity in sport?
> **Question Again:** Which factors are relevant and which irrelevant to fairness in sport?

Chapter Review

Summary

Like civilization itself, sport is an invention of human beings who seek certain benefits from their participation. Since philosophical athletes are members of social as well as sports communities, they should seek to understand and improve their role as citizens in both. Issues of justice, fairness and equality affect all communities. Philosophical athletes can learn to respect the aspects of sports and society that seek to enhance these civic virtues; they can also act as stewards for their sport as it faces corrupting influences from society.

Civic responsibility is as much a part of being an athlete as personal responsibility is. This book has worked outward from the athlete's individual concerns to the concerns and virtues of the community. In the end, however, we find them all to be related. Good communities depend on good individuals and good individuals depend on their communities.

Further Reading

Philosophy

De Beauvoir, Simone. 1952. *The Second Sex*. Translated by H.M. Parshley. Originally published in French in 1949. New York: Bantam Books. Often called the bible of the feminist movement, this text is a great classic of women's studies that remains eerily relevant even today.

Nozick, Robert. 1974. *Anarchy, State, and Utopia*. New York: Basic Books. A colleague of John Rawls' at Harvard University, Nozick provides a conservative counterpoint to Rawls' conception of justice. This is his key work.

Wollstonecraft, Mary. [1790] 1967. *A Vindication of the Rights of Woman*. New York: Norton. An early feminist response to Rousseau, Wollstonecraft uses the French philosopher's own principles to contradict the troublesome claims he makes about women's education.

Philosophy of Sport

English, Jane. 1978. "Sex Equality in Sports." *Philosophy and Public Affairs* 7: 269–277. Reprinted in Morgan and Meier, ed. (1995), 284–288. English offers an insightful and ground-breaking analysis of the masculine bias of modern sports combined with a proposal to reconfigure sport to accept traditionally feminine qualities.

Journalism and Literature

Burton-Nelson, Mariah. 1991. *Are We Winning Yet? How Women are Changing Sports and Sports are Changing Women*. New York: Random House. Examines the relationship between women and sport from a variety of perspectives through interviews and examination of various issues.

Marantz, Steve. 1998. "A Man's Appreciation for Women Athletes," In Littlefield, ed., 376–387. This well-intentioned tribute to female athletes nevertheless reveals patriarchal biases in our attitudes toward women in sport.

Conclusion

The Game of Life

"You never conquer the mountain, you only conquer yourself."
—Jim Whitaker, Mountaineer

As athletes, we spend much of our time trying to perfect our ability to play a game. But the games themselves are meaningless. The Greek soldiers who ran great distances to help armies prepare for war had a purpose since lost in the modern "marathons" that commemorate their feats. The really "big game" that we prepare for in athletics is in fact the game of life.

The object of the "game of life" is, quite simply, happiness. We all seek a good life full of challenge, satisfaction, friendship, and meaning. What's wonderful about these meaningless games we play is that they help us to develop skills useful in the "big game" with its ultimate payoff.

As philosophical athletes, we use our sports experience to develop self-knowledge, to take responsibility, to respect ourselves and others, and to understand our function in various communities. That is, we use our sports experience to increase our understanding of life and, hopefully, to lead better and happier lives.

Clearly, the connection between training for sport and performing well in the "game of life" is not automatic. An individual may be exceptionally successful within the meaningless realm of sport while failing miserably to achieve a thoughtful and meaningful existence outside of it.

The goal of this book has been to help bridge that gap, to help athletes understand how sports can be meaningful in their lives while remaining meaningless in themselves. In some sense, this book is a belated response to sport-philosopher Hans Lenk's call for a "program of enlightenment" to emancipate athletes from social manipulation:

Not enough has been done to take care of the 'enlightenment' and the critical capacities of the athlete to think over his role and the importance and significance of his successes or defeats as well as his athletic activity, in general.[1]

Athletes cannot "be enlightened," however, they must enlighten themselves. The transformation into a philosophical athlete takes place inside the individual. It begins as part of that vision of the kind of person you want to be, then becomes reality only through practice.

Ultimately, the goal of being a philosophical athlete depends on developing a clear idea of who you are and the life you want to live, then taking the initiative to go out and live it. It's not unlike performance in sport—know what to do then go out and do it. It's as simple—and as complicated—as that.

---

1. *Lenk* (1979, 116).

Twelve Questions for the Philosophical Athlete

Being a philosophical athlete takes practice. The following questions will remind you of the concepts and principles contained in this book.

1. Do you view sport as an opportunity to learn about yourself, to distinguish yourself from others, and to discover your authentic personality?
2. Do you see yourself as an embodied whole, whose intelligence can be expressed both mentally and physically, and who focuses on the mind-body connection?
3. Do you value the experience of freedom in sport and understand its connection to conscious, exercised choice?
4. Do you understand that what you do, how things appear to you, and how you interpret events are all choices for which you are responsible?
5. Do you recognize the realities of losing and death, understanding the connection between risk and learning the truth?
6. Do you recognize your responsibility for choosing your life's meaning, clarifying your values, and setting goals accordingly?
7. Are you clear in your head about the kind of person you want to be, and able to make ethical decisions that show respect for that ideal?
8. Is your treatment of others, in sport and out, guided by universal principles, such as the Golden Rule, plus a thoughtful understanding of particular relationships?
9. Have you reflected upon the "internal goods" of your sport, and used this understanding as a guide for personal conduct and care-taking of the activity?
10. Do you understand that your right to benefit from the goods of sport comes with an obligation to others and to the community itself?
11. Do you take the "perspective of the ball" in seeking to avoid social and cultural prejudices about race, ethnicity, and gender?
12. Do you understand the relationship between equal opportunity and merit-based distribution and how it applies to women and the handicapped in sport?

Selected Bibliography

A Kokomo High School Student. 1909. "The Value of Girl's Basketball." *The Kokomo Kamera*. Reprinted in Sandoz and Winans, ed., 78.

Abrahamson, Alan. 2000. "Runner Is a Symbol of Aboriginal Freedom." *Los Angeles Times*, September 26.

Alkemeyer, Thomas and Bernd Broskamp. 1996. "Strangerhood and Racism in Sports." In *Sport Science Review*, v. 5, n. 2: 30–52.

Alvarez, A. 1967. "I Like to Risk my Life." *Saturday Evening Post* 240, September 9, 10–12. Reprinted in Gerber, ed. (1972), 203–5.

Andre, Judith and David N. James, ed. 1991. *Rethinking College Athletics*. Philadelphia: Temple University Press.

Annas, Julia. 1993. *The Morality of Happiness*. New York: Oxford University Press.

Aristotle. 1984. *Complete Works*. Edited by Jonathan Barnes. Princeton, NJ: Princeton University Press.

Armstrong, Lance. 2000. *It's Not About the Bike*. New York: Putnam.

Baier, Kurt. 1994. "The Meaning of Life." Inaugural lecture (1957) Canberra University College, Australia. In Klemke, Kline, and Hollinger, ed., 378–388.

Battista, Garth, ed. 1994. *The Runner's Literary Companion*. New York: Breakaway Books.

Begley, Sharon. 2000. "The Stereotype Trap." *Newsweek*, November 6, 66–68.

Belaief, Lynne. 1977. "Meanings of the Body." In Vanderwerken and Wertz, ed., 414–434.

Bentham, Jeremy. 1789. *An Introduction to the Principles of Morals and Legislation*. London: T. Payne.

Berlin, Isaiah. [1969] 1996. "Two Concepts of Liberty." In *Readings in Social and Potlical Philosophy*, ed. Robert M. Stewart, 90–97. Oxford: Oxford University Press.

Bessier, Arnold R. 1967. *The Madness in Sports: Psychosocial Observations on Sports*. New York: Meredith Publishing Co.

Bjerklie, David. 1993. "High Tech Olympians." *Technology Review*, January, 23–30.

Bradley, Bill. 1998. *Values of the Game*. New York: Broadway Books.

Brentano, Franz. [1874] 1960. "The Distinction between Mental and Physical Phenomena." In Chisholm, ed., 39–61.

Burton-Nelson, Mariah. 1991. *Are We Winning Yet? How Women are Changing Sports and Sports are Changing Women.* New York: Random House.

Burton-Nelson, Mariah. 1994. *The Stronger Women Get, The More Men Love Football: Sexism in the American Culture of Sports.* New York: Harcourt Brace.

Butcher, Robert and Angela Schneider. 1998. "Fair Play as Respect for the Game." *Journal of the Philosophy of Sport* XXV: 1–22.

Cahn, Steven M., ed. 1997. *Classics of Modern Political Theory: Machiavelli to Mill.* Oxford: Oxford University Press.

Camus, Albert. 1955. *The Myth of Sisyphus and Other Essays.* Translated by Justin O'Brien. New York: Vingate.

Chisholm, Roderick, ed. 1960. *Realism and the Background of Phenomenology.* New York: Ridgeview Publishing Company.

Choron, Jacques. 1963. *Death and Western Thought.* New York: MacMillan.

Churchland, Paul. 1981. "Eliminative Materialism and the Propositional Attitudes." *Journal of Philosophy,* LXXVIII, 2: 67–90.

Clifford, Craig and Feezell, Randolph. 1997. *Coaching for Character: Reclaiming the Principles of Sportsmanship.* Champaign, IL: Human Kinetics.

D'Agostino, Fred. 1981. "The Ethos of Games." *Journal of the Philosophy of Sport* VIII: 7–18. Reprinted in Morgan and Meier, ed. (1995), 42–49.

De Beauvoir, Simone. 1952. *The Second Sex.* Translated by H.M. Parshley. New York: Bantam Books.

Deford, Frank, ed. 1993. *The Best American Sports Writing 1993.* Boston: Houghton Mifflin.

Delattre, Edwin J. 1975. "Some Reflections on Success and Failure in Competitive Athletics" in *Journal of the Philosophy of Sport* II: 133–139. Reprinted in Morgan and Meier, ed. (1995), 188–192.

Descartes, Rene. 1993. *Meditations on First Philosophy.* Translated by Donald A. Cress. Indianapolis: Hackett.

Dixon, Nicholas. 1992. "On Sportsmanship and Running up the Score." *Journal of the Philosophy of Sport,* XIX: 1–13.

Douillard, John. 1994. *Body, Mind and Sport.* New York: Harmony Books.

Du Bois, William Edward Burghardt. [1903] 1995. *The Souls of Black Folk.* New York: Penguin.

Eassom, Simon. 1998. "Games, Rules, and Contracts." In McNamee and Parry, ed., 57–78.

Edwards, Paul, ed. 1967. *The Encyclopedia of Philosophy.* New York: MacMillan.

English, Jane. 1978. "Sex Equality in Sports." *Philosophy and Public Affairs* 7: 269–277. Reprinted in Morgan and Meier, ed. (1995), 284–288.

Ermler, Kathy L. 1982. "Two Expressions of Failure in Sport." In Vanderwerken and Wertz, ed., 761–765.

Esposito, Joseph L. 1974. "Play and Possibility." *Philosophy Today* XVIII: 137–146. Reprinted in Morgan and Meier, ed. (1995), 114–119.

Feezell, Randolph M. 1999. "Sportsmanship and Blowouts: Baseball and Beyond." *Journal of the Philosophy of Sport* XXVI, 68–78.

Feinstein, John, ed. 1996. *The Best American Sports Writing 1996.* Boston: Houghton Mifflin.

Felshin, Jan. 1972. "The Socialization of Sport." In Gerber, ed. (1972), 227–9.

Ford, Gerald R. with John Underwood. 1974. "In Defense of the Competitive Urge." Originally appeared in *Sports Illustrated.* In Vanderwerken and Wertz, ed., 247–256.

Ford, Richard, ed. 1999. *The Best American Sports Writing 1999.* Boston: Houghton Mifflin.

Fraleigh, Warren P. 1984. *Right Actions in Sports: Ethics for Contestants.* Champaign, IL: Human Kinetics.

Frankfurt, Harry G. 1971. "Freedom of the Will and the Concept of a Person." *Journal of Philosophy* 66 (January): 5–20.

Frankl, Viktor E. 1959. *Man's Search for Meaning.* New York: Beacon Press.

Galvin, Richard F. 1991. "Aesthetic Incontinence in Sport (a response to Wertz)." In Vanderwerken and Wertz, ed., 519–524.

Garrett, Roland. 1976. "The Metaphysics of Baseball." In Vanderwerken and Wertz, ed., 643–663.

Gerber, Ellen W., ed. 1972. *Sport and the Body: A Philosophical Symposium.* Philadelphia: Lea and Febiger.

Gerber, Ellen W. and William J. Morgan, ed. 1979. *Sport and the Body: A Philosophical Symposium,* second edition. Philadelphia: Lea and Febiger.

Gilligan, Carol. 1982. *In a Different Voice: Psychological Theory and Women's Development.* Cambridge: Harvard University Press.

Gopink, Adam. 1998. "Endgame." In Ford, ed. (1999), 29–38.

Gough, Russell. 1997. *Character is Everything: Promoting Ethical Excellence in Sports.* Fort Worth, TX: Harcourt Brace.

Greenfield, Karl Taro. 1999. "Life On The Edge." *Time,* September 6, 29–36.

Halberstam, David, ed. 1991. *The Best American Sports Writing 1991.* Boston: Houghton Mifflin.

Hall, Kermit L. 1992. "Affirmative Action." In *Major Problems in American Constitutional History,* vol. II. Lexington, MA: D.C. Heath and Company, 356–357.

Hardman, A., L. Fox, D. McLaughlin, and K. Zimmerman. 1996. "On Sportsmanship and Running up the Score: Issues of Incompetence and Humiliation." *Journal of the Philosophy of Sport* XXIII: 58–69.

Hare, R.M. 1970. *Freedom and Reason.* London: Oxford University Press.

Harper, William. 1969. "Man Alone." *Quest,* XII: 57–60.

Harrison, William. 1973. "Roller Ball Murder." Originally appeared in *Esquire.* Reprinted in Vanderwerken and Wertz, ed., 31–42.

Hatab, Lawrence J. 1991. "The Greeks and the Meaning of Athletics." In Andre and James, ed., 31–42.

Heidegger, Martin. 1962. *Being and Time.* Translated by John Macquarrie and Edward Robinson. Originally published in 1927. New York: Harper and Collins.

Heidegger, Martin. 1977. "The Question Concerning Technology." In *Basic Writings*, edited by David Farrel Krell. New York: Harper and Row, 287–317.

Herodotus. 1954. *The Histories*. Translated by Aubrey de Selincourt. Middlesex: Penguin.

Hobbes, Thomas. [1651] 1958. *Leviathan*. Indianapolis, IA: Library of Liberal Arts.

Hoberman, John. 1986. "Sport and the Technological Image of Man." In Morgan and Meier, ed. (1995), 202–208.

Hoberman, John. 1992. *Mortal Engines: The Science of Performance and the Dehumanization of Sport*. New York: The Free Press.

Hoberman, John. 1997. *Darwin's Athletes: How Sport has Damaged Black America and Preserved the Myth of Race*. Boston: Houghton Mifflin.

Holowchak, M. Andrew. 2000. "Aretism and Pharmacological Ergogenic Aids in Sport: Taking a Shot at the Use of Steroids." *Journal of the Philosophy of Sport* XXVII: 35–50.

Homer. 1990. *The Iliad*. Translated by Robert Fagles. New York: Viking.

Hoose, Phillip M. 1989. *Necessities: Racial Barriers in American Sports*. New York: Random House.

Huang, Chungliang Al and Jerry Lynch. 1992. *Thinking Body Dancing Mind*. New York: Bantam.

Huizenga, M.D., Rob. 1994. *You're Okay, It's Just a Bruise: A Doctor's Sideline Secrets about Pro Football's Most Outrageous Team*. New York: St. Martin's.

Huizinga, Johan. 1949. *Homo Ludens: A Study of the Play-element in Culture*. London: Routledge and Kegan Paul.

Hume, David. [1739] 1978. *A Treatise of Human Nature*. Edited by L. A. Selby-Bigge, second edition. Oxford: Clarendon Press.

Husserl, Edmund. [1929] 1960. "Phenomenology." In Chisholm, ed., 118–128.

Hyland, Drew A. 1972. "Athletic Angst: Reflections on the Philosophical Relevance of Play." In Gerber, ed. (1972), 87–94.

Hyland, Drew A. 1978. "Competition and Friendship." *Journal of the Philosophy of Sport* V: 27–27. Reprinted in Gerber and Morgan, ed. (1979), 133–139.

Hyland, Drew A. 1979. "Playing to Win: How Much Should It Hurt?" Originally appeared in *The Hastings Center Report*. In Vanderwerken and Wertz, ed., 280–290.

Hyland, Drew A. 1984. "Opponents, Contestants, and Competitors: The Dialectic of Sport." *Journal of the Philosophy of Sport* XI: 63–70. Reprinted in Morgan and Meier, ed. (1995), 177–182.

Hyland, Drew A. 1990. *Philosophy of Sport*. New York: Paragon House.

Hyland, Drew A. 1991. "When Power becomes Gracious: The Affinity of Sport and Art." In Andre and James ed., 71–80.

Issacson, Walter. 1997. "In Search of the Real Bill Gates." *Time*, January 13, 44–57.

Jackson, Phil. 1995. *Sacred Hoops: Spiritual Lessons of a Hardwood Warrior*. New York: Hyperion.

Jackson, Susan A. and Mihaly Csikszentmihalyi. 1999. *Flow in Sports*. Champaign, IL: Human Kinetics.

James, William. [1902] 1991. *The Varieties of Religious Experience.* New York: Triumph Books.

Jaspers, Karl. 1957. "Limits of the Life Order: Sport." In *Man in the Modern Age,* translated by Eden and Cedar Paul. Garden City, New York: Doubleday. Reprinted in Gerber, ed. (1972), 118–119.

Jerome, John. 1980. *The Sweet Spot in Time.* New York: Summit Books.

Jones, Charlie, compiler. 1997. *What Makes Winners Win.* Secaucus, NJ: Carol Publishing.

Kahn, Roger. 1959. "The Crucial Role Fear Plays in Sports." In Plimpton, ed., 329–336.

Kant, Immanuel. 1948. *Groundwork for the Metaphysic of Morals.* Translated by H. J. Paton. New York: Harper and Row.

Kaufman, Walter, ed. 1975. *Existentialism from Dostoevsky to Sartre.* New York: Meridian Books.

Keating, James W. 1964. "Sportsmanship as a Moral Category." *Ethics* LXXV: 25–35. Reprinted in Morgan and Meier, ed. (1995), 144–151.

King Jr., Dr. Martin Luther. 1992. *I Have a Dream: Writings and Speeches that Changed the World.* New York: Harper Collins.

Klemke, E.D., A. David Kline, and Robert Hollinger, ed. 1994. *Philosophy: Contemporary Perspectives on Perennial Issues.* New York: St. Martin's Press.

Kolak, Daniel and Raymond Martin, ed. 1996. *The Experience of Philosophy.* Belmont, California: Wadsworth.

Kolak, Daniel. 1993. "Finding Our Selves: Identification, Identity, and Multiple Personality." In Kolak and Martin, ed., 94–113.

Krakauer, Jon. 1997. *Into Thin Air.* New York: Random House.

Kretchmar, R. Scott. 1975. "From Test to Contest: An Analysis of Two Kinds of Counterpoint in Sport." *Journal of the Philosophy of Sport* II: 23–30. Reprinted in Morgan and Meier, ed. (1995), 36–41.

Kretchmar, R. Scott. 1982. "Distancing: An Essay on Abstract Thinking in Sports Performances." In Vanderwerken and Wertz, ed., 87–102.

Kretchmar, R. Scott. 1994. *Practical Philosophy of Sport.* Champaign, IL: Human Kinetics.

Lambert, Craig. 1998. *Mind over Water: Lessons on Life from the Art of Rowing.* Boston: Houghton Mifflin.

Lasch, Christopher. 1979. *The Culture of Narcissism.* New York: Warner.

Lehman, Craig. 1988. "Can Cheaters Play the Game?" In Morgan and Meier, ed. (1988), 283–288.

Leibniz, G.W. 1902. *Discourse on Metaphysics.* Translated by George Montgomery. La Salle, IL: Open Court.

Lenk, Hans. 1976. "Herculean 'Myth' Aspects of Athletics: A Mythological Interpretation of the Fascination with Top Level Sport." In Vanderwerken and Wertz, ed., 435–446.

Lenk, Hans. 1979. *Social Philosophy of Athletics.* Champaign, IL: Stipes.

Leonard, George. 1974. *The Ultimate Athlete: Revisioning Sports, Physical Education, and the Body.* New York: Viking.

Littlefield, Bill, ed. 1998. *The Best American Sports Writing 1998*. Boston: Houghton Mifflin.

Locke, John. [1689a] 1975. *An Essay concerning Human Understanding*. Reprint. Edited by Peter H. Nidditch. Oxford: Clarendon Press.

Locke, John. 1689b. "Second Treatise on Civil Government." In Cahn, ed., 217–292.

Lucas, J. R. 1972. "Because You Are a Woman." *Philosophy* 48: 166–171.

Lucretius. 1946. *On the Nature of Things*. Translated by Charles E. Bennett. Roslyn, NY: Walter J. Black.

MacIntyre, Adasdair. 1981. *After Virtue*. Notre Dame, IN: University of Notre Dame Press.

MacIver, R.M. 1952. "The Deep Beauty of the Golden Rule." In Klemke, Kline, and Hollinger, ed., 455–462.

Marantz, Steve. 1998. "A Man's Appreciation for Women Athletes." In Littlefield, ed., 376–387.

Marcel, Gabriel. 1952. "If I Am My Body." In Morgan and Meier, ed. (1995), 87–88.

McGuane, Thomas, ed. 1992. *The Best American Sports Writing 1992*. Boston: Houghton Mifflin.

McNamee, M.J., and S.J. Parry, ed. 1998. *Ethics and Sport*. London: E and FN Spon.

McPhee, John. 1965. *A Sense of Where You Are: A Profile of Bill Bradley at Princeton*. New York: Farrar, Straus, and Giroux.

Mechikoff, Robert A. and Steven G. Estes. 1998. *A History and Philosophy of Sport and Physical Education*, 2nd edition. Boston: WCB/McGraw-Hill.

Meier, Klaus V. 1979. "Embodiment, Sport, and Meaning." In Gerber and Morgan, ed. (1979), 192–199.

Meier, Klaus V. 1980. "An Affair of Flutes: An Appreciation of Play." *Journal of the Philosophy of Sport*, VII: 24–45. Reprinted in Morgan and Meier, ed. (1995), 120–135.

Meier, Klaus V. 1988. "Triad Trickery, Playing with Sport and Games." Originally published in *Journal of the Philosophy of Sport* XV: 11–30. Reprinted in Morgan and Meier, ed. (1995), 23–35.

Merleau-Ponty, Maurice. 1962. "The Body as Expression." In *The Phenomenology of Perception*, translated by Colin Smith. London: Routledge and Kegan Paul, 198–199.

Metheny, Eleanor. 1968. "The Symbolic Power of Sport." Presented to the Eastern District Association for Heath, Physical Education and Recreation in Washington D.C., April 26, 1968. Reprinted in Gerber and Morgan, ed. (1979), 231–236.

Milgram, Stanley. 1974. *Obedience to Authority*. New York: Harper and Row.

Mill, John Stuart. [1859] 1978. *On Liberty*. Reprint. Edited by Elizabeth Rapaport. Indianapolis, IA: Hackett.

Mill, John Stuart. [1869] 1975. "On the Subjection of Women." In *Three Essays*. Oxford: Oxford University Press, 427–529.

Mills, Charles. 1997. *The Racial Contract*. Ithaca, NY: Cornell University Press.

Montville, Leigh. 1993. "Triumph on Sacred Ground." *Sports Illustrated,* October 18, 86–98.

Morgan, William J. 1987. "The Logical Incompatibility Thesis and Rules: A Reconsideration of the Formalist Account." *Journal of the Philosophy of Sport* XIV: 1–20. Reprinted in Morgan and Meier, ed. (1995), 50–63.

Morgan, William J. 1994. *Leftist Theories of Sport: A Critique and Reconstruction*. Urbana and Chicago, IL: University of Illinois Press.

Morgan, William J. and Meier, Klaus V., ed. 1988. *Philosophic Inquiry in Sport*. 2nd edition, 1995. Champaign, IL: Human Kinetics.

Morris, Herbert, ed. 1961. *Freedom and Responsibility: Readings in Philosophy and Law*. Stanford, California: Stanford University Press.

Moulton, Janice. 1991. "Why Everyone Deserves a Sporting Chance: Education, Justice, and College Sport." In Andre and James, ed. 210–220.

Murphy, Michael and White, Rhea A. 1995. *In the Zone: Transcendent Experience in Sports*. New York: Penguin.

Netzky, Ralph. 1974. "Playful Freedom: Sartre's Ontology Re-appraised." *Philosophy Today* XVIII: 125–136. Reprinted in Gerber and Morgan, ed. (1979), 88–91.

Noriyuki, Duane. 1990. "Let the Games Begin." Originally published in *The Detroit Free Press Magazine*. In Halberstam, ed., 48–61.

Novak, Michael. 1988. *The Joy of Sports: End Zones, Bases, Baskets, Balls, and the Consecration of the American Spirit*. Lanham, NY: Hamilton Press.

Nozick, Robert. 1974. *Anarchy, State, and Utopia*. New York: Basic Books.

Packer, Billy and Roland Lazenby. 1998. *Why We Win: Great American Coaches Offer Their Strategies for Success in Sports and Life*. Chicago, IL: Masters Press.

Parfit, Derek. 1987. "Divided Minds and the Nature of Persons." In *Mindwaves,* edited by C. Blakemore and S. Greenfield. London: Basil Blackwell, 19–25.

Pascal, Blaise. [1662] 1966. *Pensées*. Translated by A.J. Krailsheimer. Middlesex: Penguin.

Pateman, Carole. 1988. *The Sexual Contract*. Stanford, CA: Stanford University Press.

Pearson, Kathleen M. 1973. "Deception, Sportsmanship, and Ethics." *Quest* XIX: 115–118. Reprinted in Morgan and Meier, ed. (1995), 183–184.

Plato. 1992. *Republic*. Translated by G.M.A. Grube. Indianapolis, IN: Hackett.

Plato. 1997. *Apology, Crito, Euthydemus,* and *Phaedo*. In *Plato: Complete Works,* edited by John M. Cooper. Indianapolis, IN: Hackett.

Plimpton, George, ed. 1992. *The Norton Book of Sports*. New York: Norton.

Polidoro, J. Richard. 2000. *Sport and Physical Activity in the Modern World*. Boston, MA: Allyn and Bacon.

Porter, Kay and Foster, Judy. 1986. *The Mental Athlete*. New York: Ballantine Books.

Price, S.L. 1997. "What Ever Happened to the White Athlete?" *Sports Illustrated,* December 8, 30–51.

Price, S.L. 2000. "Tunnel Vision." *Sports Illustrated,* April 3, 83.

Prouty, David F. 1988. *In Spite of Us: My education in the big and little games of amateur and Olympic sports in the U.S.* Brattleboro, VT: Velo-News.

Rawls, John. 1955. "The Practice Conception of Rules" excerpted from "Two Conceptions of Rules." *The Philosophical Review* 64 (January): 3–32. Reprinted in Gerber and Morgan, ed. (1979), 294–296.

Rawls, John. 1971. *A Theory of Justice.* Cambridge, MA: Harvard University Press.

Reddiford, Gordon. 1998. "Cheating and Self-deception in Sport." In Mc-Namee and Parry, ed., 225–239.

Reid, Elwood. 1998. "My Body, My Weapon, My Shame." In Littlefield, ed., 118–131.

Reid, Thomas. [1788] 1969. *Essays on the Active Powers of Man.* Cambridge, MA: M.I.T. Press.

Rodman, Dennis with Tim Keown. 1996. *Bad as I Wanna Be.* New York: Delacorte Press.

Ross, W.D. 1967. *The Right and the Good.* Oxford: Clarendon Press.

Rousseau, Jean-Jacques. [1762] 1967. *The Social Contract and Discourse on the Origin of Inequality.* Edited by Lester G. Crocker. New York: Simon and Schuster/Pocket Books.

Rousseau, Jean-Jacques. 1761. "Of the Social Contract." Translated by Charles M. Sheroverj. In Cahn, ed., 421–485.

Russell, Bill. 1979. *Second Wind.* New York: Random House.

Sandoz, Joli and Joby Winans, ed. 1999. *Whatever It Takes: Women on Women's Sport.* New York: Farrar, Straus and Giroux.

Santayana, George. 1972. "Philosophy on the Bleachers." In Gerber, ed. (1972), 233.

Sartre, Jean-Paul. 1956. *Being and Nothingness.* Translated by Hazel E. Barnes. New York: The Philosophical Library, Inc.

Schopenhauer, Arthur. 1883. *The World as Will and Idea.* Translated by R.B. Haldane and J. Kemp. London: Trubner.

Sheehan, George. 1975. *Dr. Sheehan on Running.* New York: Bantam Books.

Sheehan, George. 1978. *Running and Being: The Total Experience.* Red Bank, NJ: Second Wind.

Shulman, James L, and William G. Bowen. 2001. *The Game of Life: College Sports and Educational Values.* Princeton, NJ: Princeton University Press.

Sillitoe, Alan. 1959. *The Loneliness of the Long Distance Runner.* New York: Alfred A. Knopf.

Simon, Robert L. 1984. "Good Competition and Drug-Enhanced Performance." *Journal of the Philosophy of Sport* XI: 6–13. Reprinted in Morgan and Meier, ed. (1995), 209–214.

Simon, Robert L. 1991. *Fair Play: Sports, Values, and Society.* Boulder CO: Westview Press.

Skillen, Anthony. 1998. "Sport is for Losers." In McNamee and Parry, ed., 169–181.

Slusher, Howard S. 1967. *Man, Sport, and Existence: A Critical Analysis.* Philadelphia: Lea and Febiger.

Solotaroff, Paul. 1992. "The Power and the Gory." Originally appeared in *The Village Voice.* In McGuane, ed., 176–196.

Spicker, Stuart F., ed. 1970. *The Philosophy of the Body: Rejections of Cartesian Dualism.* New York: Quadrangle/New York Times Book Co.

Spinoza, Benedict. [1677] 1955. *The Ethics.* Translated by R.H.M. Elwes. New York: Dover.

Suits, Bernard. 1978. *The Grasshopper: Games, Life, and Utopia.* Toronto: University of Toronto Press.

Suits, Bernard. 1988. "Tricky Triad: Games, Play, and Sport." *Journal of the Philosophy of Sport* XV: 1–9.

Suits, Bernard. 1973. "The Elements of Sport." In Osterhoudt, ed. *The Philosophy of Sport: A Collection of essays,* 48–64. Reprinted in Morgan and Meier, ed. (1995), 8–15.

Swaddling, Judith. 1980. *The Ancient Olympic Games.* Austin, TX: University of Texas Press.

Telander, Rick. 1993. "Headlong and Headstrong." *Sports Illustrated,* October 11, 42–45.

Tolstoy, Leo. [1905] 1994. *My Confession.* Translated by Leo Wiener. Reprinted in Klemke, Kline, and Hollinger, ed., 389–397.

Vanderwerken, David L. and Spencer K. Wertz, ed. 1985. *Sport Inside Out: Readings in Literature and Philosophy.* Fort Worth: Texas Christian University.

Voltaire, Francois-Marie. 1949. *The Portable Voltaire.* Edited by Ben Ray Redman. New York: The Viking Press.

Voy, Robert. 1991. *Drugs, Sport, and Politics.* Champaign, IL: Human Kinetics.

Weiss, Paul. 1969. *Sport: A Philosophic Inquiry.* Carbondale, IL: Southern Illinois University Press.

Wenz, Peter S. 1981. "Human Equality in Sports." Originally appeared in *The Philosophical Forum.* In Vanderwerken and Wertz, ed., 208–221.

West, Cornel. 1993. *Race Matters.* Boston: Beacon Press.

Williams, Melvin H. *Beyond Training: How Athletes Enhance Performance Legally and Illegally.* Champaign, IL: Leisure Press, 1989.

Wollstonecraft, Mary. [1790] 1967. *A Vindication of the Rights of Woman.* New York: Norton.

Index